A War on People

A War on People

Drug User Politics and a New Ethics of Community

Jarrett Zigon

UNIVERSITY OF CALIFORNIA PRESS

University of California Press, one of the most
distinguished university presses in the United States,
enriches lives around the world by advancing
scholarship in the humanities, social sciences, and
natural sciences. Its activities are supported by the
UC Press Foundation and by philanthropic
contributions from individuals and institutions.
For more information, visit www.ucpress.edu.

University of California Press
Oakland, California

Library of Congress Cataloging-in-Publication Data

Names: Zigon, Jarrett, author.
Title: A war on people : drug user politics and a new
    ethics of community / Jarrett Zigon.
Description: Oakland, California : University of
    California Press, [2019] | Includes bibliographical
    references and index. |
Identifiers: LCCN 2018017687 (print) | LCCN 2018021810
    (ebook) | ISBN 9780520969957 (ebook) |
    ISBN 9780520297692 (cloth : alk. paper) |
    ISBN 9780520297708 (pbk : alk. paper)
Subjects: LCSH: Drug control—Citizen participation. |
    Drug abusers—Political activity.
Classification: LCC HV5801 (ebook) | LCC HV5801 .Z54
    2019 (print) | DDC 363.325/15613—dc23
LC record available at https://lccn.loc.gov/2018017687

28 27 26 25 24 23 22 21 20 19
10 9 8 7 6 5 4 3 2 1

For all of those who fight against wars on people.

It has to be living, to learn the speech of the place.
It has to face the men of the time and to meet
The women of the time. It has to think about war
And it has to find what will suffice. It has
To construct a new stage. It has to be on that stage . . . .

—Wallace Stevens, "Of Modern Poetry"

Contents

Acknowledgments

This book would not have been possible without the help and support of what I call the *anti–drug war movement,* so before anything else I need to begin by thanking everyone who is a part of it, not only for their help with this research, but, much more importantly, for their tireless fight to end this war on people. I would like to single out a few individuals and organizations, however, who were particularly helpful in the research that led to this book: Matt Curtis, Daniel Wolfe, Mark Townsend, Russell Maynard, Sarah Evans, Fred Wright, Jeremy Saunders, Terrell Jones, Robert Suarez, Elizabeth Owens, and everyone at VOCAL-NY, the Portland Hotel Society, and the Danish Drug Users Union—for active drug users.

The research and writing of this book were made possible from funding provided by a Vidi grant from the Dutch Science Foundation (NWO) and the European Research Council under the European Union's Seventh Framework Programme, ERC grant agreement n° 281148. I would like to thank everyone at the University of Amsterdam who helped administer these grants and provided much-needed and helpful support along the way. Special thanks for this go out to José Komen and Janus Oomen.

Parts of this book have appeared either partially or as earlier drafts in the journal *Cultural Anthropology* (chapter 1) and the book *Disappointment: Toward a Critical Hermeneutics of Worldbuilding* (New York: Fordham University Press; introduction and chapter 1).

Many people over the years have in one way or another stimulated my thinking and thus took part in the emergence of this book. I thank the following persons for important conversations around the topics and ideas explored in this book or for reading versions of it, whether in part or in whole, all of whom have been essential to its outcome: Talal Asad, Jason Throop, Patrick Neveling, Martin Holbraad, Robert Desjarlais, China Scherz, Charles Stewart, Thomas Schwarz Wentzer, Rasmus Dyring, Alessandro Duranti, Megan Raschig, Lex Kuiper, Oliver Human, Stine Grinna, Annemarie Samuel, Michael Jackson, Niko Besnier, Jonathan Lear, Cheryl Mattingly, Elizabeth Povinelli, Oskar Verkaaik, Henrik Vigh, Joshua Burraway, Kabir Tambar, Ghassan Hage, Samuele Collu, Miriam Ticktin, Joe Hankins, James Laidlaw, Brian Goldstone, Elinor Ochs, and Joel Robbins. I also thank Natalie Frigo, Eric Werner, Steve Chaney, and Mark Francis for their ever-important friendship. For their ceaseless support, I thank my parents: Sandy, David, Janelle, and Chris. The final version of this book took shape thanks to the editorial guidance of Reed Malcolm and the helpful comments of the reviewers. I also thank all those whom I may have forgotten.

Lastly, as always, Sylvia Tidey is the key to everything. Without her with me, nothing would be possible.

Introduction

On War and Potentiality

War is the health of the State.
—Randolph Silliman Bourne

The novelty of the coming politics is that it will no longer be
a struggle for the conquest or control of the State, but a
struggle between the State and the non-State (humanity), an
insurmountable disjunction between whatever singularity and
the State organization.

—Giorgio Agamben

Recently, political anthropologists and theorists have begun to address
two interrelated problematic concerns. The first is the seemingly widespread lack of motivation for participating in political activity.[1] The
second is the political and intellectual focus on critique rather than
offering alternatives for possible futures.[2] Addressing these two problematics of politics seems increasingly urgent in a time characterized by
anxiety and precarity. Across the globe a predominantly—and thus by
no means exclusively—right-wing-led populist response to this has been
a nostalgic return to a past greatness that never actually was. Thus, for
example, the 1950s seems to be the best imagined future for many in
both the United States and Russia today, while in the United Kingdom
and much of Europe there is a strong desire to return to an ethnonation-
alist purity that supposedly existed sometime before the European
Union arrived on the scene. If history did end with the Cold War, then
it increasingly seems that many do not consider it to have been a happy
ending and are eager to restart it, this time as farce.

While this nostalgic nationalist imperative may be to turn back time, many on the political and intellectual left hope to begin to create worldly conditions that are more open and inclusive than they have been in the past, reduce economic inequality and precarity as much as possible, and do all of this in a way that avoids the existential threat of climate change. Despite this hope, the political and intellectual left has offered very little in terms of a political vision of what that future might be like or how to get there.[3] Confronted with this contemporary condition in which many clearly seek an otherwise but without a vision of what that might be, political anthropologists and theorists have come to recognize the dual problem of this lack of political motivation and alternative visions. Notwithstanding the now increasingly common recognition of these lacks and a few important attempts to offer theoretical alternatives to traditional political thinking, the actual articulation of what a possible future might be and how it may be achieved remains largely missing from this growing body of literature.

This book is an attempt to address this lacunae by offering a glimpse at one of these possible futures and showing the political process by which its potential is being ushered into existence by some unlikely political actors: active and former users of heavy drugs such as heroin and crack cocaine. I call these political actors *unlikely* because for over a century drug users around the globe have been systematically excluded not only from political processes but, as will become clear throughout this book, from humanity as well. What I hope to show and consider in this book, however, is that despite this unlikelihood, the globally networked anti–drug war political movement organized and run by drug users is, in fact, at the forefront of offering an alternative political and social imaginary. In particular, I will focus my considerations on how this anti–drug war imaginary and political activity is enacting nonnormative, open, and relationally inclusive alternatives to such key ethical-political concepts as community, freedom, and care.

For many it may seem odd that so-called addicts and junkies could show us an alternative social and political vision. But as I hope becomes clear throughout this book and as I will emphasize in chapter two, such a response is more a result of what anti–drug war agonists call the "fantasy world" created through drug war propaganda than it is indicative of the lives and capacities of most drug users.[4] I would therefore like to ask readers to set aside any preconceived notions they may have of drug users and invite them to consider instead that in fact the lives of drug users and the war waged against them illustrate well the contemporary condition within which many of us now find ourselves. This condition, I will argue shortly, is best considered one of war as governance. If the drug war is just one particularly clear example of this global condition of war as governance, then the wager of this book is that the ways in which the anti–drug war movement fights against the drug war—and the alternative worlds they are creating in doing so—may offer us some guidance in rethinking some of our most basic political and ethical motivations, tactics, and aims.

This book draws from an ethnographic archive accumulated from nearly fifteen years of research I have done on the drug war and the ethical, political, and therapeutic responses to it in various parts of the globe (chapter 1). In particular, I draw from this archive in order to hermeneutically interrogate the ways in which the global anti–drug war movement is currently building new worlds through political and ethical activities and relations. What I call the *anti–drug war movement* is a pluralist assemblage of diverse—and sometimes seemingly contradictory—groups and organizations that have created a counterhegemonic alternative to what I describe below as the global condition of war as governance.[5] While in this book I focus primarily upon the political and ethical activity of unions of active drug users and their most immediate allies, such as drug policy organizations, harm-reduction advocates, and housing-reform organizations, the global anti–drug war movement also consists of such unexpected participants as organizations of law enforcement against the drug war, right-wing libertarians, and the parents of those who have died drug war deaths. Many of these unions, groups, and organizations have become globally networked, regularly meet to share ideas and experiences, and have come to agree on a long-term strategy for ending the drug war.

In addition to this network of political activity, the anti–drug war movement has also established a global information and "ideology" dissemination machine to counter drug war propaganda (chapter 2). This includes, for example, a number of websites; Facebook pages and Twitter feeds; intellectuals and journalists who produce books and articles for the general public; good relations with a number of mainstream and alternative media outlets; and conferences and workshops that regularly occur at the international, regional, national, and local levels. The anti–drug war movement, then, has established a global infrastructure for the transmission, dissemination, and enactment of a counterhegemonic alternative to the contemporary global condition of war as governance.

Despite the global reach of this political movement, much of the activity is done at the local or regional levels, addressing what in chapter one I call the localized situations of the more widely diffused complexity of the drug war. Nevertheless, because these localized situations are the situated manifestations of the globally diffused complexity of the drug war, these agonists find themselves in a shared condition of war that, as I show in chapter one, is more or less the same no matter where it manifests. As a result, although tactics and strategies differ to some extent according to the differences of the situated manifestations, overall the global anti–drug war movement has been able to construct a coherent long-term strategy because those involved have been able to recognize that they are all, in fact, caught up in shared conditions despite the local differences.

In my hopes to present as clearly as possible the political response to this widely diffused complexity of the drug war, I primarily focus upon three localized anti–drug war groups. Thus, agonists in the Downtown Eastside of Vancouver, Canada; in New York City, United States; and in Copenhagen, Denmark, will take the forefront of this book. This is so for various reasons, the most important of which is that in these three locales we can most easily discern the emergence and endurance of the kinds of new worlds I will argue the global movement in general seeks to build. These three locales also illustrate the different scales that worlds can take—from the intersubjective to the neighborhood and ultimately beyond—and thus help us see that transforming worlds does not occur all at once from the center outward or from the top down. Instead, that transformation spreads by means of persistent political activity and across networks of relationality through processes of attunement that hermeneutically affect and intertwine others in transformative ways.[6] It is important to emphasize that this transformation is not temporary prefiguration but is actually happening and sticking. The anti–drug war movement is actually changing worlds, slowly but surely.

The success of the anti–drug war movement is, in part, a result of its organizational structure and the political activity this allows. Unlike the fetishization of horizontalist full participation that now dominates much of what has come to count as left political activity today, the anti-drug war movement, for the most part, combines a hierarchical, or vertical, structure with some aspects of horizontalism, such as autonomous groups, diversity, networking, and temporally limited full participation. In contrast to the long-term instability of horizontalist politics, this "combination of horizontal and more centralized organizational models," as Jeffrey Juris has speculated, allows for a broad-based, effective, and sustainable political movement.[7] To be clear, however, the centralized organizational model of most anti–drug war groups that I did research with is an open and inclusive political leadership that, much like Hannah Arendt's notion of political activity and the community of whoever arrives (chapter 3) they seek to build,[8] welcomes anyone who wishes to participate. Thus, many of these organizations have a decision-making and leadership process that closely resembles that of democratic centralism,[9] through which all of those who wish to participate in the political leadership debate, discuss, and come to consensus on, for example, tactical and strategic decisions, which are then carried out by the participants or members of the organization at large. The result is a politics of action that has lasting and sustainable effects. Consequently, this politics of worldbuilding has been able to go beyond the momentary prefiguration, spectacle, and protest that have come to characterize much left political activity today and is now actually building new worlds,[10] which include not only infrastructure, values, and social and worldly interactive practices but the onto-ethical grounds for such worlds.

WAR AS GOVERNANCE

What does it mean to say that the contemporary condition is one of war as governance? And how does the drug war help us notice this? Responding to these questions will help us understand how it is that the anti–drug war movement is ultimately a political movement seeking to build new worlds open and inclusive "to everybody who walks by" (chapter 3), as one agonist put it to me. No doubt much of the political activity is aimed first and foremost at making the lives of drug users more bearable. But no matter where my research took me, political agonists were clear that ultimately their political vision of an open community, freedom, and care includes everyone. This is so because ultimately they understand the drug war in terms of what I call *war as governance*, a form of governance that in one manifestation or another affects everyone. They call this contemporary condition a *war on people*.

"It's a war on people, it's a war on communities, it's a war on entire segments of cities." This is how a New York City anti–drug war agonist once described the drug war to me and how it is understood and articulated by innumerable other such agonists around the globe. When representatives of governments, states, and international institutions speak of the drug war, they speak as though it is a quasimetaphorical description of the benevolent attempt on their part to protect national and global populations from apparently dangerous substances. This rhetoric suggests that the war is waged on these substances, and this, along with the medicalization of the disease model of addiction and its therapeutic treatment, results in the contemporary dominant discourse of the war on drugs as protective policies more akin to public health initiatives than any actually fought war. When, on occasion, the drug war is articulated as an actual war, the enemy is, for the most part, officially marked as the dealers, the cartels, and the bad guys who threaten communities. Populations, in this narrative, must be protected.[11]

This is *not* how the anti–drug war movement understands the drug war, and it is not how innumerable drug users around the globe experience it. For them it is indeed a war on people. This war, as far as they can tell, does not protect a population as much as it *creates* two populations—one to be "protectively" normalized, the other to be inclusively excluded. For it is only by means of the discursive, structural, and physical violence enacted against certain kinds of people—in this case, drug users—that a normalized and protectable population comes into being. Put another way: a protectable population never exists prior to the enactment of a biopolitical will that creates that population through acts of exclusionary violence against another and covers over that violence with the rhetorical discourse of security.[12] Whether as mass incarceration in the United States and elsewhere,[13] which is historically intertwined with the drug war and has grown steadily worse as the drug war has escalated; or the dehumanization of drug users that excludes them from such things as jobs, housing, education, and medical treatment, as well as intimate relations of love and care; or both the active and passive state-sponsored physical violence against drug users that results in over two hundred thousand deaths a year globally,[14] the biopolitical will enacted through the drug war is indeed best understood as a war on people.

Increasingly, social and political theorists consider our contemporary condition one of war. For example, Giorgio Agamben has characterized our contemporary political paradigm as that of civil war,[15] and Michael Hardt and Antonio Negri provide perhaps the most sustained theoretical analysis of how this is so.[16] Yet the primary example utilized in both cases is the war on terror. I agree with these and other thinkers who argue for the existence of this global condition of war.[17] But if we want to understand what war as a form of governance entails, then we must go beyond analyses of the war on terror, counterinsurgency, or other forms of perpetual war between and within nation-states and those groups that seek to overthrow or harass them. As I show in chapter one, the drug war illustrates well that in the contemporary condition of things, war as governance is primarily a war on people fought potentially anywhere and against anyone. If we want to understand this contemporary condition of war, then we must interrogate the ways in which this war is waged against ordinary people right here in the midst of everyday life by means of both active and passive violence, a global carceral system, propaganda, surveillance, and even chemical warfare.[18] In this book I will do just that and show how some of those against whom this war is waged fight back.

In his *Society Must Be Defended* lectures, Michel Foucault famously inverted Clausewitz's claim that "war is politics by other means,"[19] and this has been an influential move for many of those who now study such phenomena as the war on terror or the security state. But Foucault's inversion—"politics is war by other means"—in fact may have been redundant. For Clausewitz already understood well that war is a form of governance. Thus, Clausewitz writes that

> war is simply a continuation of political intercourse, with the addition of other means. We deliberately use the phrase "with the addition of other means" because we also want to make it clear that war in itself does not suspend political intercourse or change it into something entirely different. In essentials that intercourse continues, irrespective of the means it employs . . . Is war not just another expression of [political intercourse], another form of speech or writing? Its grammar, indeed, may be its own, but not its logic.[20]

War and politics for Clausewitz, then, are essentially the same phenomenon. The Foucauldian inversion is not necessary because as Clausewitz has already made clear, war and politics already share a logic and are merely aspects of the same process. The respective grammar of war and politics may differ; their forms of speech or modes of writing power into the fabric, bodies, and beings in worlds may differ. But what Clausewitz sought to clarify is that war is and never has been separable from politics, just as politics is and never has been separable from war.[21] War has always been one of the—if not the primary—instruments of political power,[22] whether waged abroad or domestically.

Clausewitz begins his *On War* with a definition: "War is thus an act of force to compel our enemy to do our will."[23] He continues by clarifying this definition. Force is what he calls "the *means* of war." The political object of war is what Clausewitz describes as the imposition of "our will on the enemy." He then goes on to make a distinction between the political object, which he also calls the "original motive" of any war, and what he calls the aim of warfare, which is rendering the enemy powerless.[24] Ultimately, however, once the aim of warfare is realized (that is, once the enemy is rendered powerless by means of force), the political objective returns to the fore so that the victor can impose its will on the defeated.[25] Thus, while the aim is internal to the grammar of the instrument of war, this instrument is wielded according to the logic of the political object.[26] It is this distinction between the aim—rendering the enemy powerless to resist—and the object—the imposition of will— that allows us to begin to see how war has today become a form of governance. For as political objects change—that is, as the will to power of politics changes—so too do the instruments of war. "Thus," Clause- witz concludes the section on the political object of war in book one, "it follows that without any inconsistency wars can have all degrees of importance and intensity, ranging from a war of extermination down to simple armed observation."[27] As will become clear in this book, particu- larly in the first two chapters, the drug war as a war on people covers the range of these intensities.

If the political object of war is the imposition of will, it should be no surprise that as biopolitics has become the dominant form of politics on the globe today, war as an instrument of politics has increasingly become a condition of everyday existence. To be clear: I entirely agree with Paul Rabinow and Nikolas Rose that biopower should not be con- ceived as an all-encompassing and epochal form of power.[28] I also agree with Elizabeth Povinelli that our analytic fascination with biopolitics has partly blinded us to other forms of power and politics and most particularly that which governs the distinction between life and non- life.[29] Still, it is difficult not to acknowledge that despite these caveats, biopower and biopolitics remain dominant today. It is important to recognize, however, that dominance does not entail a universal, all- encompassing power. Rather, similar to how Talal Asad employed the notion of "strong language,"[30] the claim that biopolitics is the dominant form of politics on the globe today is simply to recognize that other forms of power and politics, more often than not, still remain (at least for now) less able to be fully exercised in relation to biopolitical alterna- tives. The contention of this book is that one of the ways in which this biopolitical dominance is exercised is through war as governance in the form of wars on people, such as the drug war, and that the anti–drug war movement offers an example of an alternative to this dominance.

THE POLITICS OF WORLDBUILDING

If the political objective of war as governance is the violent imposition of a biopolitical will such that victory is measured by the normalization, or perhaps better put, the rectification of being-human with an extremely narrow a priori definition of what, who, and how to count as human, then the struggle against this war is primarily fought as a nonnormative attempt to become human and worldly otherwise.[31] To put it plainly, if war on people is meant to force persons to become what counts as human today and to exclude all those who will not or cannot be counted as such, then the struggle against this war entails not only remaining uncountable but doing so in a manner that discloses the violence of the count and through that disclosure brings into the open new possibilities for becoming human and worldly otherwise. This is precisely what I will show those in the anti–drug war movement doing through their political and everyday ethical activity. For by means of this political struggle against a global condition of war as governance, the anti–drug war movement is allowing potentialities to emerge as new possibilities for nonnormative political and communal ways of being-with.

This is a politics, then, as a process of worldbuilding. In *Disappointment* I described a politics of worldbuilding as the political activity done within particular situations, the aim of which is altering the range of possibilities that limit a world and its existents.[32] In that book I argue against the single-world ontology increasingly advocated by some anthropologists and instead posit a relational ontology of multiple worlds.[33] In doing so I begin from the position set out by the philosopher Andrew J. Mitchell, which he articulates as "there is no 'world' in the abstract but always only [populated and articulated ones] of particular situations at particular times, and likewise no encapsulated things, but always these outpouring gestures of relationality."[34] Because this conception of world is so central to this book and the politics of worldbuilding I am trying to critically hermeneutically describe, I will quote at length from *Disappointment* so as to make it as clear as possible for our purposes here:

> By *world*, then, I intend a multiplicity of situations structured by nothing other than this very multiplicity,[35] and because worlds are structured by these situations that are never contained within one world, these situations constitute a link or a bridge between *multiple worlds*. The fact of multiple worlds and their linkage by situations entails not just that worlds can exist separately, as it were—although, to be clear, they are always potentially connected through the "wormhole" of a situation. But also, importantly,

some of these worlds can partially overlap such that we have "worlds within worlds,"[36] as Elizabeth Povinelli has put it echoing the words of Malinowski, which can and do slip into one another, even if temporarily. In this sense, both worlds and the situations that structure and link them can be described as ecstatically relational and emergent multiplicities. Such a notion of world is ripe with sites of potentiality, and thus open for a politics of worldbuilding.[37]

Thus, in that book and in this one, I intend worlds as a multiplicity of situations ontologically structured by ecstatic relationality. As a result, a politics of worldbuilding begins from a situation (chapter 1) and is aimed at opening possibilities for what worlds can become and how to dwell (be-with openly) within them by means of altering the relationalities between those existents that populate a world.

Michael Hardt and Antonio Negri, in contrast, have famously responded to the condition of war as governance with a call to the multitude to resist by means of what they call *biopolitical production,* or the immanent creation of "social relationships and forms through collaborative forms of labor."[38] But the question must be asked: Why fight the imposition of biopolitical will with more biopolitics? Because it remains within the plane of *bios,* or socially qualified life, does biopolitical production not risk a differential reproduction of the same that I have argued elsewhere is characteristic of reformist politics?[39] In contrast to this call for more biopolitical production, I will argue and show throughout this book that today we need to think, conceive, and act beyond biopolitics and begin thinking in terms of an onto-ethical politics of worldbuilding. It is my contention that the anti–drug war movement offers a glimpse of such a politics, by which new forms of social relations are created *because* new worlds and ways of being-with are created. This is recognition that worlds and social life—including labor—as well as, human-nonhuman relations always have a particular onto-ethical grounding, and so a desire to change the former demands the political and intellectual experimental creation of the latter.[40]

As I hope to make clear, a politics of worldbuilding is quite different from what most left-leaning political activity has become today. This difference is best understood in terms of the necessity of offering a political vision and the tactics for realizing this vision in a lasting manner. Although there are certainly some left-leaning movements that have clear and articulated aims with a variety of tactics well suited to meet them, this is clearly not the case for the Left in general and especially so for the most visible of left political activity today. To a great extent this political activity—perhaps the epitome of which was the horizontalist prefiguration of Occupy and other similar "activity"—has become limited to temporary spectacular and carnivalesque protest, increasingly combined with some form of occupation, that emphasizes process over results, tactics over strategy, intimate locality over abstract globality, identity over conditions, and individualizing simplicity over complexity.[41] This has led to a current state of affairs in which it often seems as though the only aim of political activity is little more than performative rituals for voicing dissatisfaction,[42] oftentimes articulated in the register of moralism,[43] symbolic occupation of buildings or public space, and a temporary prefigurative enactment of a localized process with no long-term strategy for any actual transformation.[44] Far from actually changing worlds, this prefigurative politics of performative ritual primarily results in a seemingly endless process of network building and the realization of affective solidarity.[45] Such a "politics," then, has come "to be about feelings of personal empowerment, masking an absence of strategic gains."[46] To paraphrase Lauren Berlant's assessment of a similar form of political activity: this may feel good but it does very little to change anything.[47]

In contrast, a politics of worldbuilding rejuvenates one of the essential features of political thinking and activity—that is, the articulation of and attempt to realize a political vision.[48] As Srnicek and Williams rightly put it, such a political vision and a sense of how to realize it is precisely what is missing in contemporary Left politics, and therefore, "articulating and achieving . . . better world[s] [should be] the fundamental task of the left today."[49] While there is no doubt that articulating a vision of postcapitalism and postwork worlds is vital, what is missing from Srnicek and William's political imaginary is the fact that worlds do not change through the mere alteration of relations of production, labor, and exchange. Rather, these alterations must be accompanied by, if not preceded by, alterations in the onto-ethical relationalities that constitute these worlds. If nothing else, then, the primary argument of this book—and what I hope to show the anti–drug war movement is doing through political activity—is that worlds are built first and foremost through the creative and experimental enactment of such relationalities of being-with, which give way to new modes of labor and exchange, and that it is only through these newly acquired habits of being-with that new worlds can stick and endure.[50]

Sticking and enduring is key to a politics of worldbuilding. For the demand to build a new world is a demand to build one that persists, and if it does not, then it must remain as a resource for yet another new world to come. Imagination is key for this. But imagination must be *enacted*—and not merely discussed and debated—if there is any hope of turning a vision into an actual new world.[51] To the extent that prefigurative politics creates such worlds of duration and potential, then I would consider these examples of worldbuilding. Perhaps the Paris Commune or prerevolution Russian workers' councils (*sovety*) are the best-known examples.[52] Unfortunately, however, because so much contemporary prefigurative politics has become primarily limited to process,[53] as well as temporal and spatial immediacy, it has rendered itself little more than spectacle. That is, its "effectiveness" is primarily limited to a self-referential affective moment that has very little, if any, lasting effect on anything or anyone other than those who participated.

Process is also important to a politics of worldbuilding, but it is not an end in itself. Rather, it is the first step to action that changes worldly conditions: "Freedom of discussion, unity of action," as Lenin once described democratic centralism.[54] Thus, a politics of worldbuilding is first and foremost concerned that the effects of political activity endure and are always relationally linked to other globally dispersed situations (this will become clear throughout the book). In order to accomplish this, anti–drug war political agonists have become keen political actors who simultaneously do pragmatic policy-oriented political engagement while also experimentally enacting alternative relationalities, values, and thus, possibilities. Far from a reformist agenda, however, the pragmatic policy engagement is better understood as deploying potentiality time bombs within the "system" that open more sites of potentiality for future experimentations with new worlds. Thus, for example, the policy, legislative, and judicial work that was necessary to open Insite—the first legally sanctioned safe-injection site in North America—in the Downtown Eastside of Vancouver was the opening that allowed for the eventual transformation of that neighborhood into an entirely new world (this worldbuilding process and how it is now expanding beyond the Downtown Eastside and across the globe will become clear throughout the book). The consequence, so I hope to show, is that anti–drug war political activity is effectively creating and experimenting with potentialities, out of which a future with radically different forms of sociality and politics can emerge.

The ultimate aim of a politics of worldbuilding, then, is the actual building of new worlds, which include not only infrastructure, values, and social and worldly interactive practices but, first and foremost, the onto-ethical grounds that allow for such worlds—that is, the relation-alities of being-with that onto-ethically sustain new possibilities of community, freedom, and care. A politics of worldbuilding as agonistic experimentation with an otherwise, then, entails *actually enacting* this otherwise so that it begins to *stick and endure,* rather than dissipate as if it never was, as much prefigurative horizontalism tends to do.[55]

AN ANTHROPOLOGY OF POTENTIALITY AND CRITICAL HERMENEUTICS

A politics of worldbuilding is a form of politics that seeks to allow potentiality to emerge as new possibilities for being-with, thus laying the onto-ethical grounds for new worlds. To understand such a politics, we need a theoretical-analytic that is attuned to this link between potentiality and possibility. One such theoretical-analytic, and the one that I take up in this book, is what I call *critical hermeneutics,* which is one approach to an anthropology of potentiality. An anthropology of potentiality differs in significant ways from anthropology as a field-work-based science focused on the descriptive analysis of the actual.[56] If the discipline has become one that primarily focuses upon the thick empirical description of that which is, then an anthropology of potentiality is perhaps best understood as a hermeneutics of the emerging contours of a not-yet.[57]

In this sense, an anthropology of potentiality is not very different from how some have recently described a newly developing philosophical anthropology. For example, the anthropologist Michael Jackson has described the contemporary challenge of philosophical anthropology in terms of resisting the intellectual reproduction of what already exists and instead, allow our thinking to point beyond itself.[58] Perhaps, in this sense, following Vincent Crapanzano,[59] we could consider philosophical anthropology as the analysis of imaginative horizons. Similarly, Jonathan Lear describes philosophical anthropology as an inquiry into possibilities.[60] In contrast to empirical studies of the actual that might ask questions such as "what historical trajectories or cultural order have brought such and such about and rendered it meaningful," Lear's philosophical anthropology asks, "What are the conditions of its being possible?" or "What would it be?" for such a possibility to have been the case. For philosophers such as Thomas Schwarz Wentzer and Rasmus Dyring—both of whom have collaborated closely with some anthropologists—these questions are best taken up by considering the responsivity and therefore the openness of the human condition.[61] Similar to these, an anthropology of potentiality seeks to disclose the conditions of the not-yet by hermeneutically considering enactments of an incipient otherwise in the here and now of everyday life. As a result, fieldwork and other forms of empirical research remain important to an anthropology of potentiality.[62] But as will become clear throughout this book, the importance of these methods is not that they provide the "data" for a quasipositivist "thick description" of ordinary life but rather that they offer an entrée into the hermeneutic processes already underway within various worlds, from which critical hermeneutic analysis can begin.

Such an approach can be understood as similar to other recent anthropological work that has sought to go beyond the actual in its consideration of the incipient not-yet. I am thinking here, for example, of the work of Robert Desjarlais on image in relation to perception, memory, and fantasy;[63] or Cheryl Mattingly on the possibilities invoked through moral striving and Jason Throop on the in-betweenness of moods;[64] or Ghassan Hage on alter-politics and Elizabeth Povinelli on the otherwise and more recently on geontologies;[65] or Anand Pandian on speculative anthropology and Stuart McLean on fictionalizing anthropology.[66] Each of them in their own way have acknowledged the necessity, as Joel Robbins has put it, "to be attentive to the way people orientate to and act in a world that outstrips the one most concretely present to them."[67] Such attentiveness, I would argue, is precisely what is needed for those who wish to respond to recent calls both within and outside anthropology for new and creative attempts to be made in the analysis of the worlds we engage as researchers and intellectuals, as well as the concepts and models we might offer for further engagement in these worlds.[68] A key component of this attentiveness and engagement, I would argue, and one that with few exceptions has not (yet) been embraced by anthropology,[69] is concept creation and reconceptualization. As will become clear, concept creation and reconceptualization are central to critical hermeneutics.

So, then, what is critical hermeneutics? An adequate answer to such a question, I suggest, can only be found through a close reading of this book, in combination with my previous, more theoretically focused book *Disappointment: Toward a Critical Hermeneutics of Worldbuilding*. But in short, a critical hermeneutics can be understood as at one and the same time an ungrounding and an opening. Thus, the critical ungrounding aspect can be considered in light of Foucault's description of critique as "seeing on what type of assumptions, or familiar notions, of established, unexamined ways of thinking the accepted practices are based ... uncovering that thought and trying to change it."[70] Put another way, the critical component of critical hermeneutics is an analytically self-aware process of deconstructing the a priori that limits being and becoming to a narrow range of possibilities, or what we might alternatively call the a priori that grounds normalization. The hermeneutic aspect of critical hermeneutics, on the other hand, is a process of opening possibilities by disclosing the potentialities that always already have been but that have been foreclosed by the limiting assumptions of the a priori. Here we see how potentiality and possibility are always linked and that hermeneutics is the process of clearing and activating, as it were, this linkage. For on the one hand, potentiality can be understood as the always-already-have-been-possibility that is not-yet. Hermeneutics, on the other hand, is that which ushers potential into the possible, whether we consider hermeneutics as a theoretical-analytic or as an ontological condition.

This is so because a fundamental assumption of hermeneutics is that existence—human and otherwise—is always ahead of itself and as such is constantly engaged in an existentially responsive process of becoming in the attempt to catch up with that which it never is,[71] a process that creates gaps of being that can never be filled.[72] As such, hermeneutics as a theoretical-analytic understands being as an onto-hermeneutic process of becoming. Seeking to tap into, as it were, this flow of onto-hermeneutic becoming, critical hermeneutics as a theoretical-analytic is best described as disclosing, tracing, and describing the contours of the not-yet. As such, critical hermeneutics as an anthropology of potentiality does not simply take fieldwork "data" as that complicated empirical stuff that must be made sense of. But rather it asks, for example: What potential for becoming is trying to be enacted? Or, what other possibilities of being are pointed toward? In doing so, critical hermeneutics not only discloses the normalizing limits of ordinary everyday existence but, more importantly, participates in the opening of new possibilities for thinking, saying, doing, or being. Critical hermeneutics, then, is a theoretical-analytic of the otherwise.[73]

In the rest of this book, therefore, I begin with a basic starting assumption of which I am (critically) aware and which can be articulated as the following: if the kind of political activity done by the anti–drug war movement attempts to allow potentialities to emerge as new possible modalities of being-with one another in new worlds, then an anthropology of potentiality can participate in this emergence, and critical hermeneutics would be one, but certainly not the only, way of doing so. This book, then, is best *not* read as an ethnographic thick description of a social movement but rather as a critical hermeneutics as an anthropology of potentiality.[74]

A BRIEF SUMMARY OF THE BOOK

What are these political agonists doing, and what can they teach us as intellectuals and as politically concerned beings? That is to ask: What potential are these agonists ushering into possibilities? Furthermore, what can I do as an intellectual to participate in their worldbuilding activity? Several years ago I was lucky enough to be welcomed by a number of anti–drug war agonists around the globe to observe and participate in their political and everyday activity. Many of them were already quite used to having researchers around and, frankly, had grown a bit wary of them. As I was told on more than one occasion, "we have researchers here all the time but they usually just tell us what we already know." From the beginning, however, I was clear that I have no interest in telling them or anyone else what they already know they are doing. Rather, my concern is what they are trying to do; what possibilities they are trying to bring into being.[75] That is, I told them that I am interested in the ways in which their political and everyday ethical activity opens new possibilities for being and acting together and, as such, may provide a model for a new form of politics and ethics in our time. This intrigued them. This, they wanted to hear. And this is what I hope to have done in what follows.

I could have written this book as yet another account of a rights-based social movement looking to make reformist legislative change. To write such a book, however, would be to break my collaborative promise of disclosively articulating the potentialities this political movement is trying to turn into possibilities. Thus, by critically hermeneutically *thinking with* the anti–drug war movement, in this book I disclose and articulate three interrelated but analytically separable interventions that I contend these agonists are already living out, even if some of them may not yet be aware of this fact and most certainly would not articulate as I do here.[76] What I hope becomes clear is that these three interventions are not only important for understanding what it is the anti–drug war movement is trying to do through political and ethical activity but, perhaps more importantly for our purposes, how they point us toward what both an anthropology of potentiality and a politics of worldbuilding could become.

Widely Diffused Complexity

The first intervention is in terms of addressing the widely diffused complex phenomena that constitute our contemporary condition (chapter 1 and throughout). Intellectually, this condition demands that we question just how it is that we can conceive of, articulate, and study widely diffused and nontotalizable complex phenomena that can potentially emerge at any time and at any point on the globe. Anthropologists are already excellent at analyzing the complicated intricacies of locality. But complexity is not complicated intricacy. Given enough time and information, complications can be figured out. Complexity, in contrast, can never be fully grasped since the nonlinearity of its dynamics resists totality, predictable causal relations, stability of being, and spatial and temporal contiguity and limitation.[77] All of this combined with the assemblic nature of complex phenomena makes them ripe with potential. In order to remain relevant in an increasingly complex global condition, anthropology would do well to begin to develop new methods and conceptual apparatuses for the study and analysis of these widely diffused complex phenomena, part of which would entail tracing the contours of their potential not-yet. Throughout this book I hope to have contributed to this in some small way by showing how such concepts as *situation, assemblic ethnography, hermeneutics, community of those without community,* and *attunement* can begin to help us conceptualize a contemporary condition constituted by widely diffused complex phenomena ripe with potential.

Comprehending, analyzing, and addressing globally diffused complexity is also necessary for any political activity today that expects to have actual transformative effects on our worlds.[78] The simplification of global complexity by the contemporary "folk politics" of the Left, through its emphasis on temporal, spatial, and conceptual immediacy, is in large part responsible for the Left's recent failure to bring about any large-scale transformation and even to imagine what a possible alternative future might be like.[79] As Srnicek and Williams argue,[80] the Left today not only needs a new political imaginary or vision but must accept, comprehend, and learn to address the complexity of our global condition for it to come about. It is my contention that this is precisely what the anti–drug war movement has done, and this, at least in part, accounts for the successes those involved have so far realized in changing the worlds in which they are attempting to dwell. Recognizing and politically addressing this widely diffused complexity, then, is one essential achievement of the anti–drug war movement that the political Left in general could learn from.

Concept Creation and Reconceptualization

The second intervention I seek to make concerns the rethinking of concepts, most particularly those ethical concepts that have political implications. Over the course of the last decade or so, anthropology has gone through a so-called ethical turn, by which anthropologists have increasingly and explicitly taken up ethics and morality as objects of research and theorization.[81] Unfortunately, however, much of this work has done very little to actually rethink morality, ethics, and their concepts. Instead, for the most part, anthropologists of moralities and ethics have tended, for lack of a better way of putting it, to socialize already well-established traditional Western moral and ethical concepts. As I have argued elsewhere,[82] the ordinary ethics approach is perhaps the most obvious example of this, but no matter where one looks these days, it is not very difficult to find an anthropologist writing about such things as the good, the right, or concerns with dignity. It is as if we already know what morality and ethics are, what motivations and aims are related to them, and more or less how these are done, so the task of the anthropologist has primarily become to show how all of this plays out in localized social relationships. If an anthropologist writing about divination, for example, interpreted this phenomenon utilizing concepts from the Catholic catechism or biomedical therapeutics, most would no doubt simply find this to be bad scholarship, if not inappropriate. Yet for some reason, it has become perfectly acceptable, for example, to write about our informants in terms of doing "what they think right or good" and "act[ing] largely from a sense of their own dignity."[83] This general acceptance I find interesting, and we might consider its relationship to a broader moralism that seems to have become prevalent within the discipline, most obviously so with an overwhelming concern with suffering while simultaneously turning a blind eye to the foundations of this concern within political liberalism.[84]

In contrast, much of my previous work has sought to rethink morality, ethics, and their concepts by recursively engaging my ethnographic work with both moral philosophy and post-Heideggerian continental philosophy so as to reconceive moral and ethical motivations, processes, and aims in terms of relationalities and thus to move beyond thinking and being in terms of the qualified behavior of good and evil individuals.[85] In this book I continue this project through an explicit reconceptualization of being-with in a community of whoever arrives (chapter 3), freedom as the openness of letting-be (chapter 4), and care as attunement and hospitality (chapter 5) and do so by showing that these new ways of being-in-the-world emerge through the political activity of the anti–drug war movement.

As I argue throughout, transformative political activity is onto-ethical activity, and this becomes clear in the ways in which through explicit political activity new worlds emerge through the very process of this acting. Therefore, a key part of the argument I will make is that in a global condition of war as governance that is primarily fought on the two fronts of normalization and dehumanization, a central aspect of the counterattack is the invention and enactment of new ethical ways of being-with that can provide the onto-ethical grounds for actually transforming worlds, and not only prefiguratively. My contribution to this counterattack is the intellectual articulation of this reconceptualization of the onto-ethical grounding of these new worlds.

Otherwise

The third intervention I will make concerns the question of the otherwise. A good deal of what I will show throughout this book is the slow emergence of an otherwise. In this global condition of war as governance, thinking through and ethnographically showing how an otherwise emerges through sustained and organized political activity with a vision are crucial tasks both intellectually and politically. Since it has become abundantly clear that the horizontalism of the contemporary Left is incapable of making any actual and lasting political impact beyond personal empowerment, it is now a political and existential imperative to begin to imagine and do political activity that eschews the spectacular for the nitty-gritty of the long-term struggle of worldbuilding. The difficulties arise, however, when we realize that the otherwise of new worlds is not simply "measured" by change or transformation. As Giorgio Agamben puts it, the otherwise is not merely the fact that the dog outside has stopped barking or, in terms closer to this book,[86] that populations are no longer incarcerated at extraordinary rates. Indeed, oftentimes the otherwise may not at first even be empirically observable. It is, again as Agamben puts it, in the "tiny displacements" of the sense and limits of things that the otherwise begins to emerge.[87] This is why political activity must always be sustained over the long term. For "tiny displacements" do not occur and stick through spectacle or consensus but rather only through the sustained and grueling excavation of possibilities out of the seemingly impossible. This is the kind of onto-ethical-political activity I will consider and show throughout this book.

And here we return to the anthropology of potentiality. In a contemporary intellectual context in which academics are increasingly asking how they can contribute to the becoming of an otherwise, this book's response is that our best bet is to do what intellectuals have traditionally always done: think, imagine, creatively experiment, and articulate the emergence of possibilities along with the worlds we find ourselves in. The great privilege of being an anthropologist is that we, more than most other academics, begin from worlds that we have been invited into. This hospitality, I suggest, is more than an invitation to record the happenings of everyday life or to make sense of their complicated intricacies. Rather, perhaps it is time to begin to understand these as invitations to enter the *thresholds* of possibilities within these worlds. In doing so, we may be able to understand these worlds better or perhaps even make a political contribution to the otherwise of those worlds. But ultimately and more importantly, we might be able to make a contribution to the ongoing openness of existence as such. This book is an attempt to do just this.

CHAPTER I

The Drug War as Widely Diffused Complexity

Recent decades have seen an increasing complexity in the dynamics that impinge upon politics.

—Nick Srnicek and Alex Williams

What do certain military missions in Afghanistan, domestic spying in the United States, therapeutic interventions in Russia and Denmark, torture and rape in an Indonesian police station, and stop-and-frisk policing in New York City all have in common? The answer is that they are just a few of the local situated manifestations of the widely diffused phenomenon named the *drug war*. Having roots in the nineteenth century and gradually emerging throughout the twentieth, the drug war was officially "declared" in 1971 by Richard Nixon and only became a full-blown global war in the 1980s, when it became militarized and intertwined with the Cold War through initiatives of the Reagan and then Bush administrations. Today what is named the *drug war* is responsible for hundreds of thousands of deaths a year globally and the social and political "death" or exclusion of many more people.[1] But the drug war has potential effects that go well beyond these numbers. Whether by means of military interventions, policing and incarceration strategies, international and national surveillance, and the overblown budgets to pay for them or by means of biopolitical therapeutics, national and international legislation, and the normalization of labor regimes and discipline, all of which and more constitute aspects of the drug war, this is a war that potentially affects every human on the planet.[2]

How can the drug war have such widespread effects, and how do we conceptualize it? In this chapter and throughout this book, I hope to begin to offer an answer to this question. I will argue that the drug war should *not* be conceived as something like a singular policy issue or a totalized strategy, and neither should it be limited, as it often is in public discourse, to its localized manifestation in parts of Colombia, Mexico, or the inner cities of the United States. Rather, the drug war is best conceived as a nontotalizable and widely diffused complex phenomenon that manifests temporarily and locally as a situation. If the primary task of this book is to do a critical hermeneutics of the contemporary condition of war and the political possibilities the anti–drug war movement enact by addressing this condition, then a secondary, though still considerable, task is to show that the concept of a situation as a widely diffused phenomenon significantly adds to the anthropological conceptual apparatus. This is so because the concept of situation allows us to consider that which is widely diffused across different global scales as a nontotalizable assemblage yet in its occasional and temporary local manifestation allows us to understand how persons and objects that are geographically, socioeconomically, and "culturally" distributed get caught up in the shared conditions that emerge from a situation. Becoming "caught up" in the shared conditions of a situation, in turn, significantly affects the possible ways of being-in-the-world of those persons and objects that "get caught up." The concept of situation, then, allows us analytically to recognize that in the current global configuration, complexity is at least as knotted nonlocally as it is locally, and thus, increasingly—so I contend—local complexity emerges within the shared conditions set by this diffused complexity.

Although they do not describe it quite like this, this is how those in the anti–drug war movement that I have been doing assemblic ethnography with view the drug war and their political activity. Anti–drug war politics is a politics of agonistic and creative experimentation with the otherwise, and as such it has had to define well what it is against and what it intends to transgress.[3] Unlike many post-1968 political movements that self-define as addressing issues or identities that tend to be conceived as totalized, closed, and located,[4] anti–drug war politics has defined its political agonist as a globally diffused phenomenon that locally manifests differentially and temporarily. Although there are some similarities between this and what is now known as intersectionality— most particularly in terms of recognizing the intertwining of various "factors" in the constitution of a phenomenon—intersectionality, nevertheless, assumes the existence of the same preconceived and totalized issues and identities—for example, class, race, and gender—as do other post-1968 approaches, even if these are now understood as "work[ing] together and influenc[ing] each other."[5] In contrast, the concept of a situation as the local and temporary manifestation of a widely diffused, complex phenomenon does not assume such preconceived and totalized issues and identities but rather articulates that these are themselves complex, emergent, and open phenomena that nevertheless provide the conditions for the being-in-the-world of those and that which have become caught up within them.

In this chapter and throughout this book, then, I would like to explore how what I have learned from the anti–drug war movement in terms of what those within it see themselves addressing, how they address it, and how they organize may help anthropologists, political theorists, and political agonists rethink their own objects of study. In so doing, I hope to go beyond a notion of globalization and the tracing of global connections across a closed and totalized globe, as Anna Tsing's notion of friction could be read.[6] Instead, I seek to explore how situations as widely diffused assembled phenomena that are differentially distributed participate in the ontological conditioning of our contemporary worlds and yet as assemblages always hold the potential to become otherwise.[7] The drug war is one such phenomenon.

ASSEMBLIC ETHNOGRAPHY

The study of widely diffused assembled phenomena requires an ethnographic method and style of writing that I call *assemblic ethnography*. Assemblic ethnography as a method shares some similarities with multisited ethnography as George Marcus originally and schematically articulated it.[8] But in practice and true to its name, most multisited research has tended to focus on a few, oftentimes prechosen, sites and the connections between them. In contrast, assemblic ethnography is a method of chasing and tracing a complex phenomenon through its continual process of assembling across different global scales and its temporally differential localization as situations in diverse places. Just as one never knows if, when, and where she or he will get caught up in a situation, so too the anthropologist doing assemblic ethnography can never know beforehand when and where the research will lead. For example, in 2006 I began research at an Orthodox-run rehabilitation program in Russia,[9] during which I became attuned to the political struggle there for harm-reduction services. This led me to the central role of user unions in this struggle, which had been initially funded by the Open Society Foundation based in New York. While in New York researching this initiative, I became attuned to Voices of Community Activists and Leaders (VOCAL-NY),[10] a local political organization dedicated to fighting the drug war and its pernicious consequences, and how they politically address their drug war situation, which, I came to learn, was partly informed by the successes in Vancouver, where I then went before going on to Copenhagen, Denpasar, and elsewhere.

Unlike the traditional ethnographer, then, the assemblic ethnographer realizes that research focused on any one site—and in practice, most multisited research as well—results in a *decomplexification* of the situation under study. This is so because the assemblic ethnographer recognizes that complexity is knotted nonlocally at least as much as it is locally. Perhaps most significantly, to do an assemblic ethnography is to recognize that this knotted complexity is the consequence of the temporary emergence of nontotalized assemblages, and thus a primary characteristic of this method is *tracing the various assemblic relations* that constitute the assemblage. Thus, my research did not simply move from one site to the next but rather *moved along diverse assemblic relations* of the drug war. For example, when the aspects of carceral political economics and state-based surveillance revealed themselves in New York, I traced those assemblic relations and their differential distribution to Denpasar and back again to Russia; when the aspect of biopolitical therapeutics revealed itself, I traced it from Russia to New York to Vancouver to Copenhagen. In contrast to a project with one or several fieldwork sites, then, this research unfolded along assemblic relations as they became differentially distributed. Thus, in order to consider anthropologically the contemporary condition, it is not enough to note the various frictions that constitute local intricacies;[11] we must ourselves travel along the assemblic relations that constitute the nonlocal complexity that sets the shared conditions for ways of being in diverse locations across the globe.

Assemblic ethnographic writing seeks to mirror this method in that it describes horizontal thickness, as it were, just as much as vertical thickness. In other words, assemblic ethnographic writing gives as much attention to tracing the widely diffused complexity of a situation across its various assemblic relations as it does to localized complexity. This book is an attempt at such assemblic ethnographic writing. For through my analysis of the ways in which the anti–drug war movement fights the drug war through political experimentations for being-together otherwise, I will also analytically describe the widely diffused complexity of the drug war that becomes differentially distributed across the globe and that in large part constitutes the shared conditions of those who get caught up within it.[12] Primarily, I will do this through a number of localized drug war manifestations where this widely diffused complexity has become particularly knotted and the response of the anti–drug war movement has been particularly intense; that is, in New York City, Vancouver, and Copenhagen.

But because assemblic ethnography traces assemblic relations and does not focus on sites, I will also occasionally follow these relations so as to better understand just how truly complex this nontotalizable assemblage has become. Because the anti–drug war movement, in a sense, has already been doing assemblic analysis of that against which it fights, this book will primarily follow those involved in their endeavors to win this now forty-plus-year-old "war on people" so as to disclose some of the contours and limits of the complexity named the *drug war* and how it affects the being-in-the-world of those who have become caught up in its situated manifestations. In the rest of this chapter, then, I will begin by disclosing, in very broad strokes, some of the assemblic relations that constitute the drug war. In the first section, I try to show the widely diffused complexity of the drug war by briefly tracing some of its various assemblic relations as they become manifest as situations in diverse parts of the globe. After a brief interlude in which I attempt to clarify the concept of situation, I turn to Vancouver in the final section for a closer analysis of one localized and rather intense manifestation of the drug war situation and the political response to it. By briefly illustrating how anti–drug war agonists in Vancouver started doing a situation-based politics of worldbuilding and how this kind of political activity has influenced the global anti–drug war movement, I hope to provide a hermeneutic entrée into the rest of the book so the reader can better understand how the political and ethical experimentations of the anti–drug war movement unfold within the interstices of variously localized drug war situations.

WIDELY DIFFUSED COMPLEXITY AND THE SHARED CONDITIONS OF THE DRUG WAR

In October 2013, while doing research with anti–drug war agonists in the Downtown Eastside of Vancouver, I attended a public anti–drug war event on the Movimiento por la Paz con Justicia y Dignidad (Movement for Peace with Justice and Dignity).[13] The Mexican poet Javier Sicilia, who was the guest of honor at this Vancouver event, organized the Movimiento as a response to the death of his son by drug war violence, and it now consists of thousands of family members of persons similarly killed or disappeared in the violence of the drug war situation in Mexico. This is a situation in Mexico that has taken its current form in large part by means of American funds, equipment, support, and training to carry out a war in and on the border of Mexico. This is a war in which over one hundred thousand people have been killed since 2006,[14] many of whom, if not the majority, were not drug users, traffickers, cartel members, or police. Rather, most of these drug war dead were simply "average" people who happened to get caught up in this drug war situation.[15]

The Movimiento today is most known for the traveling protests it organized called the Caravan for Peace. In 2012 the Caravan traveled throughout Mexico and the United States disclosing the violence of the drug war through stories and performances they enacted in public protest of the unnecessary deaths brought on by the drug war. Through the stories told and performances given by the Caravan, the public image of the drug war as a war against dangerous cartels that seek to harm "our children" is deconstructed, and instead a "war on people" is disclosed as an assemblage partly constituted by militarism, border security, and inequality. The hope of such deconstructive political activity is that it can dislodge hegemonic views and practices and thus provide a clearing from which political possibilities for conceiving, doing, and becoming otherwise emerge.

While this localization of the drug war situation in Mexico, like that of the localization in Colombia, tends to dominate public discourse, such localizations far from exhaust this widely diffused and differentially distributed phenomenon. Consider, for example, the short poem read at the opening of this Vancouver event by Bud Osborn,[16] the Vancouver-area user-agonist-poet and one of the founding members of that city's user union. I choose to begin with Bud's poem, which is called "Ironic" and depicts an experience he had while hitchhiking in the United States, because it offers a hermeneutic entrée into the drug war-situated assemblage and discloses the complex, widely diffused nature of this phenomenon. Much like the deconstructive political activity of the Caravan for Peace, so too does Bud's poem disclose a complexity that goes well beyond a closed issue defined by policy and legislation and that is located in some fixed place like "isolated drug wars" in Mexico and Colombia or "isolated drug addicts" in American inner cities. Rather, this poem reveals that the drug war is a complex assembled phenomenon that manifests situationally and is constituted by aspects of other assemblages such as global militarism, state-based surveillance and control, border security, carceral political economics, biopolitical therapeutics, and international and national inequalities.

Through this disclosure we also see how the concept of situation opens analytic possibilities that allow us to move between located manifestations and the widely diffused phenomena that provide the conditions for this emergence. In other words, a critical hermeneutic reading of Bud's poem discloses how the situation he found himself in along a California highway can only be understood as one local manifestation of a widely diffused assemblage that potentially can be distributed differentially and localized anywhere. Beginning from the entrée Bud's poem provides, then, in the rest of this section, I trace multiple aspects of the drug war as revealed in the poem and do so through various ethnographic knots that have emerged from my ongoing assemblic ethnography. What I hope becomes clear is that the local emergences that Bud's poem and the ethnographic knots depict—or what some might call the *drug war reterritorialization*—can never be preknown in terms of their location, form, affect, or temporality; nevertheless, they reveal a range of possibilities provided by a globally diffused, shared condition that becomes differentially distributed. I begin by reproducing the transcript of his reading in full:

Hitchhiking from Los Angeles to San Francisco, I stand in front of a highway sign. "No hitchhiking beyond this point." So I am legal, and the traffic is heavy. Two police cars pull in front of me. A short cop wears a big grin. The other cop is tall and grim. I assume they just wanna check my identification, but the first thing the short cop says is: "from the other side of the road I didn't know whether to come over here and jump you or rape you." I freeze, silent and wary. "Take everything out of your pockets." I put some change and cigarettes on the hood of his car. I reach to pull a book out of an inside coat pocket. Both cops pull their guns and aim them at me. The tall police says, "what's this?" as though he has never seen a book before. The short glowing cop tells me, "we can take you out in the desert and shoot you and no one would ever know." I remain speechless, as if any word I speak has very thin ice across it. They sort through a small traveling bag I have with me, and the short cop says, "what if I find some drugs?" I tell 'em, "I don't have any." The short cop replies, "but what if I find some?" "Well" I say, "there isn't any." "Yeah", the cop presses on, "but what if I find some?" I finally get the message. The cop's liable to magically materialize drugs where none previously existed. The tall cop pulls a notebook out of the bag, they read a couple of pages of poems and laugh out loud, and one of them snaps the binding and pages flutter and float and are blown away by onrushing traffic. Next they each examine my cigarettes and break them into pieces. The short cop says, "get in the car. We're going to have to strip you bare-ass naked." I'm shoved into the front seat between the two cops. The beaming big-bellied cop grabs my long hair around his fist, slams my head against the steering wheel. The other cop hauls my pants down to my ankles. He forces a slender metal flashlight up my ass. It hurts. The fat cop says, "nothing huh?" The other one shakes his head. He gets out of the car. The engine starts. The cop tells me "to never come back to [name of place inaudible] and get that shit off the hood of my car or I'm gonna take it with me." I leap from the police car, grab my pants with one hand; sweep my wreckage off the hood with my other hand. The squad cars roar away, spitting gravel into my face. A steady stream of staring faces passes me. I finally fasten my pants and cover my genitals. I gather what I can from the ground. I look up at the blank blue sky. The longing shredded, threatened with execution, raped, reduced to nothingness. The drug war.[17]

Reduced to nothingness, indeed. But, in fact, Bud and the many drug users I have met and come to know are already reduced to nothingness prior to such encounters. As I have been told in the various places my assemblic ethnography of the drug war has taken me and as I will explore in more detail in the next chapter, drug users all around the globe are considered, for example, to be "rubbish," "waste," and "shit." For within the conditions of the drug war, drug users do not count as a recognizable part of whatever it is one feels a part of— society, culture, nation, family, or whatever. This is normally what drug user agonists and social scientists call *stigma*. But this is more than stigma. It is exactly what Bud calls it: a reduction to nothingness. It is this nothingness, this nonbeing, that provides the possibility not only for the police violence Bud experiences but also for the lack of care from those who stare at Bud as they pass him standing pantsless on the side of the highway.

As Giorgio Agamben recognizes with his concept of bare life, this nothingness has affect as the double move of inclusive exclusion.[18] For it is as the nothingness in the midst of something—the drug user on a busy highway, the drug user in a city park, or as I've heard about and witnessed many times, the drug user in a hospital—that this nothingness has affect in the world. Indeed, it is partially by means of such nothingness that worlds are constituted. In this sense, the drug war situations that render drug users nothing in the midst of everything partially constitute the various worlds we ourselves inhabit. Worlds, that is, that are partially conditioned by the widely diffused phenomenon of the drug war with its differentially distributed situated affects.

Police officers raping and torturing persons on the sides of American highways may be a relatively rare local manifestation of the drug war (although not nearly as rare as the reader might think).[19] But as I have been told several times while doing research with user agonists in Denpasar, Indonesia, it is a fairly frequent occurrence in Indonesian police stations.[20] The vast majority of these occurrences never become public, but such stories circulate widely among drug users, who all seem to have had such experiences or know someone who has. One such occurrence that did become public through media exposure was that undergone by Merry Christina, who was raped by police officers for five days in a Jakarta police station, as her boyfriend was in the next room being tortured.[21] After having been arrested while shooting heroin in a South Jakarta slum, Merry was given the choice to either be charged for heroin possession and use—a charge that could have resulted in a fifteen-year prison term for each of them—or to "sexually service" the police officers and be released without charge and with their drugs. It is common knowledge among drug users in Indonesia that this "choice" is regularly offered to women users and that men and women alike can expect a variety of tortures from beatings, to cigarette burns, to electrocution. Often the only hope of escaping this rape and torture is through bribery payments in an amount that is generally well beyond what might be readily available to most drug users. These police tactics of the rape, torture, and extortion of drug users have become common practice around the globe and constitute a significant aspect of the widely distributed conditions for the being-in-the-world of drug users everywhere.[22]

Another common threat made by Indonesian police meant to extort a bribe for users is that they will charge a drug user with trafficking if they do not pay. Indonesia today is one of the few countries left in the world where drug traffickers are put to death, and visitors are warned of this fact on their visas, where it can be read that the "death penalty for drug traffickers" can be instituted "under Indonesian law." Indeed, just a few weeks prior to this writing, Indonesia put six persons to death,[23] five of whom were foreign nationals. Widespread international and national pleas by anti–drug war agonists and their allies to have these sentences commuted fell on deaf ears as the Indonesian government continues to implement what it calls "shock therapy" in its attempt to deter drug trafficking. Indeed, openly practiced extreme violence has been a central aspect of the drug war waged in Indonesia for some time. Thus, for example, Joey, one of the founders of a Denpasar syringe exchange and a member of the city's user union, told me that once when they were protesting against the illegality of harm-reduction practices and the kinds of violence the police often use to enforce these restrictions, riot police attacked their peaceful demonstration and broke it up with batons and tear gas. As a result of this police attack, Joey spent over a month in the hospital with a shattered skull. Such brutality toward drug users thus is not uncommon in Indonesia and occurs not only in the streets but also in the back rooms of police stations and in front of the world as the government continues its shock therapy of executions.

Recently, the Indonesian government has attempted to "soften" its stance on drug users by offering them the possibility of registering as drug users. This form of self-disclosure, or self-imposed surveillance, is considered a lenient approach because if (or does the registration turn this *if* into a *when?*) the registered user is someday arrested for use/possession, then he or she will be sent to rehabilitation instead of prison. No doubt most users would prefer rehabilitation over prison, but the very idea of rehabilitation is increasingly recognized by the anti–drug war movement as questionable at best and at worst potentially life-threatening. By tracing the assemblic relations of biopolitical therapeutics to, for example, Russia and then Denmark, we can consider these potentially life-threatening effects of abstinence-based rehabilitation.

Consider, for example, Andrei, who was found dead by his mother in their Saint Petersburg apartment. His mouth full of his own vomit, Andrei had overdosed on heroin soon after returning home from an abstinence-based rehabilitation center run by the Russian Orthodox Church.[24] As they say, "heroin can wait," and when Andrei could no longer avoid the lingering patience of heroin, he experienced an unfortunately fairly common effect of reacquaintance with the drug, an overdose. It is well known that a significant number of heroin overdoses occur when those attempting abstinence-based rehabilitation begin to use again. This startling fact is the result of the oftentimes fatal combination of such phenomena as the loss of tolerance, the enthusiasm to use again, the lack of knowledge of the potency of the specific heroin bought this time—a lack that can at least be mitigated by maintaining a relationship, which is often broken when abstinence rehabilitation is attempted, with a regular dealer—and likely solitary use because of the isolating combination of shame, guilt, and a possible loss of former using networks. This correlative fact of overdose after attempts at abstinence, combined with the overwhelming failure of abstinence-based rehabilitation programs (the failure rate of twelve-step programs is 90–95 percent),[25] suggests that the biopolitical-therapeutic aspect is one of the most fatally dangerous aspects of the drug war.[26]

Lone, a user agonist in Copenhagen, has been trying to communicate this danger to the Danish government and public for several years. In Denmark, Narcotics Anonymous and other such abstinence-based programs comprise over 90 percent of the available drug rehabilitation/ therapy programs. And just as Andrei was limited in his options for rehabilitation to a church-run abstinence program because very few other options exist in Russia, so too in Copenhagen Lone's husband, Nils, had no other option but an abstinence-based program when he decided to try to stop his regular heroin use. Although he did not feel that he needed to completely stop his drug use, Nils did know that to be the kind of husband and father he wanted to be he needed to significantly limit his use. But unfortunately, the very concept of a recreational use–based rehab program does not exist, and therefore when Nils wanted some help with his heroin use, he had to go all in, as it were. Abstinence or nothing, and in this case, as with Andrei and so many more, it turned out to be abstinence and death. Just like Andrei, Nils could not—in part because he actually never wanted to—remain abstinent. And when he used again—having bought some heroin from a dealer he did not know—he happened to inject an unusually potent fix and died. By all accounts Nils was a good husband and father and wanted to become a better one. But in the limitations of drug war situations, within which abstinence is the only "legitimate" therapeutic alternative to the abjection of drug use, Nils had his possibilities limited—not entirely but significantly—to becoming just another casualty of the drug war.

One thing that does not have its possibilities for becoming limited by the conditions of the drug war is heroin. Drug war propaganda creates the imaginary that drugs are dangerous substances in and of themselves. Heroin, for instance, is represented as a singular substance that has naturally negative effects because of its self-same attributes. Nothing could be further from the truth.[27] Drug war situations provide the ontological conditions for the very being of heroin, and this being, in fact, is always becoming otherwise. Heroin in and of itself—a thing that is more or less impossible to find in the worlds of most users today—is not the cause of most of the substance-related harm that users experience, including that of overdose. Rather, most of this harm only exists because of the unknown and unknowable substance heroin has become that the user happens to be able to purchase. As the substance that we call *heroin* travels through the unregulated, informal, and underground drug market—from source, to trafficker, to dealer, to the next dealer, to the user—heroin becomes another substance as each person along this underground commodity chain attempts to stretch his or her inventory by cutting it with yet more contaminants. Once the user finally purchases the "heroin," she has no idea what the purity of the substance is or what contaminants have been used in the cutting process. In other words, she actually has no idea what kind of entity she is about to inject. Only if the user has a good and long-lasting relationship with a dealer might she know what *her* dealer cut the substance with. But she will not know what it had been cut with prior to this dealer. It is precisely this uncertainty—nay, this impossibility of knowing precisely what substance, and its potency, that one is injecting—that oftentimes results in overdose.

Just as drug war situations affect the being of heroin, so too they affect the being of other objects. Syringes become deadly objects capable of delivering infectious diseases. They also become objects that signify to police officers that the person carrying the object may also be carrying heroin. Cigarette butts lying on sidewalks become sources of cotton that can act as filters as one prepares the heroin for injection. The dirt that may have been on that cigarette butt and now gets mixed with the substance just injected into one's arm will likely contribute to the abscess that will appear there. A building where they give out syringes, cotton, sterile water, and other such *works* to help users avoid the open-ended and dangerous possibilities of the becoming of these found elsewhere has itself now become an object of interest for police. Police will now regularly watch this building, take note of who enters and leaves, and use this as an excuse to stop, question, and frisk those who do so. In the situations of the drug war, then, the being of all of these objects and more has become something entirely different than what it is in other situations. Situations, then, are also constituted by aspects of diverse nonhuman objects and affect and alter the being of those objects in turn.

The way in which the drug war situation turns certain buildings, streets, parks, and neighborhoods into objects of surveillance returns us along the assemblic relation of state-based surveillance and control back to Bud's poem. After having traveled some way along the various assemblic relations disclosed in the poem, we can perhaps now come to see that although spectacularly disturbing, rape, torture, and other forms of police violence may not be the most insidious situated manifestation of the drug war revealed in Bud's poem. For the intertwining of the carceral political-economic and the surveillance and control aspects of the drug war are most clearly disclosed in the very fact that the police stopped Bud in the first place. This is a variant of what has come to be called *stop-and-frisk*. Stop-and-frisk essentially means that police officers with so-called reasonable suspicion can stop any individual to question and frisk. This tactic, which initially aimed to get weapons off the streets, has morphed into a means of controlling and watching populations. As Terrance, a fifty-year-old African American man from the Bronx, a former crack user who has been incarcerated twice, and now a leader of VOCAL-NY, once told me: stop-and-frisk tactics make him feel as if "I'm trespassing in my own neighborhood." He continued with a description of his experience with stop-and-frisk:

> If I'm coming out of my building, like I been many times, and stopped and frisked because I'm a person of color and I don't have my sneakers tied or I'm wearing, you know, or I have clothes on that are related to gangsters or whatever, which are the clothings that a lot of people in the neighborhood wear, you know, and I'm going to work and I'm still being stopped. And I got my bag and everything, my ID is out, you know, come on. You're not giving me no freedom to walk in my own neighborhood, but if I was in another neighborhood, another color, you wouldn't be stopping me. So why am I, at this point right here, being profiled?

Terrance's question is one increasingly asked by African American and Latino American persons who are systematically watched by this and similar forms of surveillance.[28] In 2012, for example, over five hundred thousand individuals were stopped and frisked in New York City alone, 87 percent of whom were either African American or Latino American. Perhaps most disturbing about this form of surveillance is that 89 percent of these stops turned up nothing. Yet the highest number of arrests (over five thousand) were for possessing personal-use quantities of marijuana, which under New York City law is not an offense unless shown in public, which occurs when a police officer asks you to empty your pockets. Overwhelmingly, those stopped, frisked, and arrested are young African American and Latino men, and this tactic is predominantly carried out in the neighborhoods where these men live.[29] The result, as illustrated by Terrance, is that this very real possibility of stop-and-frisk that many African Americans and Latino Americans must live with every day in New York and elsewhere has left many feeling that their neighborhoods, their streets, and even their own front stoops are no longer places where they can dwell.[30]

Stop-and-frisk is likely the most "successful" police tactic in the war on drugs. This is particularly so in New York City, although similar tactics are used in other cities in North America, Great Britain, Russia, and likely elsewhere. As we saw with Bud, this police tactic is also used on a lonesome California highway. It is not only responsible for a significant amount of the surveillance the drug war allows to be placed on neighborhoods and individuals—it also contributes to the vast increase of incarceration rates in the United States and other countries, particularly for those carrying small, personal-use amounts of marijuana. Indeed, the policing and surveillance techniques of the drug war are largely responsible for the mass incarceration of nonviolent and low-level drug users around the globe, as the global prison population has skyrocketed in the last three decades to over ten million persons.[31] Thus, for example, when Thailand renewed its war on drugs with vigor in 2003, in addition to the over two thousand extrajudicial killings done by the police and military, over seventy thousand people were also rounded up and detained without due process.[32] Although the government claims that these were all drug dealers, reports by various nongovernmental organizations and anti–drug war organizations show that most of them were simply drug users. Furthermore, prison population numbers alone do not accurately depict the total number of drug users who are incarcerated, as millions more around the globe are held against their will in the prison-like conditions of various rehabilitation and detention centers. Thus, for example, it is estimated that up to a half million people are held in drug detention centers in China, where they are systematically exposed to "beatings, lack of medical treatment, and rape," as well as forced labor up to sixteen hours per day, oftentimes in centers that have labor contracts with private companies.[33] Similar conditions can be found in such centers across Russia.[34]

But no country incarcerates drug users, and its population in general, like the United States, which now has the highest level of incarceration on the planet and, for that matter, the highest level in modern history approached, but not surpassed, only by the Soviet gulag system under Stalin.[35] The drug war and its often racialized tactics have fed this mass incarceration such that, for example, in 2012, 1.55 million people were arrested on nonviolent drug charges, the vast majority of whom were African American or Hispanic.[36] Indeed, those who profit from this carceral political economics recognize the centrality of current drug policy and laws to their corporate success. Thus, for example, in a 2010 report to the United States Securities and Exchange Commission, the country's "largest owner and operator of privatized correctional and detention facilities" highlighted changes to current drug law as one of the primary risks to its growth and profit.[37] This recognition and concern is not surprising since in the last thirty years (or, as we will see shortly, since the militarization and law enforcement aspects of the drug war have become fully knotted) the prison population in the United States has increased by 500 percent, and stop-and-frisk and other forms of drug war surveillance have been key factors in these skyrocketing numbers. Thus, for example, in 1980, a total of 41,000 drug offenders were in all state and federal prisons and local jails, while in 2011 this total stood at 501,500.[38]

If we follow the assemblic relations of the drug war from these situated manifestations of stop-and-frisk through the hyperaggressive act depicted by Bud of "both cops pull[ing] their guns and aim[ing] them at me," we are able to disclose how such policing that takes the form of intense violence, intrusive surveillance, and excessive incarceration are in fact intertwined with another aspect of this assemblage. That is, the global militarism aspect. The link between these localized police tactics and global militarism is the militarization of the police. Although police militarization had already slowly started to occur in the 1960s in response to increased civil unrest and urban rioting, it finally emerged as the phenomenon it is today in the 1980s as just one part of what at the time was called a "total war" against drugs. From the 1981 Congressional Military Cooperation with Law Enforcement Act; to the 1986 National Security Decision Directive 221 that not only instructed the U.S. military to further assist law enforcement agencies but also mandated that it train and help foreign militaries carry out antidrug operations;[39] to the 1988 bill authorizing the National Guard to assist local police in drug interdictions; to the 1989 policy that established regional task forces within the Pentagon to work closely with local police in antidrug efforts; to "the 1033 program" of the National Defense Authorization Security Act of 1997, which established the Law Enforcement Support Program to more easily transfer military equipment to local police—all of this resulted in the close cooperation between the military and the police, including the training of the latter by the former, and thus the militarization of police equipment and tactics.[40] As was recently revealed by the events in Ferguson, Missouri, American local police are now armed with machine guns, tanks, and military-style surveillance equipment and trained in military-style siege, combat, and "interrogation" tactics, enabling them to control and occupy entire neighborhoods and regions in military fashion. Indeed, those weapons manufacturers who sell to both the military and local police recognize the intertwining of global militarism and militarized policing within the drug war assemblage. Thus, for example, the German defense manufacturing company Heckler and Koch advertises the MP5 semiautomatic weapon with: "From the Gulf War to the Drug War—Battle Proven."[41]

This militarization of the police as one aspect of the larger militarization of the drug war has its origins in the 1980s, despite the overwhelming media claim that this is an offshoot of the war on terror. As Radley Balko has convincingly shown, to a great extent the war on terror—like the hostage and rioting scenarios before it—has largely been used as a convenient excuse for the militarization of the police.[42] For the overwhelming majority of the actual use of militarized police since the 1970s and right up to the writing of this book have been in drug war situations, such that most of the over one hundred SWAT raids that occur daily in the United States are drug related. And, for example, of the fifty thousand to sixty thousand times in 2005 that SWAT teams "violently smash[ed] into private homes,"[43] oftentimes in the middle of the night with machine guns blasting, they were not for the purpose of taking down cartels or breaking up a trafficking ring but rather "to enforce laws against consensual crimes," such as the personal use of some drug.[44] To the extent, however, that police militarization has increased in response to the war on terror, this is best understood as a tighter intertwining knot of the surveillance and control, carceral political-economic, and global militarism aspects of the drug war assemblage. How this intertwining became knotted can be seen in the development of the latter aspect of the drug war and particularly in the increasing link between counternarcotics and counterterrorism.

The global militarism aspect of the drug war has been significant from the war's declaration by Nixon in 1971. For not only did this declaration result in the increased funding for domestic law enforcement training and cooperation between enforcement agencies and the creation of new state and federal legislation in support of this law enforcement, but Nixon also used military and economic aid to force countries "to reduce the manufacture and trafficking of narcotics within their borders."[45] Beginning from this decisive moment, the drug war assemblage increasingly became—and particularly so during the Reagan and Bush years—partially constituted by an intertwining of national and international legislation, economic aid and development, and military aid and eventually intervention, all of which rested on the international inequalities that characterized Cold War politics.[46]

As the 1980s came to an end, it became increasingly difficult to discern precisely the distinction between drug war and Cold War military operations. This was particularly so throughout Latin America and the Caribbean as the U.S. military became fully entangled with counternarcotics operations. Senator Bob Dole was just one of many at the time to call for a "total war" against drugs and asserted that it was "time to bring the full force [of] military and intelligence communities into this war."[47] It was only a matter of time before the George H. W. Bush administration fully committed the U.S. military to the drug war, which was clearly demonstrated in the 1989 invasion of Panama. Although many of the top military brass had resisted the military's increased role in counternarcotics operations abroad, with the end of the Cold War, many of them came to see the military's participation in such operations as a means to secure the inflated budgets they had enjoyed over the past decades. Economic analysts who feared the onset of a recession if military expenditures were cut echoed this concern. William Taylor, a military expert at the Center for Strategic and International Studies, offered one solution to this concern that would prove prescient. Arguing that with the "Soviet threat" eliminated the U.S. military would need to "develop some social-utility arguments" in order to defend its standing reserve of personnel, equipment, and funding, Taylor recommended that the so-called Third World might offer a solution in the form of "insurgency, terrorism, and narcotics interdiction."[48]

If one of the initial intertwinings of the drug war assemblage was that of counternarcotics operations, global militarism, and the Cold War, then by the late 1990s and the 2000s this would morph into counternarcotics operations, global militarism, and counterterrorism.[49] Just as the U.S. government claimed that Communist insurgents in Latin America funded their operations with drug trafficking—a claim that at times was tenuous at best—so too it currently makes similar claims about terrorist organizations.[50] And just as such claims in the 1980s and 1990s allowed for the increased intertwining of economic and military aid, military and law enforcement operations, and military interventions in drug war situations, so too today have these become tightly knotted and manifest in locations such as Afghanistan; Mexico; Central Asia; Southeast Europe; and increasingly, parts of Africa; as well as continuing what had already begun in the 1980s in the United States.[51] At both the national and international levels, then, counternarcotics and counterterrorism often intertwine and emerge in the form of either military intervention as in Afghanistan, Special Ops in Latin America, or militarized police in the United States and elsewhere.

It is primarily this particular emergence of a drug war situation in Mexico that Javier talked about that evening in Vancouver and that the Movimiento focuses its political activity on. This is also the "drug war" that gets most of the media and other public discursive attention. Bud's poem, however, disrupts this narrow public discursive focus and discloses the nonlocalized complexity that is the drug war. Beginning with his poem as a hermeneutic entrée, I have tried to trace the assemblic relations of the drug war to show that it goes well beyond these localized and situated emergences, which, it should be noted, typical anthropological ethnography tends to focus upon, and that any comprehensive analysis of the drug war must recognize this widely diffused and complex assemblic phenomenon. In other words, in this section I have tried to show that the drug war can only be understood as a complex assemblage of, among other things, state-based surveillance and control, biopolitical therapeutics, carceral-political economics, militarized police violence, and global militarism in its various forms over the past forty years, *and*, as a consequence, all of these can only be understood in terms of their relation to the drug war.

INTERLUDE—A SITUATION THEORETICALLY DESCRIBED

So far I have been trying to show that the way in which the global anti–drug war movement conceives of, experiences, and addresses the drug war is best analyzed as what I am calling a *situation*. By situation I mean a nontotalizable assemblage widely diffused across different global scales that allows us to conceptualize how persons and objects that are geographically, socioeconomically, and "culturally" distributed get caught up in shared conditions that significantly affect their possible ways of being-in-the-world. This might become clearer if we consider what we normally mean when we say something like, "We found ourselves in this situation" or ask, "What can I do in this situation I'm in?" These are ways we articulate the recognition that "to be in a situation" is at one and the same time something that falls upon us, or perhaps better put, we get caught up in, and to a great extent, but not entirely, provides the conditions for possible ways of being, doing, speaking, and thinking within that situation. Thus, this is recognition that a situation is both a singularity of which one has become a part and a multiplicity that both preexists one's participation in it and as already having been, exceeds this localized instance of it. The multiplicity of a situation, however, denotes more than its durative and widely diffused existence. It also indicates its multiaspectual nature; for a situation is not a closed and totalized occurrence that appears as if from nowhere. Rather, and as I have been trying to show, a situation is constituted by diverse phenomena that become intertwined and emerge temporarily as localized manifestations. It is in these ways, then, that a situation can be described as a singular multiplicity that provides widely diffused but shared conditions.

Recently, some nonanthropological scholars have also recognized the significance of widely diffused phenomena with localized affect and have reconceived analytic and political concepts accordingly.[52] Timothy Morton, for example, has done this to address global warming, which he conceives as a hyperobject.[53] Morton defines *hyperobjects* as "things that are massively distributed in time and space relative to humans." As a result, hyperobjects are nonlocal because any local manifestation of a hyperobject is not directly the hyperobject itself, or at least not the totality of the object. A hurricane or a tsunami, for example, may be a local manifestation of the hyperobject of global warming, but it is not global warming as such. Similarly, although the drug war locally emerges differentially in various forms, such as the surveillance-induced oppression experienced, for example, by Terrance in New York City, Bud in California, or Joey in Denpasar, these are not the drug war as such.

Despite this and other similarities, however, there are real differences between hyperobjects and situations as I am trying to articulate them. The most significant difference is that Morton conceives a hyperobject as a real object, or a unit unto itself that withdraws from other objects as well as itself and thus can never fully be known or touched by another object. This is how the object-oriented ontology to which Morton subscribes defines objects,[54] and within this perspective everything, including humans, are objects with just these qualities. But this raises the question: if objects cannot touch or influence each other,[55] except for perhaps in aesthetic ways, then what are we left to do politically when confronted with a hyperobject such as global warming? Although the notion of a hyperobject as "massively distributed in time and space" is compelling and in some ways similar to a situation, it is difficult to imagine the kind of politics to be done by those who cannot "touch" and against that which itself cannot be "touched." In contrast, because situations can be described as ecstatically relational, assembling, and thus emergent multiplicities, they can and do slip into one another. This makes situations ripe with sites of potentiality and thus open for political activity.

A similar concern arises with Alain Badiou's notion of situation. In the most recent explication of his ontology, Badiou replaces the concept of situation with world, but for our purposes we can still think of this as his rendering of situation.[56] For Badiou, a situation/world comes into existence, maintains that existence, and is recognizable as such because it has a particular and unique logic that orders it. If for Badiou "being qua being is thought by mathematics," then a situation/world as "appearing, or being-there-in-a-world, is thought by logic."[57] Indeed, as he goes on to put it, situations/worlds are not simply thought by logic, they *are* logic.[58] And this logic is not a procedure that a human subject utilizes to understand a situation/world, so argues Badiou, but rather this logic that fundamentally *is* situations/worlds "is altogether anterior to every subjective constitution."[59] A situation/world for Badiou, then, is the local emplacement of a logical operation that occurs regardless of human existence.[60] This is clearly *not* what I intend by a situation, and in fact, it is precisely the kind of metaphysical humanist thinking and politics that I am trying to argue against.[61]

If the concern of these and other contemporary ontologists is the explication of a posthumanist politics, then it seems odd to do so in logicomathematical terms or by simply reversing the subject/object distinction and thus perpetuating a metaphysical humanist approach. In contrast, the critical hermeneutic approach begins with Heidegger's notion of phenomenon ("what shows itself in itself") and through analysis discloses that humans are always already intertwined in various situations, and this intertwining both precedes and exceeds any possible humanist projection onto it. To be in any world at all, and the situations that structure them, is always already to be so intertwined and as such always becoming that which situations make possible.[62] But this alone does not make a situation a more compelling analytic and political concept. In the rest of this section, then, I consider further the phenomenon of situation as it "shows itself in itself." In so doing I delineate the fundamental characteristics of a situation, which in turn will set the background for the following section, in which I consider some of the political activity of the anti–drug war movement as a way of setting the scene for the rest of the book. So as to make this analytically clear, I will delineate the various characteristics of situations in numbered subsections.

1. *A Situation Is a Nontotalizable Assemblage*

As we have already seen, the drug war is a complex assemblage of diverse aspects of other assemblages, such as global militarism; state-based surveillance and control; border security; carceral political economics; national and international inequalities; and as I will show in the next section, biopolitical therapeutics. What is called the *drug war,* then, is no "thing" in itself but rather is assembled aspects of other assemblages that together create a widely diffused situation that is differentially distributed with very real effects in worlds. Here we can begin to see how the concept of assemblages can be helpful for thinking the complexity of situations about which I wrote in the opening paragraphs of this section and how this differs from Morton's hyperobjects and Badiou's situations/worlds.

Anthropologists are likely most familiar with the notion of assemblage through Ong and Collier's rendering of it in terms of global assemblages.[63] There is little doubt that their edited volume has made an important and influential contribution to the development of the discipline since its publication. And to the extent that Ong and Collier's global assemblage articulates the basics of a general theory of assemblages most fully developed, for example, by Deleuze and Guattari, Latour, and DeLanda, there are similarities with what I am calling a situation, which is a nontotalized assemblage. I differ significantly from Ong and Collier, however, in that despite claims to the contrary, they seem to conceive global assemblages as supplements to what they variously refer to as "social and cultural situations," "spheres of life," "environments," and "context."[64] In contrast, over the course of the last decade I have been thinking through the concept of nontotalizable assemblages—whether in terms of moral and ethical assemblages[65] or worlds and situations[66]—in such a way that entails that they not be thought of in terms of a supplement. In some ways my thinking of assemblages has paralleled that of Paul Rabinow.[67] But while Rabinow seems to conceive of assemblages as primarily localized and temporary (thus, not unlike how I conceive of situations), I have come to think of our worlds as nothing other than densely intertwined knots of several much more widely diffused and nontotalizable assemblages that constantly flow together and slip apart in a potentially infinite number of combinations. This flowing and slippage of the singular multiplicity of situations defies totalized categorization or identification. This is precisely why as nontotalizable assemblages situations cannot be thought as supplement, for there is nothing other than traces of other such assemblages to "supplement."

Thus, for example, the diverse aspects of the drug war situation can easily slip into other nontotalized assemblages and thereby defy easy identification with either. As we saw in the previous section, the global militarism aspect of the drug war situation can be foregrounded and reconceived as the war on terrorism or a defense against Communist insurgents, and police militarization and carceral political economics can be repositioned as being tough on crime. As a result a situation is quite slippery since it never all at once can be fully grasped because part of its very nature is the capacity for its constitutive aspects to be temporarily refigured. Such refiguration can occur "naturally," as it were, since aspects of situations take on different signification as they are represented, experienced, or considered differently. Or, this refiguration can be done intentionally and strategically, as certain persons may wish to emphasize one particular "interpretation" of an aspect over others—for example, mandatory minimum prison sentencing as being tough on crime rather than judicial procedures with clear racial and class prejudices. Indeed, this slippery intertwining is one of the primary characteristics of the robust complexity of the drug war that makes resisting it so difficult and that an assemblic ethnography seeks to disentangle. Because of this complexity, I am trying to argue that we must begin our anthropological analyses not at so-called global assemblages that supplement a preexisting context but instead with the situations that make evident that we are always already caught up in singular multiples that provide the widely diffused but yet shared conditions that significantly affect our possible ways of being-in-the-world.

2. A Situation Is Not Singularly Locatable

Because a situation is never isolable and only exists as a singular multiple—that is, as always intertwined with other assemblages, a situation is never located. Rather, as I have been emphasizing so far, a situation becomes temporarily localized. Thus, for example, the situation of the drug war is not simply located in the veins of heroin users crouched under American highway overpasses or in the jungles of South America or the borders between the United States and Mexico or the poppy fields of Afghanistan; nor is the drug war simply located in the substance called *heroin* that is actually a range of potentially infinite kinds of beings as opium derivatives get cut with more contaminants every step they move through the underground commodity chain; nor is the drug war simply located in American, Russian, or Thai prisons or in the infectious disease wards of hospitals around the globe. Rather, the drug war emerges—at times but not always—in all of these locales and more. Notice, however, that these locales are not always and only caught up in the drug war. For example, there are people in prisons, infectious disease wards, and under bridges who are there for reasons unrelated to the drug war. Thus, only by attending and being attuned to each of these situated manifestations of the drug war, and their unique, similar, and shared potentialities and emergent actualities, can this situation be effectively politically addressed or anthropologically analyzed. It is precisely this attunement that characterizes an assemblic ethnography.

3. Sites of Potentiality for Political Activity Arise from the Interstices of Situations

The conglomeritic and flowing nature of assembled situations leaves them with interstices of noncohesion. As we saw in the previous section, these interstitial sites disrupt any possibility for an actually existing totality of a situation and therefore, any possibility for thinking or articulating the totality of a situation. At these interstices, problematics of a situation likely occur, and sites of potentiality can be found, from which possibilities for political activity emerge.[68] This differs significantly from the "untouchable" hyperobjects of Morton or even the bounded issues or identities that dominate most contemporary politics. To some extent this rendering of situations as sites of potentiality is similar to Max Gluckman's[69] classic articulation of situations as moments of paradox, confrontation, conflict, process, and potential change.[70] Despite this similarity, however, I entirely reject the Gluckmanian claim that they disclose social structure conceived as a transcendental. Indeed, the argument I am trying to make is that situations allow us to begin to conceive shared conditions that are widely dispersed across various levels, horizontally and vertically, as it were, without the necessity of any transcendental at all, whether this be thought of in terms of social structure, culture, Badiou's logic, or Ong and Collier's "context." In the next section and throughout this book, I will show how the anti–drug war movement is now addressing such sites of potentiality in their experimental political activity without the need of such "bannisters."

The Situationists similarly conceived of situations as nontranscendentally structured sites of politics, at which experiment and play could be done in the attempt to bring about an otherwise.[71] But if Situationists saw the first political task as the construction of situations from which political experiment and play could begin,[72] then the anti–drug war movement begins by disclosing *already existing* situations that must be permanently transformed so as to build new worlds in which drug users and nonusers alike can dwell. The conceptual, analytical, and methodological problem the complexity of situations presents, then, is how precisely to trace and articulate the movement, force, and limits of the intertwining so as to initiate this transformation. Similarly, I submit that these problems are central to anthropology and the other human and social sciences today, as they struggle to address the increasingly complex contemporary global configuration of things. Thus, I have been attempting to delineate the concept of situation and the method of assemblic ethnography as possible ways of addressing this complexity.

In the next section, I turn to a brief example of how some actors in the anti–drug war movement show us how a politics that begins from a situation can be done. What I want to emphasize is how this political activity does not begin from a "problem" singularly conceptualized, and thus it does not focus its energy on simply trying to "change policy" or laws—although there is, of course, some effort aimed at this—or to become included into that which already is. Rather, because of their recognition of the complexity of the drug war, anti–drug war agonists focus upon interstitial potentiality, from which they can begin to clear and open new possibilities for other ways of being and, eventually, for other worlds to emerge. In the final section of this chapter, then, I consider how this has started to occur from the interstitial site between the surveillance and control aspect and that of biopolitical therapeutics.

A POLITICS THAT BEGINS FROM A SITUATION

Bud read his poem at a public anti–drug war event held at a university annex that is part of a recently constructed public-private housing complex on the border of the Downtown Eastside neighborhood in Vancouver, where a politics of worldbuilding has been going on for twenty years. By 1997 an estimated six thousand to ten thousand drug users, over half of whom were HIV positive, were concentrated in just a few square blocks; over six thousand persons lived in single-room occupancy (SRO) hotels; a constant police presence resulted in regular and random harassment and arrests; and the death toll mounted. The potential for a situation-focused politics was all around and in fact was already emerging in 1993 when what would eventually become one of the key housing and drug user organizations in the neighborhood was formed and made harm reduction—and particularly the provisioning of clean syringes and works—an inseparable part of its political activity related to housing. As one of the cofounders of the organization put it, at the time this was quite radical and experimental, and now it is fairly common practice. The key political point here is that these anti–drug war agonists recognized that in the Downtown Eastside the housing problem, drug use, police harassment, and HIV and other infectious diseases were inextricably intertwined, and thus addressing only one in isolation would be more or less as if they were not addressing anything at all. This was the recognition of the necessity of a politics that addresses situations and not isolated issues, and it would be this recognition that would become characteristic of the global anti–drug war movement.

Indeed, well beyond Vancouver the anti–drug war movement is a global political movement that mirrors the characteristics of the situation it addresses. Just as the drug war is an assemblage of diverse aspects of other assemblages, so too is the anti–drug war movement an assemblage of diverse collaborators[73] that mobilize to address, for example, local, national, and international antidrug legislation and policy; fatally dangerous therapeutics; carceral-political economics; and punitive policing, among other items. The kind of politics done by those in the anti–drug war movement, then, recognizes the multiple ways in which the drug war touches and affects their and most others' ways of being and mobilizes accordingly. This is the kind of political movement that William Connolly argues is needed today to address what he calls the "contemporary condition," a movement he describes as "anchored entirely in no single class, gender, ethnic group, creed or generation" and taking "the shape of a vibrant pluralist assemblage acting at multiple sites within and across states."[74] This is precisely what the anti–drug war movement is, and it takes this form because it is addressing one of the most widely diffused situations that significantly shapes the "contemporary condition" no matter where one might be.

Despite these early attempts by Vancouver agonists to initiate a situation-focused politics, throughout the 1990s the overdoses in the neighborhood continued to pile up—to two hundred in 1993 alone. Finally, however, in 1997 a kind of tipping point—an event—occurred that issued a demand from this world that could no longer be avoided. A public health survey of drug users in Vancouver revealed that the Downtown Eastside had the highest HIV rate in the "developed" world.[75] This report, which articulated something that many of those living in the neighborhood had already felt and experienced, motivated some to act. Bud was just one of those who did. Bud approached the housing organization mentioned above, and together they organized the political event that would become known as 1000 Crosses. This event, for many, marks the true beginning of the experimental political activity that has come to make the Downtown Eastside famous the world over among anti–drug war agonists. It is so named because of the one thousand crosses planted in a neighborhood park, which stood in place for each of the drug users who had died in British Columbia since 1993, the vast majority of whom were in the Downtown Eastside. But the event was more than this. Drug users also occupied parts of East Hastings Street—the main thoroughfare through the neighborhood where all the commuter buses run—and stretched a steel chain across the street with a sign on it that read THE KILLING FIELDS. With this event the users of the Downtown Eastside and their allies began to respond to the political demand that emerged from the interstices of their drug war situation. Motivated by an ethics of dwelling,[76] the users and inhabitants of this neighborhood began the long and difficult political process of transforming their "Death Zone," their "killing fields," into a world where they could once again begin to dwell.

In just a few months, the now globally famous Vancouver Area Network of Drug Users (VANDU) would be formed by Bud and others, and this union, along with the housing and other allied organizations, would begin a political process that is still ongoing today. The result has been the transformation of the Downtown Eastside into an attuned world in which drug users can now dwell in a world designed for them as drug users. This world consists of, among other things, a neighborhood bank organized specifically for the needs of active drug users and those with precarious housing; social enterprise businesses that employ drug users and adapt to their schedules and ways of being; art studios and galleries where users and other neighborhood inhabitants can create and show their works; and increasing numbers of public housing, some of which, like where the anti–drug war event took place, are combined with private housing. Each of these are networked with the others, as well as with various health and therapeutic services in the neighborhood, such as Insite, the safe consumption facility Vancouver has become famous for; a trial heroin prescription program; a health and dentistry clinic; and detox.

These agonists have, in other words, built a world that is attuned to itself and its inhabitants and as a result remains open to ever-new possibilities for becoming as it continually maintains this attunement.[77] In this new world of the Downtown Eastside, for example, a bank is no longer an exclusionary profit-driven establishment but a place open to anyone no matter their credit history, their residence status, how they smell, or what they say. As we will see below, it is also a place where one can get a crack pipe, and as I will show in chapter five, see an opera and get a free meal. In this new attuned world, drug users are no longer excluded from employment possibilities; rather, the social enterprise employers negotiate and adjust their hiring and work expectations to the vicissitudes of users' variously stable lives. In this new world created by experimental, situation-focused politics, drug users no longer die at extraordinary rates because, as I will make clear below, the entire neighborhood has essentially become a "safe zone" for drug use. All of this and more have become possible, I suggest, because the Vancouver agonists were able to, as other anti–drug war agonists elsewhere are beginning to, tap into the sites of potentiality of their drug war situations. As I hope is clear, this form of politics underway in Vancouver is beginning to allow new conditions of existence to emerge that challenge and counter those of the drug war.

This experimental politics has become possible because of the sites of potentiality these agonists have actively disclosed within the interstices of their drug war situation. This is perhaps most clearly seen in the way in which they have mobilized political action around harm reduction, which sits right at the interstice between the state-based surveillance and control aspect and the biopolitical-therapeutic aspect of the drug war assemblage. In nearly every country, the drive to manage the normalized health of a working population by controlling what can and cannot be put into a body has increasingly resulted in the institutionalization of harm-reduction programs that were once organized by those people who used the drugs themselves. This has shifted what was once a political project of drug users and their allies to a state-funded therapeutic intervention run by bureaucrats, "college-educated" managers, and public health therapists and thus largely out of the hands of drug users, who are now mostly left in the position of docile beings who must normalize or wait until they are able to do so. Additionally, the attempt by both international and national harm-reduction organizations to convince governments to accept harm reduction is regularly posed in terms of supporting security and economic development.[78] Harm reduction, then, falls directly in the interstice of biopolitical therapeutics and state-based surveillance and control.

Whereas this institutionalization of harm reduction has in most cases led to the isolated clinic as the only location where a drug user can acquire clean works, the political activity in the Downtown Eastside has resulted in an entire neighborhood that is now essentially a safe zone of harm reduction. As one user agonist in Vancouver described it to me, unlike the typical harm-reduction model that is linear and isolated, the Downtown Eastside is networked so that there is nowhere one can be where clean works or a safe consumption facility are not close at hand. A crack-pipe vending machine in the bank lobby; the now world-famous safe-consumption facility called Insite in the geographical center of the neighborhood; several other unsanctioned facilities spread out across the neighborhood; and syringe exchange in numerous community centers, clinics, and housing units—no matter where one is at any given time, it is nearly impossible to be further than a minute or two from harm-reduction services in the neighborhood. Unlike many of the other places my assemblic ethnographic research has taken me, harm reduction in Vancouver is beginning to become disentangled from its biopolitical-therapeutic and surveillance and control aspects and is simply becoming part of ordinary life. In so doing it is slowly transforming the possibilities for living that life.

As a result, Vancouver has become a model and inspiration for anti–drug war agonists around the world. No matter where I go or with whom I talk, everyone asks if I have been to Vancouver and always compares themselves negatively with the successes there. Increasingly, though, these other user agonists are beginning to mobilize to wrest control of harm-reduction practices from state-based and funded institutions. Consider the example of safe-consumption facilities, which is one of the most radical initiatives enacted by anti–drug war agonists around the globe and what Vancouver is best known for. Initially conceived for heroin injectors but increasingly for smokers and snorters of various kinds of drugs, safe-consumption facilities are locations where people can use these drugs under the supervision of trained personnel who are on the lookout for potential overdose. Where officially sanctioned, such as in Vancouver, Amsterdam, Copenhagen, and various other European cities, these facilities are recognized as being responsible for significant decreases in overdoses. Globally, however, there are many such facilities run underground, and although there are no official statistics to confirm this, hearsay suggests that these have been just as successful in reducing overdoses as the sanctioned sites.

Despite the clear evidence that safe-consumption facilities work, the political tactics for enacting them differ according to the peculiarities of any particular drug war situation. In Copenhagen, for example, where the BrugerForeningen, or the Danish Drug Users Union for active users (from here on referred to as the BF), and its allied organizations convinced the government to fund and support a range of initiatives, safe-consumption facilities being just one, the tactic tends to be engagement with legislators, and the strategy is quickly shifting toward decriminalization. In Moscow and Saint Petersburg, on the other hand, in a country that has one of the fastest-growing HIV rates in the world—a rate driven by heroin use—and yet where the government, along with police and medical personnel, persecute, imprison, and leave many drug users to die,[79] this drug war in Russia currently is more effectively fought—though dangerously so—using illegal and underground tactics to offer such things as safe-consumption facilities. In New York City, I have found that combinations of these two tactics are regularly used depending on the relata or aim being addressed. For example, legislative and judicial tactics are utilized for policing issues, illegal and underground tactics for consumption facilities, although recently VOCAL-NY has been leading a national campaign to initiate such facilities across the state and country—a campaign that is beginning to have positive effects.

Harm reduction, particularly safe-consumption facilities, is just one example of the transformative possibilities available at the interstitial site of potentiality between state-based surveillance and control and biopolitical therapeutics. Although much harm reduction has been folded into these two aspects so that from a particular perspective it remains part of the drug war problem, anti–drug war agonists have found that from a situation perspective harm reduction does in fact hold much potential for politically experimenting with and opening possibilities for an otherwise. Inspired by the transformations underway in Vancouver, anti–drug war agonists and their allied organizations have begun to politically experiment with harm reduction as they respond to the particular situational emergence of the drug war in their locale—some of them by necessity acting outside the law—and the consequences have been real and include, among other things, communally run safe-consumption facilities, housing, and health care.

In Copenhagen, for example, the opening of a safe-consumption facility created a space—literally, a courtyard on which the facility was built—where drug users started to gather and feel safe because it was a space built for people like them. Eventually, a small café was opened in this courtyard to provide free or very affordable meals and food to those who gathered there. A few days a week, an organization of lawyers who offer free legal support to drug users and other precarious persons set up an information table in the courtyard and provide coffee and snacks. And as I am writing this chapter, another safe-consumption facility was recently opened down the block. Here, as in Vancouver, we see how harm reduction done as neither state-based surveillance nor biopolitical therapeutics, but rather as attuned care (see chapter five), provides a clearing—an opening—for new possibilities to emerge for being-together in a nonjudgmental manner (see chapter four). And just as the opening provided by the housing organization in Vancouver provided the clearing from which a new network—a new world—of attuned care emerged and eventually spread across the Downtown Eastside, so too can we see how a similarly new world is beginning to spread out from this courtyard in Copenhagen.

This kind of experimental and agonistic politics of worldbuilding has become possible, I have been trying to show, because of the way the anti–drug war movement conceives its political agonist. Unlike the bounded issues and identities addressed by many contemporary political movements, the anti–drug war movement has recognized the drug war as an assembled situation that at one and the same time discloses its widely diffused complexity and its openness to an otherwise. For unlike an isolated issue that can only be "won" or "lost," and unlike Morton's hyperobject that, as conceived, seemingly cannot be "touched," situations always hold sites of potentiality at their interstices. Beginning from these interstices, experimental political activity—as both the Downtown Eastside and Copenhagen show—can begin to transgress the situation and as such remain open to an otherwise by means of those and that which are already intertwined.

. . .

In this chapter I have followed the lead of the anti–drug war movement and conceptualized the drug war as a situation that is widely diffused across different global scales, emerges differentially in various worlds, and thus affectively conditions those and that which "get caught up" in the situation. As such, the drug war is best considered as a nontotalizable assemblage constituted by various aspects of other nontotalizable assemblages, such as global militarism, state-based surveillance and control, carceral political economics, biopolitical therapeutics, and international and national inequalities, among others. I hope to have shown that conceiving the drug war as such helps make it more analytically clear for both intellectual and political purposes. In the rest of this book, I will continue to interrogate the complexity of the drug war by tracing the contours and limits of this situation, the ways in which it conditions the being-in-the world of those who get caught up in it, and the kind of political activity currently being done to change the situation and in so doing, open new possibilities for worlds and their inhabitants to become otherwise.

CHAPTER 2

"Addicts" and the Disruptive Politics of Showing

If you think everyone who uses drugs is the enemy, then you're more likely to declare war on the people.

—Nick Pastore, Police Chief, New Haven, Connecticut

No matter where my assemblic research took me, a key aim that I heard over and over again was the need to change the conditions, or what we might also call the *onto-interpretive matrix,* through which the drug war and its consequences are understood. This was perhaps most commonly and openly articulated in the weekly meetings in New York. During the process of strategizing or planning tactics, which were always for the purpose of addressing very specific problems—for example, syringe access or police violence—there was always also an awareness that the ultimate aim of their work is addressing the conditions of the drug war. These conditions were most commonly referred to as the drug war *culture,* or *ideology,* or *mind-set* and were recognized as those that set the range of possibilities by which most of the people they engage in their political work, and most people in general for that matter, relate to and understand drug use and users. Indeed, as these leaders often put it, the conditions of the drug war produce a "fantasy world" such that people "don't live in reality" but instead live in a "prison of the mind." Because of this, these leaders, as well as every other anti–drug war agonist I spoke to about this, know that their task is, as one of the leaders put it in a meeting, "shattering the mind-set" of those who have become imprisoned by the drug war "ideology."

Trash, shit, waste, and rubbish; animals, slaves, and nothing—these are just some of the ways drug users have told me that people such as strangers on the street, police officers, and even their own family regularly refer to them. Within the "fantasy world" of the drug war, drug users figure as the less-than-human Other that stands over and against the human order of things. Or perhaps better put, and as I will show in this chapter, within the conditions of the drug war, drug users have become the inclusively excluded Other that grounds the contemporary biopolitical order. This already begins to become clear when we think of the drug user not in the most derogatory terms, such as *trash* or *shit,* but in the most common manner of categorizing the user—that is, as *addict.* While the category of addict has a complicated history that is inextricably intertwined with nineteenth- and early twentieth-century colonial imperialism, the rise of consumer capitalism, race relations, and conceptions of sexuality and gender, certainly by the mid-twentieth century, "the addict" had been rendered as the dangerous internal Other from whom the population must be defended.[1] Thus, by the time of the official declaration of the war on drugs in 1971, the user as addict had come to be that which discloses the limit of what counts as "us"; a limit that must endure so "we" can remain secure in the "who" that we claim to be. In this sense, the drug war as a war on people can be understood as a biopolitical practice for the maintenance of this limit that secures belonging and, as such, produces and reproduces "the addict" as one of the internal Others that ground the contemporary biopolitical order.

In the previous chapter, I showed that situations structure worlds and thus provide the conditions for the possible habituated ways of being in those worlds. It is just these conditions that anti–drug war agonists refer to as the *fantasy world, culture, mind-set,* or *ideology* of the drug war. But such conditions should not be understood as mental schemes of mediation or representation but rather as ontological conditions that allow for particular kinds of material, affective, and discursive intertwining. In other words, these are conditions that allow such things as human bodies, nonhuman living beings, moods, objects, ways of speaking and thinking, and built and nonbuilt spaces, among many other things, to responsively intertwine in ways that become habitual ways of being. This responsive intertwining would be one way of describing a noncognitive, nonhuman-centric hermeneutics of existence. Or put another way: an onto-interpretive matrix of being. Thus, by means of this habituated hermeneutics of existence, the "fantasy world" of the drug war becomes the "real world," not only of drug users but, in fact, for all of us, as the drug war is a significant aspect of our biopolitical contemporary condition.

Situated conditions understood in this way can be understood to some extent as similar to what Judith Butler calls *frames.*[2] For Butler, frames are the interpretive conditions that demarcate what can be apprehended as reality and are also central to the very production of that reality and who has a part in it. Whether articulated as situated conditions or frames, the point is that what comes to be recognizable as reality—that is, recognized not simply cognitively but primarily existentially—is always and only possible by means of the onto-interpretive conditions available. Despite this similarity, however, I find the notion of frames too limiting, as it suggests a kind of closed and static totality that often seems to be described as rather homogeneous and is either always already in place or must be changed in toto. Furthermore, this change only seems possible if initiated by those privileged enough to recognize the frames—those who, so it often seems, the frame has already recognized—by means of what I have called elsewhere the politics of the a priori, which mobilizes such metaphysical humanist conceptions as rights, dignity, and responsibility.[3]

In contrast to such an enframed and closed totality, situated conditions are constituted through the relational intertwining of diverse aspects of other nontotalized assemblages. Consequently, not only are dynamic shifts of interpretation possible. But so too are there always several interstices within a relationally assembled situation, from which political activity can be done that allows potentialities to emerge as new possibilities, as we saw with the Vancouver example at the end of the last chapter. Thus, despite similarities, there are significant ontological and political differences between the concepts of frames and situated conditions, or what I will simply call *conditions*.

Be that as it may, I agree with Butler that war has become one of the key conditions for structuring our world today. But as I have been arguing in this book thus far, we must understand war not simply in terms of wars against external enemies but primarily in terms of wars against internal enemies. For one of the fundamental assumptions of this book is that if modernity is best understood in terms of a biopolitics that has been primarily concerned with the care of populations and life, then this was only possible by means of war as an integral aspect of biopolitical governance.[4] And although war occasionally manifests as war against an external enemy in the form of another sovereign power, war as a necessary aspect of biopolitical governance is primarily waged as wars on internal enemies, or wars on people. Because wars on people—such as the drug war—are central to biopolitical governance, it is important to recognize that those against whom these wars are waged remain perpetually bound up with the very power that wages war against them. As

Judith Butler puts it, such internal enemies remain "in a situation of forcible exposure . . . [to] the exercise of state power freed from the constraints of all law."[5] As such, "the people," against whom such wars on people are waged, remain ever present as the necessary internal Other that provides the validating foundation of not only the truth but, more importantly, the rightness of the biopolitical order. War, in this sense, is *the* general ontological condition for the contemporary order of things.

Who, then, are "the people" that constitute the internal enemy? How are we to recognize that internal Other if she is a part of that to which we ourselves belong? Assuming that she looks, dresses, speaks, and has interests similar to ours, what criteria are available for discerning who counts as the enemy? As Butler convincingly argues, war itself provides such criteria for both recognizing and affectively relating to the internal Other, even if these come by means of a general nonrecognition and abjection.[6] Within the general condition of war, we become capable of both recognizing who counts as the enemy while at the same time not grieving their plight as those left to survive within what I call *zones of uninhabitability*.[7] In other words, war provides the conditions for "us" to become the kinds of subjects who are able to recognize "them" as unworthy of living—because they seem incapable of living—our kind of life. That is to say, war renders the internal Other as an object over and against our subjectivity. War, then, produces both the subject of belonging and the ungrievable object that is inclusively excluded from—that is, grounds, such belonging.

This production of recognition works remarkably well when turned against external enemies, for then war is openly and proudly (some call it patriotically) articulated as such. Wars on people, though, are never referred to as *war* as such but rather only as metaphor. Does anyone other than drug users and those who have gotten caught up in the cross fire actually think the drug war is an actual war? For the most part, the answer is no. This is so because wars on people are only ever presented as an essential part of biopolitical practice—"addicts" are incarcerated to keep the streets "clean," drugs are illegal to protect children, and police are militarized to protect communities. In drug war situations, then, war goes by various other names such as *health, security, care,* and *law*. We can begin to see, then, how the care of populations and life is founded upon an internal order that is maintained by a war on certain people that is articulated precisely not as war but as "keeping the peace."

In the rest of this chapter, I will interrogate this conception of the internal enemy of the "addict," whose expendability grounds the biopolitical order of things, and the way in which some of these "addicts" politically resist by seeking to disrupt this "fantasy world." I will first consider the discursive production of this "fantasy world" that the anti–drug war movement addresses because those involved understand that most people they engage with—politicians, police, medical personnel, social services, media, family members, and more or less "everyone else"—relate to and understand drug use and users through the conditions that produce this "fantasy world." I will then turn to consider some narrative articulations of anti–drug war agonists in order to emphasize that despite the fact that anti–drug war agonists speak of a "fantasy world," the worlds in which they live are not at all fantasy but very real indeed. The conditions of the drug war have not covered over some "true reality" with a false "fantasy" but rather have produced reality itself no matter how absurd it may be.

In the final section, I turn to one of the most significant tactics utilized by the anti–drug war movement in the attempt to "shatter mind-sets." As will become clear, what I call a disruptive politics of showing is a first-step political tactic by which anti–drug war agonists hermeneutically disrupt the dehumanizing "fantasy world" of the drug war by enacting the otherwise they hope one day will come to be the nonnormative norm. In doing so, they lay the grounds for the new social, political, and ontological habits this otherwise would entail. It is important to emphasize the difference between this disruptive politics of showing and prefigurative politics. While the latter can be described as political activity that attempts to foreshadow or represent an imagined and hoped-for future, the disruptive politics of showing is enacted to disrupt—or initiate a breakdown— of the "mind-sets" of those who inhabit and perpetuate the "fantasy world" of the drug war by showing them that the otherwise they cannot imagine already exists right here in front of them. This is the difference, then, between temporarily performing a political hope and doing the sustained hard work of politically building new worlds. As I hope becomes clear, this hermeneutically disruptive political tactic is the first step in the politics of worldbuilding that I will trace throughout the rest of this book.

LESS-THAN-HUMAN: THE EVIL ADDICT

With 184 parties to it, the United Nation's 1961 Single Convention on Narcotic Drugs established the now international norm of scheduling drugs and the criminalization of drug use.[8] As a result, the Single Convention is an essential part of the international drug control regime, within which the domestic drug policies of all signatories and parties are made, and the drug war is waged.[9] This document not only helped establish the criminalization of drug users as the global norm but also provides the institutional grounds for their dehumanization. Thus, the preamble of the Single Convention states that "addiction" is "a serious evil for the individual and is fraught with social and economic danger to mankind" and that it is the "duty [of all parties] to prevent and combat this evil." Here, with this institutional grounding for what would become the global war on drugs, we have the equation of "addiction" with an evil that poses a threat to the very social existence (i.e., "the social and economic order") of "mankind." And as is always the case with evil—that enemy of good and order—humankind has a "duty" to "combat" it. Thus, the drug war is institutionally grounded in a call to fight evil.

But if addiction is the evil to be fought, it must be remembered that addiction is always embodied; with addiction there is always an "addict." So, then, what is the "addict?" To begin to answer this question and, in so doing, get a glimpse at the way in which the drug war discursively conditions "addicts" as less than human, I will consider at length an online CNN article titled "Addicts Shoot Up in a Safe Haven in Canada," which is a companion piece to "Shooting Up Legally," a CNN International *World's Untold Stories* special report about Insite, the supervised injection facility in the Downtown Eastside of Vancouver.[10] Because this article is positioned as upholding so-called journalistic standards of neutrality and objectivity in its investigation of Insite, analyzing its discursive framing allows us to see more clearly the (re)production of the drug war "fantasy world" than would an analysis of an article with more obviously discriminatory and exclusionary language. For, in contrast to such obviously discriminatory media depictions as the *Irish Independent*'s "Sterilising Junkies May Seem Harsh, But It Does Make Sense" or the innumerable other such articles in which drug users are "insult[ed] and demean[ed] with a large degree of impunity,"[11] this CNN article makes an attempt to fairly portray the conditions in which drug users try to survive the war waged against them.

While both the online article and the television special certainly maintain CNN's typical attempt to give "both sides of the story," they nevertheless perpetuate the conditions by which drug users are rendered as those internal Others who are not like us because they are in significant ways less than human. For already in the title of the article, the subjects of the story are depicted as such. That is, as addicts. From the Latin *addīctus* meaning variously "assigned by decree," "bound," "to surrender," "to enslave," or "to condemn," an addict is one who has become enslaved or bound to a substance, an activity, or in some cases a person. An addict as enslaved has lost control of himself, no longer possesses sufficient will to free himself from his bondage, only desires that to which he is already enslaved, and as enslaved relinquishes any responsibility for his actions to himself or others in the sole pursuit of that to which he is bonded.[12] The addict, then, has lost all of the qualities—rational and moral—that today have come to define humanness.

The article's first lines immediately set the frame for the nonhumanity of the drug-using addict: "Heroin, cocaine and amphetamines are the kind of street drugs you expect to find in the shady corners of any city, hiding away from the glare of law enforcement. But in one small space in downtown Vancouver addicts openly inject their fixes—as medics watch on." We expect, the article assumes, to find these illicit and dangerous substances in the dark shadows of cities—in alleyways, under bridges, or behind dumpsters. This is, after all, where the abject of cities tend to gather. Note that what gathers in these "shady corners," however, are the substances—the heroin, cocaine, and amphetamines—and the reader is left to assume that the unsaid accompaniment of these substances are the addicts that are bound to them. The redundancy, apparently, would be unnecessary. For as with the slave who is simply identified by the name of an owner or lord, the addict who has surrendered herself to a substance is identified with it. The addict as enslaved has become consubstantial with the drug; the addict has become object; has become abject. Indeed, the second sentence confirms this reading, as only here the addict appears "openly" in order to be watched, as if only under the surveillance of biopolitically trained medics can "the addict" recover a part of her humanity. But this partial recovery is only momentary, for here under the watchful and responsible eye of the medic, the unsaid consubstantial being of addict and substance in the first sentence is reiterated in the second as "addicts openly inject their fixes," and so in the very "openness" of the injection, they come to embody the conditions of their being. Thus, despite the author's attempt to write an "objective" journalistic piece, the limits are already in place for how the reader should understand the subject of the article: the "addict" as consubstantially enslaved to a substance is less than human.

This assumption of the less-than-human nature of the drug user continues throughout the article, articulated in different voices. For example, the author herself continues to use the term *addict* throughout the entire article, and in one particularly telling line in describing Insite and what happens there, she discloses the less-than-human qualities of the addict: "With fluorescent lighting and lots of mirrors, the atmosphere is clinical, *even as the room fills with drug addicts focused on one task only—feeding their addiction.*"[13] Like popular images of "primitive man," who spent all of his time doing nothing other than desperately trying to find enough food to make it through the day, addicts too have only one focus—"feeding their addiction." Without will and seemingly incapable of self-control or responsibility, the addict can only focus on his singular desire; his insatiable need for more drugs. More primitive than civilized, more animal than human, the addict cannot help himself "even" in the most modern and civilized of atmospheres: the "clinical" setting.

Indeed, the second voice of the article, the voice that apparently lends the "objectivity" to the piece and provides the other side of the story, the voice of David Berner, an addiction counselor and founder of Canada's first residential treatment center, gives expert support to this depiction of drug users. He asks, sarcastically: "It's more humane to help a person stay stupid? To help a person stay enslaved? You don't need to have heroin or needles or crack pipe kits to entice people to health. You could approach people and say, 'let me look at that sore. I'm a nurse. Let's clean you up a bit.'" Clearly opposed to Insite and any harm-reduction model, Berner tells us that the humane thing to do—one could say the enlightened thing to do—is to help free the slave from his self-imposed ignorance. Like the child who brings the alley cat home to Mother, Berner seems to be saying that all a drug user really needs is a bit of care, a bath, and a good home to domesticate him. Whether in Vancouver, New York City, Saint Petersburg, Copenhagen, Denpasar, or anywhere else I have done research with active drug users, I have never met one who does not want care, a bath, and a home. But I have never met one who wants them because she thinks she is stupid, a slave, or less than human. Berner's paternalistic view of what drug users need, however, depicts them as not counting as human and only worthy of that name once they are cleaned up a bit through a therapeutic intervention. The polysemy of the word *clean* does a good bit of the work here as it refers most explicitly to the cleaning of the "sore" and also to the cleaning of the body as that which, on the exterior, may be dirty from living on the street, as well as to cleansing the body as a whole from drugs. Only a fully clean being, so it seems, can be a human being.

The third voice in the article, however, wants to remind readers that there is more to this being that we call human than cleanliness. Liane, a resident of the Downtown Eastside who has been using drugs for twenty years, told the author: "Remember us addicts, we're somebody's mothers [sic], we're somebody's sister, we're somebody's daughter." Although Liane uses the word *addict* to describe herself—and indeed, unfortunately, it is too often the case that users continue to describe and understand themselves in the terms made available within the conditions of the drug war—she also reminds us that she and her fellow users are in fact just as human as nonusers; this is particularly emphasized by referencing in a gendered manner the discursively dominant notion of the familial and reproductive dimension of humanness.

In fact, the author also attempts to emphasize the humanness of Liane when she first introduces her in the article: "In the alleys we meet Liane—another long-term user—who has used Insite since it opened in 2003. She is articulate, educated, and angry." Despite the humanizing intent, this description of Liane as "articulate" and "educated" is completely out of place in the flow of the narrative and seems to do nothing other than refer to the conditions that render and frame the drug addict as "stupid" and less than human. For the author feels no need to describe David Berner or any of the other politicians or social workers she quotes as articulate or educated. Apparently, the author only feels that she must inform the reader that someone who has been using drugs for twenty years and met the author in an alley could also be articulate and educated. Just to be sure that we do not get the wrong picture, though, Liane is also described as "angry," a passion that seems to fit our sense of those who are met in alleys.

In this one CNN article, then, we see nearly the full range of the dehumanizing discourse that is one aspect of the contemporary condition that renders drug users as one of the primary inclusively excluded Others of our biopolitical order. As such, the drug user comes to be understood and treated as—and as I will point out in the next section, they oftentimes also become—those who have lost the characteristics that today are equated with humanness: their freedom, autonomy, self-responsibility, and control. In other words, within the conditions of the drug war, the enslaved "addict" has lost her very humanity to the substance. It is here important to note that since liberalism's Lockean foundation, the condition of slavery has been understood as a state of war, the rectification of which is the foundational ground of the civil and political order.[14] But as the political theorist Andrew Dilts has argued, the founding of this order is not a singular one-time event. Rather, it is continually reenacted by means of an inclusive exclusion that makes a sharp distinction between those "who are part of the contract (and therefore understood as reasonable) and those who remain outside it (who are irrational who can justly be treated with what would otherwise be excessive punishment)," which is one of the ways Locke described the state of war.[15] This being the case, it is not difficult to understand why a biopolitical order that today is essentially a late-liberal biopolitical order (re)produces itself by means of a war of governance waged against those it renders enslaved. In other words, the drug war as a biopolitical war of governance continually produces the very object/enemy against which it fights as a means of maintaining its very existence as a civil and political order.

Yet there is something more than mere slavery about this view of the addict. For if it were merely a matter of being enslaved to a substance, then one could have his or her freedom, and thus his or her humanity, restored by being released from this enslavement. Unfortunately, this is not how it works for many of those who are former users. Rather, for many who no longer use, the mark of use remains. As Terrance, one of the leaders of Voices of Community Activists and Leaders (VOCAL-NY), once told me: "Even if I don't use anymore, it's all they want to talk about. It's all they see." Even if one becomes "clean," she remains a "former addict" or in the parlance of Narcotics Anonymous, always and forever a "recovering addict." The suspicion remains, and the question remains: "Is she really clean?"

The director of an international harm-reduction and drug policy organization once described this to me as though the person who uses drugs gets contaminated by the drug; a contamination that she can never clean herself of. When the director spoke of this contamination, he was not only talking about addiction but also about possession. The fact that the director was also speaking of possession is important, for it suggests that perhaps neither slavery nor contamination is the best way to consider the exclusionary transformation of the drug user that the drug war produces. For as I have already pointed out, the "addict" can never regain her humanity; she is forever an "addict" even if a "former" one. And even if an "addict" can become "clean" again, suggesting that she has rid herself of the impurity by which she was once contaminated, the notion of contamination suggested by the director does not help us understand how mere possession of a substance, or even of paraphernalia such as syringes or pipes, can result in incarceration. This notion of contamination does not fully help us understand how it is that in 2011 alone, the New York City Police Department arrested 50,684 people for merely possessing personal-use amounts of marijuana.[16] Or why, despite a specifically amended law to the contrary, the New York City police continue to arrest persons carrying syringes.[17]

The dehumanization that is produced by the drug war, then, cannot be thought of simply in terms of slavery as a loss of control or sovereignty, and neither can it be thought of in terms of the purity and danger of contamination. Rather, as revealed in the very first line of the CNN article, this dehumanization is best conceived in terms of a transformation of ontological status; a dehumanization as the transformation of the human subject into a nonhuman object occurs, whereby the user and the drug become one through a process of consubstantiality. *Consubstanialis* is the Latin rendering of the Greek *homoousios*, both of which can be translated as "of one being" or "of the same being" and is the concept used in the Nicene Creed to describe Christ as being "of the same being" as God the Father. It is this consubstantiality of the Father and Son that at one and the same time render them separate and distinct entities and *of* the same being, thus providing the ontological ground for the Trinitarian God.

Similarly, I am trying to argue that the conditions of the drug war render the user and the drug consubstantial. Recall the opening lines of the CNN article: "Heroin, cocaine and amphetamines are the kind of street drugs you expect to find in the shady corners of any city, hiding away from the glare of law enforcement. But in one small space in downtown Vancouver addicts openly inject their fixes—as medics watch on." The substances of the first sentence and the "addicts" of the second are linked in a relation of consubstantiality—separate and distinct entities and yet of the same being. Whether in the sentences or in our worlds, the names of the substances and the "addicts" could be interchanged, and it would not alter their sense. But unlike the sharedness of being that grounds the Christian God, the result of the consubstantiality of user and drug is not divine but rather evil.

It is through this ontological transformation by which drug users are rendered consubstantial with the substances they use that the drug war produces the Other internal to humanness itself. This, then, suggests that the "addict" is not so much enslaved to a drug as much as bound to it—*bound* being one of the other meanings of *addīctus*—bound, that is, consubstantially as "of the same being." The result is the dehumanization of a certain vector of humanness: the consubstantiality of the "addict" and the drug is understood, as the Single Convention puts it, as an evil that displaces the essential goodness of she who has been transformed.[18] As evil—or the absence of good—the "addict" is the ultimate internal Other—the Other not only of society but of humanness itself—who is indeed the internal enemy and who, as the Single Convention makes clear, it is "mankind's" duty to "combat." Having thus produced its own internal enemy, the drug war has also simultaneously produced that protectable population who must be secured. This, then, is the first inclusive-exclusionary step in the drug war as a biopolitical war of governance.

"PEOPLE WHO USE DRUGS BECOME 'EXPENDABLE' BEINGS"

I have so far been trying to trace some of the ways in which the conditions of the drug war render drug users less than human, an inclusive-exclusionary rendering that simultaneously produces a recognizably protectable population. As one director of a national drug policy and harm-reduction organization based in New York put it: "Drug users are considered subhuman." As a result, he continued, "They are internal enemies . . . So I think the war on drugs is, it falls under that thing, you know, state security. So the war on drugs is just another mechanism for, an excuse for increased state surveillance." Indeed, this assessment appears to be entirely correct when considered in light of, for example, the former U.S. drug czar William Bennett's claim that drugs and drug users are "the gravest threat to our national well-being," a sentiment supported by former Los Angeles police chief Darryl Gates, who once claimed that "casual drug use [is] 'treason,' and then recommended that users be 'taken out and shot.'"[19] This is a sentiment that is, as of this writing, being enacted in the Philippines, where state-sponsored violence carried out by its own personnel and vigilantes has resulted in the murder of nearly eighteen hundred drug users over the course of about two months.[20]

It is just this drug war ideology or mind-set that has led to, as the policy director of VOCAL-NY put it, "state or public paternalism . . . directed at drug users. Or sort of hatred, or eh, what's the word I'm looking for, controlling . . . the sort of, like, idea that these people, like, we're gonna, like, tolerate them but they have to be managed carefully for their own good. The sort of incarceration mindset that the drug war helped extend into all these other areas of life beyond the prison. So it's part of housing, it's part of all, just, walking down the street and the stop-and-frisk type of stuff." As should be clear from the previous chapter, today the drug war is one of the primary situated conditions that allows for this "state paternalism" of "control" and "management," whether in the form of extreme and overt state-sponsored violence as is currently being done in the Philippines or "softer" versions such as stop-and-frisk policing and other punitive and surveillance mechanisms or in the form of therapeutic social service interventions. This is particularly so in areas that I have elsewhere called *zones of uninhabitability*.[21] From police randomly stopping, frisking, and questioning young African American and Latino men in New York and elsewhere in the United States, to child services randomly showing up at the front door of a Copenhagen mother who has not used heroin in nearly five years, to the constant police presence in the Downtown Eastside of Vancouver, which despite the successes of the ongoing experiment in worldbuilding taking place there still gives the neighborhood the feel of an occupied territory—in all of these ways and more, the drug war does indeed offer "an excuse for increased state surveillance."[22] This is the "incarceration mind-set" that has extended into a large swath of everyday life so that even walking down the street has become a potential sign of evildoing and a cause for stop-and-frisk; or, one could lose possibly his or her public housing just for having a visitor—for example, one's son, who had once, in the past, been convicted on drug charges. For a drug user, everyday life has become an incarcerated life,[23] a part of what Martin, one of the leaders of VOCAL-NY, calls living in the void. In this void, when not being overtly controlled, one is likely being ignored and treated as a nonentity whose presence right there in front of you on the street or in the park simply does not count. Imprisoned in the void, drug users are reduced to nothingness, a nothing that as such is that much easier to control.

Perhaps more than anyone I spoke with, Terrance most regularly articulated the way in which the drug war renders users less than human, the result of which is that they do not count or matter and thus should, at best, be avoided and, at worst, be locked away, left to die, or killed. Echoing the final words of Bud's poem in the previous chapter, Terrance put it plainly: "If you're a user you just don't count, you're nothing." And this condition of not counting is indeed productive of subjectivities. For it not only provides the conditions for how nonusers feel about, interact with, and treat users, but it also conditions how users feel about themselves and act toward themselves and others. "How would you respond," Terrance continued with an example, "if you went to a doctor and was sitting across from him and he saw some track marks on your arms and he started making all kinds of facial expressions, and moving away from you a bit, and suddenly talking differently to you? You wouldn't go back there, you'd begin to feel like nothing." Indeed, this is something I have seen and heard over and over again in all the places my research has taken me: when one is continually treated as nothing, as not counting, as not being human, as being nothing other than shit and trash, then one begins to feel as though this might actually be the case and acts accordingly. Because being is an ecstatically relational and hermeneutic process, one becomes what one is treated as. As Martin put it, when users are "constantly being beaten down by that, that narrowization of not being anything, that's causing them to lose a lot of hope. They start to feel like, they start to act like they are nothing."

Not only are the subjectivities of users reduced to a nothingness that grounds their way of being, so too have our worlds become grounded on the disposal of the shit and trash; worlds that are ordered around what Martin calls the void of where those who are not counted, those who are nothing, are contained. This is what the policy director called "the incarceration mind-set" that has spread throughout much of our everyday lives such that we can say we are living in a carceral society,[24] which is just one of the more obvious consequences of the conditions of biopolitical wars of governance. Terrance, who was incarcerated twice for drug-related charges, would agree:

> Yeah, because, eh, when I was a user people never looked at me as a human being. They looked at me as a crackhead . . . just look at me and see I'm a drug user, I'm a threat to society, I'm the scum of the earth. It's wrong. Look at me as a human being first! And maybe when you come to me I can trust you and put out why I'm doing what I do. You know what I'm saying? Instead you are locking me up, throwing me in jail and throw the keys away. You know because you use drugs, automatically you are a bad person, you're a criminal, you're the scum of the earth. You are not looked at as a human being. You're looked at as something else.

I am trying to argue that this "something else" is what I am calling the *internal Other*, the internal enemy of the order of things that must be contained or killed to establish and maintain and care for "our way of life." Perhaps the "something else" that is the "addict" is best conceived as what Bataille called the *accursed share,* or that which is "destined for violent consumption" for the purpose of maintaining the order of things.[25] As the waste excreted from a restricted economy so as to maintain order, the accursed share in contemporary times, Bataille further argued, is primarily consumed, and thus order is primarily maintained, through war.[26] Whether that war takes the form of a war against an external enemy or an internal biopolitical war on people, all that matters for the maintenance of the order of things is the expenditure of wealth and resources, including that of human resources. With over one trillion dollars spent by the U.S. federal government over the past forty years and all the countries on the globe spending well over $100 billion annually, it is clear that the drug war expends wealth.[27]

So too does it expend human lives. As a war on people, it is difficult to tally the violent consumption of lives the drug war has made possible, but it goes well beyond any number of deaths related simply to actual military or paramilitary/police or cartel violence. In fact, the United Nations Office on Drugs and Crime (UNODC) does not even count these deaths as what it calls "drug-related deaths," which it defines as deaths as a result of "fatal drug overdoses, deaths due to HIV acquired through injecting drug use, suicide, and unintentional deaths and trauma, due to drug use."[28] But these so-called drug-related deaths, which in 2012 were estimated to be 183,000 for just that one year, must be understood as a direct consequence of the conditions of the drug war. While the UNODC report does not explicitly attribute these deaths to the drug war, it does rightly attribute the majority of these deaths to such things as a lack of knowledge of the purity of drugs taken; a reduced tolerance because of abstinence due to treatment or incarceration; or a lack of opioid antagonists, such as naloxone, that would reverse an overdose, all of which are the result of the drug war conditions of prohibition. Perhaps, then, these deaths, in addition to the violent deaths at the hands of militarized police, cartels, and actual militaries, would be better referred to as *drug war–related deaths.* When all of these drug war–related deaths, as well as all of the social deaths caused by the dehumanization about which I have been writing, are taken into consideration, then it becomes clear that the drug war as a war on people provides the conditions within which "people who use drugs become 'expendable' beings," as it is well put in a Canadian Drug Policy Coalition pamphlet fortuitously titled "Changing the Frame."[29]

This, then, is the war on people that has created entire worlds that have become zones of uninhabitability, where users and nonusers alike are better described as trapped in a world than dwelling there. For most, these zones of uninhabitability are not even recognized because they and those who are trapped in them do not count and do not matter; their plight is, as Butler would put it, ungrievable. And all of this is so, I am trying to argue, because as the director of the policy organization put it above, our contemporary biopolitical order needs its "internal enemies"; it needs internal Others against which wars can be waged as the grounding activity of the contemporary order of things. The "good life," or the social and economic order as it is put in the Single Convention, rests upon, depends upon, and is maintained by a war against evil—an evil that is embodied in those "expendable beings" too often referred to as "addicts."

A DISRUPTIVE POLITICS OF SHOWING

I have so far been tracing the various ways in which "addicts" are discursively and ontologically rendered less-than-human expendable beings within the conditions of the drug war. In this condition of war that renders drug users nonhuman internal enemies, how might they begin to politically fight back against this war on people? In other words, how can those who have had their very ontological status as potential political agents—that is, their status as human beings—eviscerated, begin to do political activity and become recognized as doing such? In the final section of this chapter, I will turn to what I call a disruptive political tactic of showing, by which anti–drug war agonists hermeneutically disclose the fantasy of the "fantasy world" and, in so doing, simultaneously enact, or show, the very otherwise they hope to bring into existence as the new nonnormative norm. As will become clear, both the disclosure and the otherwise are enacted through a disruption of the "fantasy world," and it is in the brief clearing made by this disruption that anti–drug war agonists show not only that other ways of being, and thus, other worlds, are possible, but that this otherwise already exists right here and now. What I want to suggest, then, is that in the contemporary condition in which wars on people have become central to biopolitical governance, this political tactic is the first step of a political struggle through which new social and political habits, and, eventually, other nonexclusionary worlds, come into being, stick, and endure.

. . .

"I think that's just basically an old way of thinking, that users are nothing, that they're a waste," Martin told me one day as we sat around the

VOCAL-NY offices waiting for the leadership meeting to begin. "That's just so not true," he continued, "and that's what we do here, that's why we meet here and meet with politicians, to show them that we are not waste, that we aren't nothing." Showing is a good deal of what anti–drug war agonists do. There is, of course, much focus on such things as policy change, legislative initiatives, and particular problems like syringe access and police oppression. All of this rests, however, on a disruptive politics of showing, a political tactic that primarily aims at disrupting drug war conditions in order to open a clearing through which new conditions for being may emerge. Indeed, if conditions are that by which worlds and their inhabitants are (re)produced, then much of the work of politics must be to offer possible alternative conditions for the worlds we *could* live in. This is something anti–drug war agonists know well. For none of their other tactics, let alone their ultimate aim of ending the drug war, are possible without this form of hermeneutic politics, by which they seek to disrupt the "fantasy world" of the drug war and open new possibilities for other worlding conditions.

Martin described to me once the effects of this hermeneutically disruptive tactic: "When I'm dressed [for a meeting with a politician] you'd think I was on Wall Street until I look you in the eye and let you know, I am one of those same people that I'm fighting for, sitting across the table from you right now is an active user. And to see their jaw drop and their eyes stretch open with, really? Yes, that's right. And there are many more just like me." Perhaps this tactic would be better called something like *shock and awe.* For its most immediate consequence is disruption, a shaking of one out of the habit of being, thinking, talking, and doing. It initiates what I have elsewhere called a *breakdown,* or a dissonance that arises when a habituated normativity is confronted by its founding exclusion, thus forcing one to reflect on and alter one's already acquired way of being-in-the-world in order to account for this confrontation.[30]

People become stupefied, Martin said another time, when he tells them that he is an active user. "They really can't help but to pay attention to what I say after I tell them, they are just so fascinated that this is even possible," he said. For example, at a drug policy event in Buffalo, New York, Martin had just finished giving a talk about his personal experiences with the dehumanization of the drug war when a state senator approached him. Apparently moved by what Martin had just said, the senator asked how long Martin had been "clean," assuming that he was a former user. Martin answered that he had not used in "about twelve hours." The senator was astonished: "Twelve hours?" Martin replied,

"Yeah, twelve hours." The senator looked at him with fascination and said, "Are you serious?" They eventually started to talk about VOCAL-NY, their aims, and the costs of the drug war, and this conversation went on for about twenty minutes. The disruption, the breakdown, initiated by the simple fact of an active drug user engaged in political activity, then, opened a possibility for political conversation and hopefully, eventually more.

Henrik, the head of the BF (BrugerForeningen) in Copenhagen, also regularly uses disruption as a political tactic when meeting a new agonist. Henrik has been using heroin several times a day, every day, for over twenty years. And as with many heroin users, you would never know it. He looks and sounds just like any other "average" fifty-something Danish man. He uses this to his advantage when meeting with politicians, bureaucrats, or any others with whom he meets regularly in his advocating and lobbying duties as the head of the BF. As he has described to me: "I'll be sitting in this meeting with them for some time, or I'll have them here at the union giving them a tour and showing them around, and after a while I'll just stop what I'm doing and turn to them and say, 'Oh, and by the way, I'm on heroin right now.' They are always so shocked. They just couldn't imagine that some 'junkie' on heroin could be standing in front of them looking so good and sounding intelligent. It really shakes them, and they really start to listen after that."

This "jaw dropping," "fascination," and "shock" of New York and Danish politicians are the consequence of a disruptive political tactic of showing meant to evoke a hermeneutic disclosure of the conditions of the drug war. If one's mind-set is that "addicts" are trash and shit, or enslaved and irresponsible beings, or consubstantially equivalent to a substance that renders them the evil internal enemy, then when the man sitting in front of you discussing drug, health, or judicial policy and legislation tells you that he is currently on heroin or was just using cocaine twelve hours ago, your mind-set will very likely be disturbed. In the midst of this disruption—or this breakdown of the "supposed to be"—the politician, or whoever it may be, sees because she has been shown not only that an otherwise is possible but, in fact, that an otherwise already exists right in front of her.

One can see, for example, that it is possible to use heroin every day for over twenty years and be, as the CNN author put it, both "articulate" and "educated" without being either "angry" or in an alley. Of course, not all drug users look as "good" as Henrik or as if they were on Wall Street like Martin (it is important to note that not all nonusers do, either). I want to suggest, however, that although their "look" may make the effect more shocking, what is ultimately disruptive about this political tactic is the disclosed fact that active drug users are doing political activity well. Because of this, Henrik, Martin, Terrance, and all of the other anti–drug war agonists I know are convinced that this form of hermeneutic politics works whether people are initially "fooled" by how the user-agonists look or not. For the point is not to show that drug users can fit into that which counts but to change what counts. The point is to enact what Derrida has called *democracy-to-come,* or "the regime of everyone, beyond all exclusionary conditions."[31]

Bringing about this regime of everyone—or as I will call it in the following chapter, a community of those without community—begins, then, with drug users doing politics themselves. If the drug war has turned us into enemies, so the thinking goes, then we must be the ones who fight back. There are, of course, many nonusing allies who participate in this political struggle, but as has become the mantra of the international drug users movement: "Nothing about us without us." As a result, it is active and former users who are at the center of the anti–drug war movement, and it is they who are showing how our worlds could be otherwise if they were no longer understood and treated as nothing. As Phil, a longtime political agonist in Vancouver, put it to me one day when describing the tactics they have used in the Downtown Eastside: "It is a way of reframing things. To show that [drug users'] existence is of worth."

As Terrance explained, this is a matter of joining the battle and showing that rather than nonhuman evil, drug users are, in fact, leading the fight against exclusionary conditions. As he went on to tell me: "This drug users union will make a big difference if it's done correctly. People start coming forth and talking about they are a user or a former user, and then make people know like, wow, look at these guys right here, look at the stuff they're doing. Going out talking to Congress, all these rallies, all these actions, and it's being brainstormed and organized by users, and it's becoming effective . . . I think that is one of the most shocking things to our government officials that these individuals that are using get this accomplished. They're no longer in the background. They are starting to come forth. They're starting to address issues; they're tired of the way we're being treated. You know what I'm saying? We're tired of being treated, not second or third class, but ninth and tenth class. You know? We deserve to be treated like humans just like anybody else."

Here we see the double nature of this hermeneutically disruptive politics. For on the one hand, this form of politics shows that drug users can, in fact, do politics. Disrupting the conditions that render them less-than-human and irresponsible beings, they show that they are indeed capable of doing the most human of all activities—that is, political activity.[32] On the other hand, by means of this very enactment they simultaneously transform the situated conditions into those by which they must count as human. For by actually doing politics themselves, drug users do not simply show that they are capable of it. More importantly, they force others to recognize this capability by engaging in political activity with them, even if the others are ultimately against them. This transformation is what those who politically interact with anti–drug war agonists find to be the most "shocking thing." For it disrupts the order of how things normally are. This transformative disruption, however, may only be temporary, as the conditions are not permanently changed by means of any singular political act. But the political wager is that over time, enough disruptions will lead to further acts that will have permanent worldly effects.

This hermeneutic politics, then, has what Simon Critchley calls a *clôtural logic,* which he sees as the ethical and political moment in Derrida's thinking.[33] Clôtural logic is that by which the limit that bounds or closes or conditions any situation is interrupted by that which exceeds that situation. This excess is not outside or beyond the situation, however, but an integral aspect of it. Thus, interruption, or what I am calling *disruption,* is possible because every situation is an open structure because of this disruptive potentiality—what Critchley calls a *clause of nonclosure*—within the situation itself. As one of the inclusively excluded grounds of the contemporary biopolitical order of things, drug users are this excess who are a disruptive source for a potential otherwise. The hermeneutic-disruptive tactic of showing is how they politically enact this clôtural logic.

Furthermore, in contrast to the assumption that political change comes about through rational conversation and debate, this hermeneutic-political tactic begins with the postulate that changing biopolitical conditions is a matter of changing habits. This is a political tactic that appreciates that if it is the case, as William James put it, that habit is "the enormous fly-wheel of society, its most precious conservative agent,"[34] then the first political task must be to disrupt and change habits so as to ultimately change society. Thus, the hermeneutic politics and the disclosive tactic of showing enacted by the anti–drug war movement recognize that the drug war culture, mind-set, or ideology, or for that matter, what we normally call *meaning, understanding,* and *interpretation,* are not a consequence of the most rational argument or the realization of the truthfulness of one position over another. Rather, they are acquired and habituated ways of being, speaking, acting, and doing that are grounded in a particular rhetoric and style framed and given legitimacy not only by institutions of power but, perhaps more significantly, by their seeming sharedness by those around us.

If this is the case, then political change does not occur by making a better argument. But rather, political change and the otherwise come about by enacting "habitual disruptions of the habitual," which makes possible "experiencing the inexperienceable."[35] It is precisely this "experiencing the inexperienceable" that anti–drug war agonists bring about when they show others that they are, in fact, exceptionally capable of exercising their humanness by being very adept political actors. Such habitual disruptions, or breakdowns, initiate not only personal but ultimately socially and politically creative attempts to imagine and enact new habituated ways of being. It is by disrupting and changing habits, then, that anti–drug war agonists attempt to politically change the conditions of the drug war and, in so doing, attempt to "invent new relations and futures."[36] Put another way, this is a politics of what Jonathan Lear calls *radical hope.*[37]

Ultimately, though, this is a long and slow political process. But within the conditions established by wars on people, it is unclear how else political and social change could come about. This is perhaps even more the case in an historical context in which military power—including that of militarized police—has surpassed any realistic hope of change brought about according to a revolutionary model based on, for example, the French or Bolshevik Revolutions. Furthermore, because liberal reformism is increasingly exposed as little more than a last-ditch effort to maintain an exhausted status quo, it seems that change can only *begin* to come about by such disruptive tactics to the conditioned and habituated "supposed to be." By showing, for example, both the willing *and* unknowing perpetrators of the drug war that they live in a "fantasy world" and how things could and should be otherwise, new habituated ways of being—indeed, new worlds, slowly come into existence.

In fact, it is just such tactics that are behind the recent victories of the anti–drug war movement in the United States, where medical and personal-use marijuana are increasingly being legalized, one result of which is the decreasing numbers of low-level marijuana arrests that have contributed to both the rise of mass incarceration and the increasing precarity of those—mostly African American and Latino young men—who have been arrested. Or in Copenhagen, where prescription heroin is now being implemented, which will increasingly lead to less crime related to street dealing and fewer overdoses as the result of users not knowing the purity of the heroin they buy on the street. Or in the Downtown Eastside of Vancouver, where an entire neighborhood has been transformed into a world in which drug users are increasingly able to dwell because, for among other reasons, it has become a world conditioned by what in chapter five I call *attuned care*.

Each of these political victories became possible because anti–drug war agonists began by disrupting the conditioned and habituated "fantasy world" produced by the drug war. The clearing these disruptions brought about allowed for—made political space for—imagining new possibilities for how to live in worlds with drugs and drug users without the latter being that world's exclusionary ground. As a result, these anti–drug war victories have significantly bettered the lives not only of drug users but of nondrug users alike. Thus, for example, with reduced policing, decreases in crime, better relations between people within certain neighborhoods, and a reduction of infectious diseases, the otherwise that the anti–drug war movement hopes to bring about is one that will be better for all. Perhaps Martin put this best: "All of this is for one goal, and that's making it better, for not just me, but for everyone. Not just for me, not just for users, but for everyone." In our contemporary condition of wars on people, then, the anti–drug war movement is showing us a model of political activity for resisting the biopolitical inclusive exclusion of internal others and how a world without exclusionary conditions could slowly come about.

In the rest of this book, I would like to show the readers just some of the ways in which these nonexclusionary conditions are being enacted. For if the first step of a politics of worldbuilding is a disruptive showing of how an otherwise can be, then the next step is actually enacting the nonexclusionary otherwise within the clearings created by this disruption. As will become clear in the rest of this book, these clearings differ in spatial and temporal magnitude depending on their location. For example, in Vancouver the clearing has, to a great extent, come to overlap with much of the neighborhood of the Downtown Eastside and has been precariously maintained now for over a decade, while in New York City clearings tend to be quite temporally fleeting and rather intersubjectively located. Nevertheless, within these clearings, no matter how small and brief they may be, the anti–drug war movement is actively creating new nonexclusionary worlds conditioned by attuned care, where whoever arrives is let-be to be and become what they will and cared for as such. In what follows I will attempt to give a glimpse—to show—what these worlds are like and how they are actively being brought into being.

CHAPTER 3

A Community of Those without Community

To remain present in the proximity of another who by dying removes himself definitively, to take upon myself another's death as the only death that concerns me, this is what puts me beside myself, this is the only separation that can open me, in its very impossibility, to the Openness of a community.

—Maurice Blanchot

On a bright and pleasant day in late July 2013, I attended a Memorial Day ceremony honoring those drug users who had died in Denmark during the past year. Having arrived early I helped Henrik and others from the BrugerForeningen (BF) insert 280 single flowers into a small patch of grass alongside a busy city street; one flower to represent each so-called drug-related death that had occurred in Denmark in the past year. This patch of grass, which to most onlookers is barely noticeable as it is little more than grass planted on a median between the busy city street and a much smaller parallel-running road, is what the city has offered the BF as a place to erect a memorial stone that reads, "In Memory of Drug Users" to honor the drug war dead. Just a few meters away, a new metro stop was being constructed. And so it was here, on a barely noticeable strip of grass and a few scattered trees in the midst of busy city traffic and the continuous clamor of urban construction, that approximately forty people gathered to honor and remember Denmark's drug war dead.

Friends, colleagues, parents, and other relatives of recently and not-so-recently deceased drug users joined union members and other anti–drug war agonists on this Memorial Day, chatting and catching up, laughing and crying, and telling stories of old friends, partners, sons, and daughters as they drank a beer or soda and nibbled on the few snacks provided. As a blues band consisting of union members set up their instruments and the sound system, Henrik and Thomas—another member of the BF leadership—put in place a podium with a transparent base filled with used syringes the union had collected during their weekly program for clearing the city streets of any potentially danger-ous used paraphernalia. A police car slowly rolled up and asked some-one what this was all about and then slowly pulled away. It would drive by two more times in the next hour, each time slowing to a near stand-still to "observe" the ceremony. Once the band began to play, the gath-ering of people unhurriedly started to attune their focus toward them, the podium, and the 280 singular flowers.

After a few songs, Henrik walked up to the podium and offered a short welcome and introduction and then announced the first guest speaker of the day, a leader of a drug user union in another European city. Each year the BF invites someone from another country to speak at the ceremony in order to emphasize that despite the symbolic emphasis of the flowers, this is, in fact, a day to remember the drug war dead around the globe. As the speaker would point out, about sixty-five hun-dred drug-related deaths occurred in Europe in 2012, and approxi-mately two hundred thousand occurred across the globe.[1] But as I pointed out in the previous chapter, these numbers do not account for the wider drug war–related deaths, which would also include all of those who died at the hands of, for example, militarized police, cartels, actual militaries, and state-sponsored vigilantism. Each of these deaths, the speaker would emphasize, was the result of a "repressive" and "moralistic" drug war that provides the widely diffused shared condi-tions that render the lives of most drug users ungrievable. It was just this conditioned and assumed ungrievability that this ceremony sought to belie. These 280, these 6,500, these 200,000 deaths counted, and they counted as more than statistics to be used in whatever way some organization or institution found fitting. As the gathering on this mar-ginal strip of grass on this day attested—as did the similar ceremonies happening in over sixty other countries on that same day—these were the unnecessary deaths of friends and lovers, and as made clear by one of the other guest speakers there that day—a mother of one of the dead—sons and daughters as well.

In many ways this Memorial Day ceremony resembled those that memorialize the dead of the wars that are recognized, such as the two World Wars or, for that matter, the annual memorial ceremony held in New York City on September 11. Among other things, those ceremo-nies can be understood as a ritualistic practice by which grievable war dead are recognized as having sacrificed their lives for the greater good of the nation.[2] In this sense, death is memorialized as the ultimate contribution to a totalized and unified community marked by sameness of identity, by a territorialized we that differ profoundly from they, a difference substantiated by these very deaths. These ritualized ceremonies transform a singular wartime death of an individual into a foundational ground for a totalized and individualized community as nation, a community that has become subjectivized through a metaphysical humanist projection. By means of this projection, the community is understood as a "property" of human subjects just as much as these subjects are understood as "property" of the community,[3] within which all become subsumed and, as such, similarly become potentially sacrificial as standing reserve.

Despite the superficial resemblance, in this chapter I want to argue that this Memorial Day ceremony in Copenhagen, and the sixty plus others that occurred on that July day, are in fact significantly different from the memorialization of those recognized and sacrificial deaths that ritualistically and repetitively found the totalized community of identity and belonging. For as unrecognizable and ungrievable deaths, the drug war dead are not ritualistically transformable into the foundational ground of any singular and individualized community of identity. Rather, like the trash on the side of the road that blows onto the small patch of grass where this Copenhagen ceremony takes place, drug war deaths are the waste the totalized community expends. Not only are drug users left to die, they find themselves in a shared condition of war by which they die at a rate per year that nears the total death count *since* 2001 in the so-called global war on terrorism.[4] And yet, unlike those who die in such recognized wars—whether they are American soldiers, Taliban fighters, or villagers in any number of countries—drug users have no totalized community that embraces and memorializes them.

So far in this book, I have been arguing and trying to show that drug users rendered as "addicts" have become one of the primary internal Others that are inclusively excluded in order to found and maintain the contemporary biopolitical order. If it is the case, as Roberto Esposito claims,[5] that community and violence have always been linked throughout human history and that the founding of any particular community is mythologized with a sacrificial death that creates a lack at the foundational core of the community, which, in turn, creates an obligation on the part of its members to sacrifice themselves for the maintenance of the community, then biopolitics as a war on people can be understood as the continuous repetition of this founding moment. For it is by means of the inclusive exclusion of internal Others, such as the "addict," that biopolitics continuously (re)founds the contemporary order of things by sacrificing this internal Other while at the same time creating an obligation on the part of the normalized population potentially to sacrifice themselves by waging this perpetual war on the internal enemy.

Perhaps, however, this widely diffused and complex condition of war creates the possibility for an entirely other kind of community to come into being. In this chapter I would like to interrogate this perhaps and in so doing begin to trace the contours of the kind of community I will explore in more detail throughout the rest of this book. This is a community that we might call a community of those without community—that is, a nontotalizable community of finite beings that is incapable of being equated with any closed and totalized community of identity and, as such, is incapable of being located in any particular locale.[6] Put another way, the community of those without community is perhaps best understood as the communal noncommunity of finite belonging as such. In the rest of this chapter, I will consider how it is that such a community begins to emerge within the contemporary biopolitical condition of war. I will do this by interrogating how in this condition of being inclusively excluded from all existing communities of identity and belonging, drug users nevertheless continually speak of and work to create a community always open to whoever arrives.[7] As this Memorial Day service in Copenhagen indicates—as do the sixty plus others that occurred around the globe that day—death is not only the means by which drug users are excluded from the closed community of identity and belonging but, in fact, is that by which this "community of those without community" comes into being. How this is so will become clear as this chapter develops.

COMMUNITY

Nearly everywhere my assemblic ethnography of the drug war took me, I heard anti–drug war agonists speaking about community. Indeed, this was the most commonly used referent for drug users in general, whether locally or globally. There is no doubt, of course, that at times that to which *community* referred was a bit ambiguous. Thus, for example, in New York City it was not uncommon that at times *community* seemed to reference the African American "community" or the poor "community"; and in Vancouver, the neighborhood of the Downtown Eastside;

and in Copenhagen, the union itself. But in each of these seemingly ambiguous utterances, I suggest, we actually see a clear articulation of drug war situations as intertwined assemblages. For in each of these particular situational manifestations, the shared conditions of the drug war have concentratedly emerged as intertwined with other situations, such as race and poverty in New York City and throughout the United States, poverty and indigenous oppression in Vancouver and throughout Canada, and the unique ability in Copenhagen and Denmark to secure funding from the welfare state to organize a drug user union that has become more akin to a familial union than a labor union. It is just such concentrated emergences of the shared conditions of the drug war that allow for the at times ambiguous equation of a community of drug users with a totalized and localized community of identity and belonging, even if the latter is one that is marginalized.

This seeming ambiguity is ultimately cleared away, however, by the fact that for the most part, drug users are excluded from these marginalized communities—for example, the African American and First Nations "communities"—just as much as they are from the dominant one. Michael Javen Fortner, for example, has shown that the harshly punitive Rockefeller drug laws of New York State were strongly advocated for and supported by working and middle-class African Americans who had increasingly become concerned about their neighborhoods.[8] Although today this support may have waned as the devastating consequences of these laws have come to fruition, this does not mean that African Americans or the neighborhoods where they live have become any more inclusive for drug users. Thus, for example, Terrance's Bronx neighbors may be more sympathetic than most to those in the neighborhood who have been caught up in the drug war situation manifest there; a neighborhood, that is, that Terrance describes as "drug infested." But this does not mean that these neighbors are any more accepting of drug use or users. Similarly, for years some non–drug using residents of the Downtown Eastside have and continue to fight against the anti–drug war politics of worldbuilding underway there—for example, by protesting the Insite safe-consumption room or demanding increased police presence and crackdowns. In this sense, then, there is no community of identity and belonging to which drug users belong because even those marginalized ones who have become intertwined with the drug war, for the most part, also exclude them.

This being the case, and yet *community* remaining one of the key concepts of the anti–drug war movement, the question must be asked:

What is this community that anti–drug war agonists regularly reference, who constitutes it, and how does it come about? To put this question in a slightly other way: How can we begin to reconceive a concept like community in a contemporary condition of widely diffused complexity that disrupts any possibility of thinking community in the traditional manner of a closed totality? Such a task is even more difficult in our contemporary condition, in which "fantasy worlds" of such communities are violently created by waging exclusionary war on internal Others such as "drug addicts." In this chapter and throughout the rest of this book, I will interrogate just how it is that in this condition of widely diffused complexity and wars on people, a contemporary condition that seems to foreclose the very possibility of community, the anti–drug war movement is politically creating new open communities by experimenting with and enacting the new kinds of values those involved consider most appropriate for a community of whoever arrives.

The question of community and how to regain it has been central to social and political theory since at least the nineteenth century. As Sheldon Wolin has put it, this concern has "largely centered on the attempt to restate the value of community" against the alienating and exclusionary fragmentation of urban and industrialized society.[9] This desire to return to a supposedly more intimate and affective bond has led to various conceptions of community that, in one way or another, have been conceived of in terms of a geographically located and closed totality that is unified,[10] if not in thought, belief, and will,[11] then certainly against others who do not belong.[12] As Zygmunt Bauman has put it, this closed community has always been—and still remains today—only possible through the violent exclusion of both external and internal Others.[13] While it may be the case that anthropologists—after generations of more or less assuming some version of this closed totality as an object of study—increasingly reject the closed, totalized, and self-identical community for a more contested and fragmented conception,[14] Rupert Stasch has convincingly shown that traces of this assumption linger in many of the discipline's most dearly held concepts and analytic approaches.[15]

Similarly, there is little doubt that in much public discourse and political practice, this notion of community as a totalized and closed unity to which one belongs remains dominant today (here we need only think about the recent rise in nationalism and other versions of exclusionary right-wing politics around the globe).[16] Through the lens of this exclusionary foundation, it is clear to see how community has become a central conceptual marker for biopolitics in the twentieth and now twenty-first centuries.[17] This being the case, it would seem particularly odd that drug users rendered as "addicts," who have become one of the primary inclusively excluded grounds of the contemporary biopolitical order, make community a key concept in their struggle against this order. But this only seems odd if we understand them to be using community in this traditionally totalized and exclusionary sense. For it is clear that drug users can never be included—or folded into—that which relies upon their very exclusion to exist. Therefore, we need to consider how it might be that the anti–drug war movement is using the concept of community differently. Just what is it that these political agonists might mean by their use of community?

Reading together Jean-Luc Nancy and Maurice Blanchot's philosophical accounts of community may be helpful for addressing this question. Nancy makes the seemingly radical claim that "community is revealed in the death of others."[18] But it is important to recognize that he does not mean this in the sense of transforming the dead into what Nancy calls a "communal intimacy" and neither does community in his sense "*operate* the transfiguration of its dead into some substance or subject," such as homeland, nation, or even humanity.[19] Recall that in the opening section, I argued that the anti–drug war movement similarly understands drug war deaths as inoperative in this way. The community of which Nancy writes, then, and that I will try to show is fundamental for understanding the kind of community enacted by the anti–drug war movement, is precisely an inoperative community in that its grounding—that is, death—cannot be worked upon to become instrumentalized for a totalizing communal project of shared identity. Death, rather, reveals the "finitude and irredeemable excess that make up finite being."[20] That is to say, the ecstatic finitude disclosed by death, while foreclosing any possibility of thinking the subject in terms of a self-totalized and autonomous individual that shares identity with other such individuals within a totalized community of identity, ultimately is what constitutes the fundamental grounding for being-with.[21]

How does this disclosed finitude and its excess—or better put, the ecstatic relationality that characterizes finitude—help us better understand the community of those without community that the anti–drug war movement politically enacts? According to Nancy, the experience of death discloses one's existence as always already outside of oneself, exceeding the subjective boundaries of the body and ego. This experience, however, does not disclose the infinity of being-human but rather the finitude of this being. For the experience of death is one that can never be appropriated as one's own. Rather, the experience of death will always exceed "me" and thus always stands as the limit of what one could become. Most importantly for our purposes, it is the disclosure of this limit—a limit shared by all finite beings—that is, a sharedness of nothing other than our disappropriation—that opens the ontological ground for being-with or community. This limit that constitutes the ontological ground of community for Nancy, furthermore, moves us closer to understanding how the anti–drug war movement enacts community. This is so because death reveals not only the ecstatic limit of autonomous and individualized existence—the limit that constitutes the condition of being-with—but also the limit of this being-with in that we can never share or stand in for the death of an other but only ever experience dying-with an other.

It is just this experience of dying-with that Maurice Blanchot considers essential to community. In his critical reading of Nancy, Blanchot argues that what is missing from Nancy's account is the demand the death of the other places upon us. For Blanchot, then, it is the experience of dying-with an other, not the awareness of one's own eventual death, that provides the ecstatic experience of finitude that grounds an open community. As Blanchot writes:

> What, then, calls me into question most radically? Not my relation to myself as finite or as the consciousness of being before death or for death, but my presence for another who absents himself by dying. To remain present in the proximity of another who by dying removes himself definitively, to take upon myself another's death as the only death that concerns me, this is what puts me beside myself, this is the only separation that can open me, in its very impossibility, to the Openness of a community.[22]

Blanchot continues by quoting Bataille: "A man alive, who sees a fellow-man die, can survive only *beside himself*." If for Nancy death discloses the human condition of being-with by revealing the ecstatic finitude of human existence, then for Blanchot death—and most especially the death of an other—discloses this essential being-with as placing a demand upon each of us to be concerned for the other.

Reading Nancy and Blanchot together, then, we can begin to understand how it is that death is so central to the notion of community articulated and put into practice by the anti–drug war movement. For Nancy and Blanchot link death and community by showing that death reveals the illusion of the normalized subject as a self-totalized and autonomous individual through its disclosure of the limit of our singular finite being. For Nancy this limit of finitude is that which humans hold in common; it is that which ecstatically pulls each of us into our relational intertwining of being-with. Blanchot, however, takes the next step and argues that the disclosure of this relational intertwining also reveals an essential interdependence among all finite beings.[23]

Recently, Roberto Esposito has built on these insights in order to offer a revived notion of community characterized, above all, by a mutual obligation to care.[24] In contrast to what he calls the *immunitary logic* of biopolitics—the logic of inclusive exclusion—Esposito has articulated an affirmative biopolitics grounded on the open vulnerability of finite existence and the necessary intertwining of a community of finite beings.[25] Esposito perhaps best describes this notion of community by considering the etymological constitution of *communitas* in terms of the *cum* of being-with and the *munus* of the obligatory care, an obligation that takes the form of a gift, that this being-with entails.[26] Thus, for Esposito, as for Nancy, Blanchot, and Bataille, the open community of those without community, ontologically grounded by what throughout this book I call *attuned care,* perhaps best describes the human condition of finite beings that are always already ecstatically intertwined with one another. As will become clear, this is what I contend those in the anti–drug war movement intend when they articulate and enact their sense of community through their political and ethical activity.

In the rest of this chapter, I want to explore how the anti–drug war movement enacts such a community of those without community. In particular, I will consider how this community emerges through the openness among those who have become beside themselves because of the experience of dying-with. This is the ground for a politics that, in the words of Simon Critchley, "repeatedly interrupt all attempts at totalization" and "maintains the community as an open community" of difference.[27] For as a thanatopolitics groundlessly grounded and motivated by the experience of dying-with, the politics of worldbuilding enacted by the anti–drug war movement brings into being a community of those who have nothing in common but their shared being-toward-death, the recognition of which discloses their essential being-with and the obligation to offer the gift of attuned care.[28] In what follows, I will show how the experience of dying-with disclosively opens anti–drug war agonists to their essential being-with-others, which in turn for many becomes a political motivation for enacting an open community. As will become clear throughout the rest of this book, such an experience and motivation lead to a politics that seeks to open worlds to whoever arrives and, in doing so,[29] attune to their singular need for care.[30]

DYING-WITH

On the morning of September 7, 2012, the Caravan for Peace about which I wrote in chapter one gathered, along with a number of local anti–drug war agonists, on the steps of New York City's City Hall. Recall that the Caravan was founded by Javier Sicilia, whose son was killed by a Mexican drug gang, and consists of family members of those who have been similarly killed as a result of getting caught up in the drug war situation in that country. As part of their tour across Mexico and the United States, the Caravan was in New York this day to bring attention to the social and physical violence and corruption wrought by the drug war in the two countries and around the globe. Voices of Community Activists and Leaders (VOCAL-NY) was one of the local anti–drug war groups there that day in support of the Caravan, and Frank, one of the staff leaders, asked Martin to represent the union by speaking at the event.

Martin had only recently started to participate in VOCAL-NY and was interested in becoming a part of the leadership. Frank, however, was not yet certain that Martin was "leadership material," as he occasionally exhibited some unreliable tendencies. Martin, for example, had gained a reputation for being undependable, as he would regularly show up late or not at all to important union events and actions, and when he did show up, he would occasionally let his jovial and chatty predilections become disruptive. Despite these tendencies, Martin had become strongly motivated to join VOCAL-NY and actively participate as a leader because of the experience he had holding his mother in his arms as she died from complications related to AIDS. Martin's mother was a heroin user who eventually contracted HIV because of the lack of clean syringes that could have easily protected her from the virus if syringe exchange programs had been available to her. This experience of dying-with his mother, a dying-with that was absolutely unnecessary and a direct result of the drug war, in the words of Bataille put Martin "beside" himself and disclosively opened him to the necessity of community. That is, community as the being-with of finite beings who have come to realize that as being-toward-death they are always already essentially intertwined with other such beings in relations of care.[31] It was this community that Martin wished to disclose to others by joining the VOCAL-NY leadership. And because the Caravan was founded and consisted of those who had had similar experiences of dying-with as a result of drug war situations, Martin's experience with his mother and the openness it created for him is precisely why Frank asked Martin to speak that day on the steps of City Hall, despite his general wariness of Martin's dedication.

Martin did speak that day, and it was a transformative experience for himself and Frank. Here for the first time speaking in public of his mother's death and the dying-with that he experienced with her, Martin exhibited the passionate public speaking that would eventually make him one of VOCAL-NY's most articulate speakers, not only at public events, but as we saw in the previous chapter, also in closed meetings with politicians and bureaucrats. As he would tell me a couple of years later, that speech that day was his "coming out." This, of course, is an interesting way of putting it. No doubt when he told me this, Martin meant something like this speech was the event that not only gave him the self-confidence to fully participate and dedicate himself to the union leadership but also opened the eyes of Frank and others to the fact that Martin was capable of it. But this phrase "coming out" indicates something more. It indicates that this speech, as an articulation of his experience of dying-with his mother, was an ecstatic experience through which he finally and fully realized his and all others' care-ful intertwining with one another. By "coming out" of himself, by becoming "beside" himself, Martin, in that moment, consciously realized that he had always already been part of a community of those without community and as such, has an obligation to disclose and open this community to others and care for them as they arrive.

Similar experiences of dying-with are perhaps the most commonly articulated motivation I heard for persons joining the anti–drug war movement and are thus central to what I have called elsewhere the *ethics of dwelling* that motivates a politics of worldbuilding being done by the anti–drug war movement.[32] We have already seen this in the example of the Caravan for Peace and Martin, but innumerable other examples abound. The guest speaker at the Copenhagen Memorial Day ceremony, for example, recalled in his speech that the union that he heads was founded as a result of the overdose death of a prominent drug user agonist in his country; as we saw in chapter one, the politics of worldbuilding in the Downtown Eastside of Vancouver often marks its beginnings with the Killing Fields demonstration and the 1000 Crosses protest that took place in 1997; each cross, as with the flowers in Copenhagen, memorializing a drug war death. Like the Movement for Peace, any number of organizations around the globe have been founded by the parents of those who have died from overdose or other drug war–related deaths. This thanatopolitical motivation at the heart of the anti–drug war movement is why in this section I want to make clear that the experience of dying-with discloses the very possibility for a community of those without community and the political possibilities such a community allows.[33]

The experience of dying-with, however, need not be a literal proximity as it was for Martin; dying-with is experienced even when not in one another's arms or side by side. The death of an other, even without copresence, can become an experience of dying-with. This is clearly seen in any number of examples of those I have come to know who joined the anti–drug war movement because a loved one or close friend died of an overdose without them having been copresent. Indeed, even for Martin this experience was central to the event of his speech that day on the City Hall steps. Just two weeks prior to this event, a close friend of his had died from an overdose, and it was this experience of dying-with, even though he was not copresent, he would later tell me, that ultimately solidified for him the need to become a serious union leader and thus give that speech. Put another way, this experience of dying-with made undeniably palpable the existential demand that he had an obligation to open community to others. Indeed, this kind of noncopresent dying-with is the most common experience of dying-with I heard about in my assemblic ethnographic research. Ultimately, then, whether copresent or not, the experience of dying-with a friend, relative, or even just the guy seen occasionally at a party or in the neighborhood, I was told over and over again, was *that* experience that disclosed the open community to many of those I came to know in the anti–drug war movement.

Perhaps paradoxically, this includes those who had an overdose themselves but did not die. What does it mean to say that one experiences their own death (or near death) as a dying-with an other? According to Heidegger we can only ever experience our own death, an experience that is precisely nonrelational and thus, that which individualizes us. For Heidegger, then, the experience of our own death is the most present at hand, self-same, and individualized experience we could ever—or better put—we *will* ever have. But several anti–drug war agonists who have overdosed and shared this with me talked about it as if it were something that had happened to an other—an other of whom some of them spoke as if they were not copresent—*and* as an experience of dying-with that they had shared with this other. To be clear, most people, understandably, preferred not to talk with me in much detail about their overdose. But the brief descriptions occasionally offered while trying to avoid the conversation suggest the line of analysis I am developing here. For example: "Uhm, yeah, they had to tell me what happened after I woke back up," or "You know, it wasn't like it was happening to me." Both of these brief descriptions strongly suggest an experienced distance between the teller and the one overdosing. This distance is reinforced in both cases by describing the overdose as "what happened" or "it was happening," a description that further distances the experience from the teller. In other words, these and the similar brief descriptions of overdoses I heard suggest that an overdose as a (near) death experience is quite similar to an experience of dying-with in that rather than being a radically individualizing experience, as Heidegger would have it, it is actually an ecstatic experience through which oneself is disclosed as perhaps the closest other.

Natalie, a staff member with VOCAL-NY, was far and away the most open with me about her several overdose experiences. She once described in detail one such experience she had while shooting up with her then boyfriend:

> And I remember he gave me a shot and I sat there for a few seconds, and it got really hot. And, like, all the heat started lifting from my feet; literally, I felt it was almost like I was burning up. Like, the heat just rising up, rising up to my head. Vision narrows down to, like, a little flicker of light, and then you're just out. That's all I can remember. Can't remember anything else. Now, I remember a feeling of being, it's almost as if being underwater, like, drowned completely, right? It's, like, very heavy, and you're underwater not really breathing and you're hearing sometimes voices. Sometimes I heard voices, and I think he tried to wake me up or put ice on me or something like that. But I don't remember feeling it, but I remember something, and then the voice would go away, and just be gone, right? So by the time I, you know, I literally remember, just like, waking up, it's almost like, you know, taking, eh, like, getting air in you, like . . . [inhales deeply] . . . kind of like waking up from whatever the fuck it was. I was in overdose but I didn't realize it at that time.

This is a very complex narrative that I cannot give justice to here. But what I would like to focus upon is the pronominal shifting that occurs throughout and how this could be read as Natalie describing her overdose as a (near) death experience similarly to that of dying-with an other.[34] Note that this pronominal shifting does not occur as a unidirectional fading away of the first person self but rather shifts several times between first and second, including the possessive form, as well as between personal and impersonal. Thus, for example, Natalie begins her narrative description using the first person singular—"I felt like I was burning up"—and the first person possessive—"my feet," "my head." Then she abruptly shifts to second person impersonal: "And then you're just out." At this point she claims, in first person, "That's all I can remember," as if she were no longer present, or at least not fully so. She then continues for a few sentences using either the second person impersonal "you" or an objective description pieced together from what her boyfriend would tell her afterward or the hazy memories she can excavate or imagine. Her narrative only returns to first person when she reaches the point in the retelling where she regains consciousness. But not, it should be noted, without first shifting back, briefly, into second person impersonal—"I literally remember, just like, waking up, it's almost like, you know, taking, eh, like, getting air in you"—before ending the narrative in first person—"I was in overdose."

What I think Natalie is telling us with this description and its grammatical structure is that having an overdose and living through it is something quite similar to the experience of dying-with an other that I have been trying to argue is central to the realization of community. Natalie's narrative describes her (near) death as the (near) death of an other that she shares. In other words, she is describing an experience of dying-with an other who is also herself. And perhaps this is the best way to describe the experience of dying-with an other that discloses community. For in the experience of dying-with an other, one also comes to experience one's own finitude as being-toward-death and the necessary relationality of concernful and caring relations this finitude entails.

To be even more precise: Natalie describes how in the experience of nearly dying she came to be "beside" herself and experience herself ecstatically as a finite being who, even in the moment of her (near) death, stretches beyond the self-same and individualized self and discloses itself as always already outside itself. Natalie, in other words, as a finite being experienced herself as other; an other with whom she is intimately intertwined in an ecstatic relationality. But this relationality is no duality. It is an open relationality that in this instance included her boyfriend, who was there trying to revive her until, as she would go on to tell me, he left her out of fear of being arrested when they would find her dead body. But note: this abandonment came only when he thought she had already died; when he thought the finitude of her existence, as it were, had ran its limit and care and being-with was no longer necessary. (Or at least less necessary at the moment than avoiding being arrested, which is just another dehumanizing decision drug users are forced to make in the conditions of the drug war).

This experience of dying-with an other who happened to also be herself was central to Natalie's motivation for joining VOCAL-NY. This experience, which gave way to the realization of her ecstatic finitude, opened her to the fact of already being a part of a community of those who have nothing in common other than their being-toward-death, as well as the obligation she had toward that community. Having been a drug user who had overdosed several times, Natalie was in a very particular position to have this experience. She knew, however, that this was not unique to drug users but, in fact, is part of the human condition. As she told me: "Human beings can find themselves in some precarious and dangerous situations and so need help . . . that's how I'm looking at it, community is all of us. That's our community." She went on to say, "That's what the slogan is about, you know—'How many people have to die?'—before some things are actually gonna change and happen. Before we begin to care for each other."

A DISRUPTIVE HERMENEUTICS OF DYING-WITH

I have been trying to show how the experience of dying-with an other, even if that other is oneself, brings about the realization that one is always already a member of an open community of those without community. For those who have had this experience with a drug-related death, it is quite easy to see that along with this realization comes an obligation, or a demand, to welcome all others as part of this community in concernful and caring relations. This is their political motivation and mandate. But it also raises the important question of how to disclose this existential fact to those who have not experienced death with one who has died unnecessarily? Or perhaps an even more difficult task: how to disclose this to those who might think that such unnecessary deaths are the result of the irresponsible behavior of "addicts." I want to suggest that at least one of the ways this occurs is trying to show, or more precisely, to empathically communicate, the experience of dying-with that has motivated anti–drug war agonists.

Consider Lone, the Copenhagen user-agonist about whom I wrote in chapter one who is mobilizing against abstinence-based rehabilitation.

Recall that Lone's husband, Nils, died of an overdose after having participated in an abstinence-based rehabilitation program despite the fact that he never really wanted to become fully abstinent. Lone had not been copresent with Nils when he died. But the fact that he was the father of her son and the love of her life made it all but inevitable that she would experience dying-with-Nils when he overdosed. Nils's death tore Lone from herself; it ruptured the secure illusion of her self-same identity as an individual being standing next to other such beings. Nils's death set Lone "beside" herself in the realization that she—like all of us—had always already been ecstatically intertwined in concernful relations of care and dependence; she became aware that she had always already been a part of a community without having known it. If it is the case, as Roberto Esposito claims, that the *cum* and *munus* of *communitas* etymologically indicates the mutual and obligatory gift of care that accompanies being-with,[35] then this is certainly a good description of what Lone felt—as did Martin, Natalie, and many others I have come to know—as a consequence of the dying-with she experienced. For as a result of this experience Lone became politically active—first by working with an organization of lawyers who defend drug users and sex workers free of charge and then eventually by organizing a group to combat the tyranny of abstinence-based programs, such as Narcotics Anonymous.

How does such political activity disclose community to others who have not experienced dying-with? One possible way is to enact the kind of disruptive hermeneutic politics that I discussed in the previous chapter, by which one's normal everyday way of being-in-the-world is interrupted and called into question. This is precisely what Lone once did, and this incident has become well known around Copenhagen for "turning" one of the local anti–drug war movement's most trenchant political enemies. Lone was asked to spend a couple of days with a conservative politician who supported many of the most repressive aspects of the drug war situation in Denmark and to have their time together filmed by a local television station as part of a film on possible safe-consumption facilities in Copenhagen. Although much of their time together was preplanned, there was also room in the filming schedule for ad lib, particularly since a good deal of the filming consisted of driving around the city.

Lone immediately took advantage of this flexibility and used it to her political advantage. On the very first day of filming, Lone arrived at the preestablished meeting spot with her son Albert, who she introduced to the politician and the film crew. As the boy skated away and the politician commented on what a well-mannered son he was, Lone turned to the politician and said she wanted to show him something, and they would have to drive to see it. A car was called, and soon she, the politician, and the camera crew were driving across Copenhagen to see something only Lone knew of. When the car finally stopped, it did so at a cemetery. The politician was hesitant but followed Lone as she walked into the cemetery. The camera was rolling, after all.

Eventually they stopped at a tombstone. Lone pointed to it, and the politician could see on the stone the words, "Albert loves you." The politician had just met her son Albert so he knew immediately, Lone told me, who was buried there. The politician stood silently and stared at her and the stone. The camera rolled. Lone started to tell him how indeed this was Albert's father and her husband, Nils, who had died because he had no other options but abstinence when he wanted some help. The politician was well known for saying that "drug addicts" need "to hit rock bottom" before they can be helped, and so Lone told him that "this is rock bottom." For the next two days of filming, Lone continued to tell the politician about Nils's death and how it was not a solitary sad case—as he at first tried to interpret it—but, in fact, a very common story. Several months later, Lone met the politician again, and he told her that "he had been thinking of what she said much more than he expected." Today he is one of the political allies of the anti–drug war movement in Copenhagen and, completely contrary to his original position on the matter, helped draft the policies that allowed the safe-consumption facilities to become possible in the city.

This is an example of the hermeneutic politics of showing that disrupts one's way of being and potentially leads one to become something otherwise, about which I wrote in the previous chapter. Here I want to suggest that this disruptive hermeneutic politics was accomplished by providing an opportunity for the politician to have what I will awkwardly call a secondary experience of dying-with. If the experience of dying-with an other sets one "beside" oneself in the realization of one's finite and groundless being-toward-death, a finite being that as such is always intertwined with other finite beings, then this secondary experience can be described as what Jason Throop calls *empathic attunement* with this dying-with experience.[36] Empathic attunement does not bring about a repetition of an experience and neither does it enact a similar experience. Rather, it allows one to imagine what an experience could be like.[37] What I want to suggest is that this imagining of an experience of dying-with can also set one "beside" oneself.[38] Thus, this empathic attunement and the imaginative process that it entails, just as much as an actual "lived" experience, can also open oneself to an awareness of the essential intertwining of community within which one has already been and thus become motivation for political action.[39]

Here I want to differentiate this empathic attunement and imagination from the kind of politics of compassion that Miriam Ticktin critically engages. For I entirely agree with her analysis of the ways in which "compassionate" humanitarianism "ultimately works[s] to displace possibilities for larger forms of collective change."[40] I would argue, however, that this displacement is the result of such compassion being based upon an assumption of the totalized and individualized autonomous, rational, and responsible subject of which I have been critical so far in this book, the result of which is the enactment of what I call a politics of the a priori.[41] In contrast, when I write here of empathic attunement and imagination, I do not intend it in a crude intersubjective sense of two self-same individualized subjects standing over and against one another magically feeling-for or -with through either empathy or sympathy. Far from it. Rather, by empathic attunement I mean becoming attuned to always already having been intertwined with other beings through the ecstatic relationalities we essentially are. Thus, one does not *have* empathy or sympathy for or with an other over against the self.[42] Instead, empathic attunement is the attuned relationality that constitutes what comes to be derivatively experienced as, for example, a "you" and an "I." Empathic attunement, then, is the coming into "awareness" of our essential relational-being; empathic imagination is the coming into "awareness," by means of this attunement, of what it might be like to be at another point in this relationality of being. Thus, to make the claim that empathic attunement and imagination are essential to community as I am describing it here, as well as the form of political activity I am describing in this book, is precisely to make the claim that "possibilities for larger forms of collective change" necessitate a rethinking in political and ethical terms of how to build worlds that express the essential relationality of existence and how it might be to live within such worlds.[43]

It is just this claim that many of the tactics used by the anti–drug war movement stand upon. For the movement relies upon this empathic attunement and imagination for changing "mind-sets," particularly for the possibility of initiating a secondary experience of dying-with. This, I suggest, is what is being done when VOCAL-NY members slam their fists on tables, interrupting some politician or bureaucrat, and yell something like, "How many more people have to die?" or "Your policy is killing people!" This is what is being done when on the front windows of the user union in Vancouver photos of recently overdosed persons and those who have died other drug war deaths are regularly posted. And this is what is being done at the Memorial Day ceremonies and the innumerable events like the ones Caravan for Peace held across Mexico and the United States, where what is trying to be communicated are not facts and figures as much as an experience. Or better put: all of these public utterances and performances are meant to initiate an empathic imaginary experience of dying-with that could potentially open others to attune to the fact that they too are already a part of the community of those without community.[44]

A COMMUNITY OF "EVERYBODY THAT WALKS BY"

What does a community of those without community look like when it is realized in a world? In this final section, I want to suggest that it looks something like the world that has begun to emerge in the Downtown Eastside of Vancouver. As I have already mentioned, community is central to the anti–drug war movement in general. But perhaps it is nowhere more prevalent than in the Downtown Eastside. No matter where you are in the neighborhood or with whom you speak, the concept word *community* will eventually be uttered or displayed. In random conversations with users on the street, interviews with anti–drug war agonists, or casual conversations with social enterprise workers and managers, *community* is used to describe both the who and the what of the neighborhood. So too is the concept displayed all around, for example, as the name of a social enterprise vintage clothing store, a Wi-Fi password at a café, or in the name of several organizations and services. In a kind of performative maneuver not unlike that of what Alexei Yurchak describes in the postwar Soviet Union,[45] community seemingly has come to be equated with the geographic and demographic limits of the neighborhood.

It is certainly understandable why many of those who live and work in the Downtown Eastside would want this to be so. With the steady economic collapse and political marginalization of the neighborhood over the past half century, it is no wonder that Downtown Eastsiders have begun to think of themselves as a community of those without community in the sense of having been excluded from a larger communal whole to which they have been systematically told and shown they do not belong. As if that were not enough, they are also regularly told that the Downtown Eastside as a neighborhood does not constitute a community. For example, once in the late 1990s, one of the key anti–drug war groups in the neighborhood had banners made, many of which explicitly named the Downtown Eastside a community, and hung them throughout the neighborhood. Because of a zoning peculiarity, it turned out that a few of the banners were actually hung in the adjacent neighborhood of Gastown, which at that time was beginning to become the gentrified area that it is today. The housing director of the group, as a result, attended one of the Gastown neighborhood committee meetings to ask permission to keep the banners where they were. The committee flatly rejected his request, and the reason given was that the Downtown Eastside is not a community, as they saw it, but rather a ghetto. In other words, the committee rejected a simple request to hang some banners that articulated the communityness of the Downtown Eastside because of the very fact that the latter was making a claim to be a community. That is, the Gastown committee refused to recognize that a socially, politically, and economically marginalized neighborhood, which at that time had an estimated six thousand to ten thousand drug users living there, counted as a community; or put another way, the committee made the judgment that the Downtown Eastside was a neighborhood of people without community. Because of experiences like this, which have been repeated in innumerably similar ways, it is little surprise that many in the Downtown Eastside want to equate community with its geographic and demographic limits.

This notion of community as a geographically locatable and closed or delimited totality to which one belongs is certainly the assumption of those, such as the Gastown committee, who seek to exclude the Downtown Eastside from any such totality.[46] In contrast, however, I want to argue that this form of the closed community is *not* being enacted in the Downtown Eastside as a key component of the politics of worldbuilding being done there. Rather, the community of those without community that has become manifest in the Downtown Eastside is precisely the kind of community that I have been trying to delineate in this chapter so far and which is, so I have been arguing, what the anti–drug war movement in general intends by community. That is, a community of finite beings who through the experience of dying-with (even if secondarily experienced) have realized their essential care-ful intertwining with all other finite beings.

The origin myth of the politics of worldbuilding now underway in the Downtown Eastside tells us that this political activity began when the agonist-poet-user Bud Osborn organized the Killing Fields and 1000 Crosses protest in 1997. Certainly for nearly a generation by that point, various organizations and individuals had been mobilizing to address various problems in the neighborhood, but for many this event marked the beginning of a new form of political activity: a politics that no longer sought to solve problems while leaving the status quo as is but rather a politics that sought to create a new world attuned to those and that which constitute it.[47] A significant part of this politics of worldbuilding was and is the opening of possibilities for community to emerge. As with most communal origin myths, this one too attempts to link the foundation of a community, as Roberto Esposito puts it, "to the blood of a cadaver that lies abandoned, on the ground."[48] But whereas those communal foundings—perhaps most famously exemplified by the murders of Abel or Remus—initiated a lack at the very origin of the community, a lack that established the original obligation that binds its members to a sacrificial debt to be paid for the community's perseverance, the Killing Fields and the 1000 Crosses events are considered the founding of a community that, rather than demanding sacrifice, offers a gift to whoever arrives.

This, then, is a community that can never be delimited either geographically or demographically; it is a community that can never be closed or totalized because until human extinction there will always be more who arrive through birth. Furthermore, this is not a community to which one belongs through some form of shared identity of sameness but rather, as Hannah Arendt might have put it, it is a community composed of finite beings that in their very birth constitute something new in existence.[49] The community that the anti–drug war movement seeks to open and that perhaps has emerged most clearly in the Downtown Eastside, then, is a community of those without community because, above all, it is a community of difference that remains open to all of those who arrive.

This community of difference, to be clear, is not a community of different identities, as a multicultural community would be. For multiculturalism is best understood as the epitome of a late-liberal politics of identity-focused difference and recognition;[50] a politics that necessitates various forms of governance and self-discipline to achieve—a process that Joseph Hankins refers to as the "labor of multiculturalism"[51]— and that too often, despite its claims, has homogenizing effects.[52]

In contrast, the community of difference about which I am writing resists any attempt at identification and homogeneity and is better understood as similar to what Giorgio Agamben means by a community of whatever beings, by which he intends a pure singularity that has no identity.[53]

This pure singularity of whatever being, furthermore, is not an individual subject, and neither is it an instance of a universal and a priori being such as a human being. Rather, a pure singularity, according to Agamben, "is reclaimed from its having this or that property, which identifies it as belonging to this or that set, to this or that class (the reds, the French, the Muslims)—and it is reclaimed not for another class nor for the simple generic absence of any belonging, but for its being-*such*, for belonging itself."[54] As I have argued elsewhere, this *belonging itself* is best described as the existential imperative to dwell in openness,[55] the enactment of which is perhaps the most radical of political possibilities. For as Agamben puts it, "The State cannot tolerate in any way . . . singularities form[ing] a community without affirming an identity, that humans co-belong without any representable condition of belonging."[56] Thus, the *cum* or being-with of community in the Downtown Eastside—as it is in the anti–drug war movement in general—is not a shared identity of sameness that has become equivalent to the identity of the community but rather emerges from the recognized finitude of our existence that has already always bound us by a *munus,* or a relationality of obligatory and attuned care, with anyone who arrives.[57]

Certainly, many of the people who currently reside in the Downtown Eastside were born there, but a significant percentage of them arrived from elsewhere.[58] It is, to a great extent, a neighborhood of those who have arrived. Indeed, for decades the Downtown Eastside has been the place where many went because they had no other place to go and had often been kicked out of those other places where they had tried to be. In other words, for quite some time the Downtown Eastside was a neighborhood of those without a neighborhood. Note that this was not a community in the sense that I am using it here. But this arrival did establish the conditions from which such a community could emerge, and this, to a great extent, is because the Downtown Eastside was a place where people oftentimes went to be left to die. Indeed, it was the extraordinary rate at which people were dying in this neighborhood that eventually led to the politics of worldbuilding that the 1997 protests are recognized as having started. For it was the experience of dying-with that occurred in this neighborhood—an experience that was and is to this day ritualistically enacted in protests, ceremonies, banners, and photos of the dead throughout the neighborhood—that brought about for many the realization that they were indeed already a community; a community of those without community.

As I will try to make clear in the rest of this book, this community of those without community, no matter where it manifests, is an open community in which its "members" are let-be to be the whatever being that they are (chapter 4) and cared for as that unique existence (chapter 5). This is precisely how it was described to me by one of the main players in the political activity in the Downtown Eastside when I asked him to describe the community that had emerged in the neighborhood: "We wanted to offer the possibility for people to just be whatever they are," he told me, with "the opportunity to breathe, and be accepted no matter what. We wanted, for example, to let someone scream if they need to scream because sometimes you need to scream and that has to be okay." There is a lot here, and in the final two chapters of this book, I will explore further the ideas of letting-people-be to "breathe" and caring for them as those who may occasionally need to scream. But in the final pages of this chapter, I want to set the scene for those final chapters by focusing on and emphasizing that this community is one of attuned connectivity and, as such, a community within which one is "accepted no matter what."

Thus, for example, once while talking with the manager of one of the social enterprise vintage clothing shops about how community is central to the running of it—indeed, the word *community* is actually in the name of the shop—she told me that they try to run the shop so that anyone would feel welcome. This hospitality includes not only the prices, which range from a few dollars for a shirt to very pricey vintage jackets, but also, for example, the general atmosphere. As she put it, "We want anyone to feel comfortable coming in here. We don't want this to be like so many other vintage shops where you need to have a 'cool card' to feel welcome. We try to be open to anyone." She went on to describe the way the shop attunes to the women it hires, all of whom reside at a nearby residence program for women who have mental health issues and are either former or current sex workers and drug users. She told me that the jobs they offer these women are not so much about job training—although that could be a part of it—but mostly about "providing a space where they can feel comfortable, and let them become a part of something." When I replied that the shop was a place where they could find "meaning," she corrected me and said, "No, where they can have a project and get connected." This notion of "getting connected" is key to understanding how community groundlessly grounds. For as I have been trying to show, this connection is not about belonging to a totalized community of identity. Rather, it is a connection to other finite beings, an ecstatically relational connectivity that, as will become clear in the remaining chapters, constitutes the *cum* out of which the gift of attuned care becomes obligatory *(munus)*. Put another way, this connection as *cum-munus* is what groundlessly grounds our being-human-together. Or at least this is how Teresa described it to me.

Teresa is in her early fifties, and after having been homeless for nearly three years, moved into the women's residence and got her first social enterprise job at the vintage shop. "It helped me to become connected, it helped me feel human," she told me about her work at the vintage shop and the job she had at the social enterprise artisan chocolate and coffee café, where she had worked when I first met her. "You know," she continued, "when I was homeless, I used to create this fantasy world of other people and things for me to be doing so I felt connected to something. Because that is the worst thing about being homeless, you aren't connected to anyone. You need that to be a person, you need to be connected to other people." Another time, when Teresa and I were explicitly talking about the idea of community, she reiterated this relation between being connected and being-human: "Being connected to a community is definitely, I think, ehm, an essential part of being a person." A couple of years later, I was walking with Teresa in one of the city parks where she used to sleep and spend most of her time when she was homeless. She told me about what she did to survive during those years and how the fantasy world she created for herself helped her get through it, at which point she stopped and turned to me and said, "There are still a lot of problems [in the Downtown Eastside], and I don't always agree with what these organizations are doing down there, but one thing I will always be grateful for is the chance they gave me to feel like a person again, to become connected again."

For Teresa this connection that was available to her through community was clearly central to her feeling as though she had regained her humanness. She is not alone. For this experience of being welcomed into an open community as the whatever being that one may happen to be—and thus becoming connected in relations of care that are essential to being-human—is central to the reimagining of politics, community, humanness, and the values that go along with these that the global anti–drug war movement is currently enacting. Unlike those who exclude drug users from any kind of predefined and totalized community of identity and belonging, including that of humanity as self-controlled, responsible, and autonomous rational agents, the anti–drug war movement opens community to all of those who arrive, whatever their way of being may be. As Natalie at VOCAL-NY once put it: "Community is all the people . . . human beings, regardless of race, gender, class, age, whatever the fuck, right? . . . That's at least my understanding. That's how I'm looking at it; community is all of us. That's our community." This community of all of us, this *cum-munus* that discloses our being-human, is then by necessity open to all who arrive. This was ultimately articulated most clearly by Ann, one of the leaders of VOCAL-NY: "Us! Everybody you put your eyes on. Everybody that walks by. Everybody you say excuse me to, or have a nice day. That's the community. The community is everybody. Everybody keeps saying you gotta be this way to belong in my world . . . where do I fit in? I'm a black, gay, ex-drug user, what else do I do? Fifty thousand other things I can't think of. So I don't fit nowhere. So for me, since ya'll had a part of making me, you're the community."

In the rest of this book, I will show how this community of "everybody that walks by" is brought into being through the politics of world-building and the creative experimentation of enacting new values done by the anti–drug war movement. In the next chapter, I will show how the *cum* of community begins to emerge through practices of freedom as letting-be. Then, in the final chapter, I will show how the *munus* of community is enacted through the gift of attuned care—that is, by offering the ontological conditions of attuned care for the being that arrives. In considering these two integral aspects of the community of those without community, or the community of "everybody that walks by," I hope to show how it is indeed the case that, as Ann put it, "Ya'll had a part of making me, [so] you're the community."

CHAPTER 4

Disclosive Freedom

The *raison d'être* of politics is freedom, and its field of
experience is action.
—Hannah Arendt

In the last week of every month, Voices of Community Activists and
Leaders (VOCAL-NY) holds its membership meeting. At the time of my
most intense research with them, these meetings were held in a large
room in the basement of a housing complex in the East Village of Man-
hattan. The number of those attending changes each month depending
on personal schedules, weather, and so forth, but normally around a
hundred people will show up. The diversity of those in the room is note-
worthy. Although there are always more men than women, the numbers are not normally that far off from half and half. Black, white,
Latino; young and old; some wearing clothes suggesting they came
directly from a well-paying job, others not; some live in stable housing
with their family, others do not; some participate intensely in the meeting, others nod off from heroin use or the exhaustion of a precarious
existence in a relentlessly unforgiving city; while others seem to have
come primarily for the free dinner that is always served. In other words,
those who fill this room every month constitute a community of whoever arrives.

These meetings usually have two components: an update of recent
union activity and a training or educational component. Since most of
the organizing, strategizing, and tactical planning is done by a core
leadership and staff, these meetings are necessary to communicate this
work to the membership and to get their feedback in terms of how the
union's activities could better reflect members' experiences and needs as

users. The meetings are also important for recruiting, as the leadership and staff are always looking to find members who are willing and able to become more active in the day-to-day work and political activity of the union. And as we will see shortly, it was about this time that it was decided that new recruits were needed to expand the leadership of the union. Such recruitment is done in a number of ways, but perhaps the most common one is through inspirational talks given by leaders that touch on such themes as the self-transformational possibilities of participating, the importance and necessity of collective political activity, and the thrills of showing "everyone" that drug users are perfectly capable of doing political activity.

Terrance may not be the most dynamic speaker of the leadership, but he does speak with an authority that is buttressed not only by his long experience with VOCAL-NY but also, as a former basketball player, by his tall and bulky frame. As he was once introduced at a meeting in November 2012, Terrance is "the strong, silent type." When he does speak, however, there is no doubt people listen. On this particular night, Terrance, along with other leaders, were talking about their experience at the recent national harm-reduction conference that had been held in Portland, Oregon. Most of the others spoke about the chance they had to meet others in the anti–drug war movement from around the country and globe, or the day trip they took to Vancouver to visit the Downtown Eastside, or about plans that had been discussed in Portland to start a national union. Terrance, on the other hand, talked about his experience of being with a group of people who, as I discussed in chapter two, show how they are more than the shit, and the waste, and the trash they are often made out to be. This hermeneutic tactic of showing, Terrance said, has had much success in recent years, one proof of which is that a lot of people are, as he put it, "waking up and smelling the fucking coffee" and becoming "aware of what fucking direction the wind is blowing into the future." The point Terrance was making that night is that slowly but surely, the anti–drug war movement is beginning to win the war against the drug war, and the situation is changing. This change is occurring, he continued, because drug users themselves are actively leading the fight and in doing so showing, as Terrance put it, that "I am not just a user, I am a person."

What is Terrance getting at with this statement? I think we can understand it as a twofold critical response to the conditions set by drug war situations. First, Terrance declares, "I am a person," and his personhood stands prior to his userhood, however that may be construed.

This priority is especially necessary to declare if, as I showed in the first two chapters, users are reduced to nothingness and have their humanness stripped away. In this case, Terrance is declaring that even as a user, "I am a person." As we have already seen, this and similar claims regarding his humanness are regularly made by Terrance. But there is also a second critical sense to his statement. Terrance can also be heard as making the much more radical claim that his being a user is just one aspect of who he is as a person, which must be understood as a multiplicity of ways of being and possibilities of becoming. As he puts it: "I am not *just* a user."

It is this second sense of Terrance's statement that I would like to begin with in this chapter. For in doing so, we can begin to interrogate not only what it might mean to oppose having one's possibility for being-in-the-world reduced, at worst, to nothingness or, at best, to a totalized one-dimensional identity-subject but, more importantly, how to begin to conceive of the human person as a nontotalizable, open possibility for being-in-the-world with others. It is this latter notion of the human person that I want to argue that not only Terrance points us to with his statement. For it is, in fact, at the heart of the anti–drug war movement and its political activity and vision for other possible worlds. In particular, I want to explore the openness of being-human as a necessary aspect of the being-with or *cum* of community through one of the keywords of the anti–drug war movement—*freedom*.

FREEDOM

In October 2013 I was sitting in a large auditorium in Denver, Colorado, filled beyond its capacity for the opening ceremony of the largest gathering of anti–drug war agonists on the globe. Similar to the diversity of VOCAL-NY's membership, this audience could be seen as a global gathering of a community of whoever arrives. It is also a gathering of a political movement that reflects the widely diffused complexity of that which it fights against. For among the audience that day and participating in the conference that week were representatives of drug user unions and drug policy organizations from around the globe, a national organization of police chiefs and other law enforcement officials from around the globe who stand against the drug war, an organization of mothers whose children have died from overdoses and who now fight against the drug war, various public health groups, and a right-wing libertarian organization.

It was actually here at this conference, among this odd mix of political agonists, that I first began to realize that the drug war is a widely diffused complex phenomenon, from which emerges a shared condition that affects the lives and ways of being of nearly everyone on the globe. The affect is, of course, differentially distributed situationally—for example, it affects a poor African American male in the Bronx differently than it does a single white mother in Denmark, both of whom use heroin; it affects a police chief in Seattle concerned with his budget and nonviolent policing differently than it does a parent who has lost a teenage son to a prescription drug overdose—but yet this distribution remains within a range of possibilities set by the situations of the drug war, a shared condition that once recognized is obvious in its sharedness. There is no doubt that the sharedness of the drug war manifests differently, for example, in Vancouver than it does in New York City and in both of these differently than in Copenhagen or Denpasar or Moscow or Amsterdam. But in each of these places and more, anti–drug war agonists speak with certainty of a globally diffused phenomenon named the *drug war* that they are all equally caught up in. Despite those differences of place and "identity" that today tend to result in more political divide than collaboration, these anti–drug war agonists recognize the sharedness of their general condition and have come together to struggle against and change it. And on occasion, many of them gather from around the globe in conferences just like this one: an International for our times.

At gatherings such as these, or even in the everyday political activity of local agonists, where advocating for such things as policy change or establishing safe-consumption rooms or doing any amount of other necessary anti–drug war work, it would be easy to miss that underlying all of this political activity is ethical activity aimed at altering ontological conditions. Indeed, as I have been trying to show in the previous two chapters, much of the political activity of the anti–drug war movement is best conceived in just these terms. For changing situations and worlds is a process of changing the ethical-ontological configuration of things and beings. This is precisely what Ethan Nadelmann, the executive director of the Drug Policy Alliance and likely the most visible spokesperson for the anti–drug war movement, tried to convey to the audience that day.

Nadelmann was nearly halfway through his talk when he asked the crowd: "What is it we are fighting for?" Someone shouted out, "Freedom!" Hoots and hollers and, eventually, a round of applause followed.

Indeed, freedom ended up being a keyword in Nadelmann's speech, and particularly so in his closing when he said, "This is a long-term struggle for freedom; for freedom, for freedom and liberty. Yes it's a passion for justice and science and health, but it is for freedom and for liberty [an audience member shouts out "Yeah!"]. Anyone of us fighting against racism, fighting for more action for drug treatment, fighting for harm reduction, if you don't say those words freedom and liberty, and that's what this struggle is about every day, then you are selling short the values that we struggle for . . . the fight for ending the war on drugs." Clearly, then, according to one of the most prominent leaders of the global anti–drug war movement, this is a movement that above all else struggles for the "values" of freedom and liberty. No matter what particular aspect of the widely diffused complexity of drug war situations one may struggle against—and here he names inequalities and biopolitical therapeutics and just previously had mentioned mass incarceration—this particular struggle as just one battle in the war to end the war on drugs is fought in the name of freedom and liberty.

This point driven home by one of the faces of the movement did not surprise me since by that time I had been told by anti–drug war agonists around the globe that freedom is what their movement is about. Such claims would most often come up in random conversations or stories told. For example, once while driving with Henrik, the head of the BrugerForeningen (BF), near the famous Little Mermaid statue along the water in Copenhagen, we passed a large modernist building with a great view over the bay. Henrik pointed to it and told me that he was not sure what the building was being used for these days; the last he had heard, it was being rented out to rich people for their fancy special events, but "once we win this war and get our freedom, I'd like to buy it for the union so we can all sit up there on sunny days, hook up to a drip of dope, and just sit back and take in this gorgeous view."

Henrik's statement, like Nadelmann's, points to the ambiguity of the way in which freedom is mobilized as a concept by the anti–drug war movement, an ambiguity I will explore in this chapter. For on the one hand, this notion of freedom harkens to the liberal notion of freedom that today has become dominant. I will refer to this notion as sovereign freedom because it begins with a sovereign and self-mastered subject who through an act of will is able to exercise this control and mastery on the world. As will shortly become clear, it would be very easy to understand many of the articulations of freedom I heard in this way. On the other hand, freedom is often mobilized—as Henrik showed—to articulate an imagined horizon,[1] a hoped-for and hopeful open future where it would not only be possible but perfectly acceptable for a union of drug users to own a location with such a beautiful view and enjoy it freely as they relax on deck chairs while connected to a drip of dope. Freedom, here, does not originate from a sovereign subject and get projected onto a world via mastery and control but instead is best considered as an openness to possibilities by which one lets worlds and their inhabitants become what they may, free of the imposition and control of categories and normalization.[2]

Thrown, as we are, into a contemporary condition dominated by sovereign freedom founded on mastery and control, it is not surprising that so many of the explicit uses of the concept that I have heard so easily resonate with this dominant notion. Consider, for example, the following from the head of another European user union: "For me this is about freedom. The freedom for anyone to do what they think is best for them as long as it doesn't hurt others. If I want to use drugs, if that is how I think my well-being is attained, then I should be free to do that. If someone else doesn't that is fine they can do what they want but that shouldn't stop me." Or Martin from VOCAL-NY: "I would love to one day see individuals having the choice to use or not use without the consequence of violating the law in any way ... to choose to relax and enjoy themselves. To choose to enjoy themselves without, as long as they're not doing any harm to anyone else." Or again from one of the main agonists in Vancouver: "Me personally, I mean, I don't, I wouldn't label it as a right to use, I would label it as a freedom of choice."

All of these utterances at first glance seem to articulate the liberal version of sovereign freedom. This is particularly so when we focus on the use of words like *choice* or phrases to the effect of "as long as it doesn't hurt others." Such utterances seem to be grounded in a notion of freedom that begins with a sovereign subject with full mastery over itself and its desires and with the ability to enact that mastery on worlds and their inhabitants. This is a subject of both negative liberty—free of external constraints, including "external" constraints that originate "within" the subject—and positive liberty—free to do what one desires or "being one's own master."[3] This "choice" that the sovereign subject is free to make is only limited by the possibility that it may harm others. Notice, however, that this limit is not imposed by a concern or care for the other. Neither is it a recognition that one's own freedom may be reduced in the face of the other. Indeed, such a possibility simply does not arise within the perspective of the sovereign subject of freedom, for this very perspective is grounded on the assumption of the boundless potency of freedom to be enacted on the world at will. As such, the limit on freedom imposed by the liberal imperative "not to hurt others" is only there so as not to impede the self-same possibility of freedom in the sovereign other. Just as Hobbes's sovereign steps in to protect society from the war of all against all, so too the sovereign subject must limit its own freedom in order to protect itself from getting caught up in a war of totally free subjects seeking to impose their will onto all others. The liberal imperative "not to hurt others," then, limits total freedom as absolute mastery of others so as to preserve the conditions by which all persons can enact their free choices within reason, as it were.

There is perhaps some irony in the fact that this liberal version of sovereign freedom seems to be so prevalent in the anti–drug war movement, considering this concept's genealogical history of being grounded in a master-slave relationship. As the political theorist Leslie Paul Thiele points out, sovereign freedom, since its inception with the ancient Greeks, has been predominantly in the service of what he calls *possessive mastery*.[4] Whether articulated as the domination of masters over slaves in Greek and Roman politics; or the mastery of the higher self over the lower in ancient philosophy; or Hegel's true freedom arising with mastery over history itself, a notion echoed in Marx; or in the possessive individualism of liberalism, the history of the contemporary dominant notion of freedom is grounded in the possessive mastery most clearly expressed in the image of the master-slave relationship.[5] It is ironic, then, that those who are caught up in conditions that render them nonhuman slaves—"addicts"—would repeat the very same notion of freedom that is grounded upon the possessive mastery that necessitates some form of slavery.

Perhaps, however, this is not necessarily the case. Perhaps this notion of freedom is used because it is the only one available in our contemporary times. As I have argued elsewhere, this certainly seems to be the case with other political-moral concepts such as dignity, rights, and responsibility despite the very real possibility that they have become exhausted.[6] As such, analytically, we may be better off accepting that although oftentimes our informants will use the political-moral vocabulary of dominant discourses, they may use this vocabulary to indicate a political-ethical imperative that exceeds that which the former can articulate because there is not yet another moral concept available. It is the gap of this "not-yet" that a critical hermeneutics attempts to fill. This is so because hermeneutic analysis assumes that humans are—as is all existence—always ahead of themselves, constantly engaged in an existentially interpretive process to catch up to their being—a being that can never completely be met. Therefore, a central task of critical hermeneutics as an anthropology of potentiality is to interrogate possibilities for thinking, doing, and being morally and politically otherwise, rather than reproducing the political-moral vocabulary that no longer clearly resonates with what it is like to be-in-this-world today. It is precisely this critical hermeneutics that I will do in the rest of this chapter and book.

DISCLOSIVE FREEDOM AS OPEN LETTING-BE

Is it possible to interpret differently the utterances above on freedom as choice and not harming others? When the head of a European user union told me, "This is about [the] freedom for anyone to do what they think is best for them as long as it doesn't hurt others . . . [and] they can do what they want but that shouldn't stop me," it would be very easy to interpret this as two sovereign subjects exerting their independent will just enough "to choose" for themselves without imposing on the other. If, however, we bracket this assumption of the self-mastery of a sovereign subject and instead begin with a notion of disclosive freedom,[7] characterized by openness and letting-be, then we end up with an entirely different interpretation of what is being said and enacted through the politics of the anti–drug war movement.

Disclosive freedom *does not* begin with two individuals standing over and against one another and exerting their self-mastery to limit their willed control over the other who is simultaneously doing the same. Disclosive freedom *does not* begin with individualized centers of power that are either imposed or controlled. *Neither* is disclosive freedom an a priori property of humans. Rather, freedom as open letting-be is a *condition* for all beings; a condition, as Heidegger put it, for which humans must be the guardians. For Heidegger, disclosive freedom "is not a particular thing among others, not something lined up as part of a row, but rather it prescribes and permeates the totality of beings as a whole. If we are to investigate freedom as the ground of possibility of human being, then its essence is more primordial than man. Man is only a guardian of freedom . . . human freedom signifies now no longer: freedom as a property of man, but the reverse: *man as a possibility of freedom.*"[8]

Disclosive freedom is not an a priori human property, as is sovereign freedom, to be exercised on the world. Rather, it is the condition of open potentiality that makes possible both humans and nonhumans alike; a condition, that is, that allows these beings always to be in a process of becoming. If humans are the "guardians" of this open potentiality, it is only because they, more than any other being, have the capacity to close the openness and restrict, if not foreclose, potentiality. Humans must be the guardians of freedom as openness because they pose the greatest danger to it. One of the ways this danger has been enacted is precisely by means of acting on the notion of sovereign freedom. For by acting as sovereign subjects, humans have done little more than impose limiting and narrowing possibilities for being onto each other, as well as nonhuman animals and things—that is to say, onto existence as such. By limiting and narrowing possibilities to such a degree—what could also be called normalization and categorization—the enactment and imposition of sovereign freedom has closed off potentiality and thus, the potential otherwise of our worlds. It is in response to this closing off that Heidegger writes of humans acting as guardians of freedom—as having a duty, if you will, to let-be so that open potentiality remains.

Disclosive freedom as open letting-be allows for a way of being-with that lets oneself and all others be to become what they may rather than imposing any particular way of being onto them. Freedom as openness and letting-be, as the political theorist Tracy Strong puts it, is "that which keeps one [and others] from becoming bound up with a single identity."[9] This freedom to become rather than to be categorized, boxed in, or imposed on by the a priori lets humans, nonhuman beings, and worlds be to disclose themselves, or perhaps better put, to become disclosed.[10] In terms of this book, such a notion of freedom as the "openness to the mystery" of becoming pertains to all such that not only the "addict" is released from the imposition of the single identity[11]—recall Terrance's exclamation "I am not just a user"—but so too is the "normal person." Freedom as open letting-be has the conceptual potential to release us and our worlds from the stifling and anxiety-provoking constraints of sovereignty. For as Hannah Arendt put it: "If men wish to be free, it is precisely sovereignty they must renounce."[12]

This is so because for Arendt freedom is not rooted in the willing of the sovereign subject but instead in the natality that characterizes being-human. One of the essential human conditions for Arendt, then, is the capacity to begin, to start anew, and to bring something otherwise into the world, and it is this that she calls *freedom*. As she put it, freedom is the capacity "to begin something new [and] not being able to control or even foretell its consequences."[13] For Arendt this freedom was only possible as political freedom enacted through political action. Indeed, her dismissal of the social as detrimental to the political is well known and has been much critiqued. And it is here that Heidegger's notion of freedom as open letting-be, a notion that Arendt was surely influenced by,[14] becomes even more important. For if Arendt limited her nonsovereign freedom to politics narrowly defined, then Heidegger's disclosive freedom entails everyday caretaking and concern.[15] As Heidegger put it, freedom as "the 'letting-be' of what-is, does not, however, refer to indifference and neglect, but to the very opposite of them. To let something be is in fact to have something to do with it."[16] Or as Leslie Paul Thiele puts it, disclosive freedom "is not tantamount to a retreat from the world. Quite the opposite: it entails the formation of worldly relationships made all the more dynamic because they are no longer constrained by the habits of possessive mastery [characteristic of the dominant notion of sovereign freedom] . . . Far from a fatalistic retreat, disclosive freedom launches us into an invigorated participation in worldly life."[17]

Unlike the dominant notion of sovereign freedom that assumes autonomous and ultimately individualized subjects standing over and against a world and one another, disclosive freedom as open letting-be discloses human and nonhuman beings as always already intertwined in worlds. Those who spoke to me during my research about freedom as choice, for example, may at first glance seem to be repeating the same metaphysical humanism that categorizes them as addicted slaves. But what I hope to show in the rest of this chapter and book is that in fact they are pointing to an openness and potentiality of an otherwise. This open potentiality, furthermore, is not found as some transcendent telos or an a priori property to be put to use but rather is found in the worlds with which drug users are already intertwined. Thus, in contrast to how some anthropologists of ethics write of freedom as a property or capacity of individual human beings[18]—a notion that even if couched as sociohistorically specific or as interactive has a very strong affinity to the sovereign freedom about which I have been writing—in the rest of this chapter, I want to consider freedom as an ontological condition for any being whatsoever. This condition of openness, however, must be released and let-be, and this is the political project of the anti–drug war movement. As will become clear, this movement enacts a kind of freedom that could be understood as combining both Arendt's and Heidegger's notions of freedom. For ultimately, this political project seeks to bring new worlds into being in which freedom as open letting-be is available to all of those who dwell in them—worlds, that is, of attuned care.

HARM REDUCTION, OR NONJUDGMENT, AS DISCLOSIVE FREEDOM

The harm-reduction philosophy is an approach to drug use that begins with a very simple premise: people use drugs, in most cases they will continue to do so until they "choose" to no longer do so, and in the meantime conditions should be such as to reduce as much as possible the potential harm (e.g., overdose and the spread of infectious disease) drug use can have on both users and nonusers alike. In most places around the globe, the enactment of this philosophy is primarily limited to rather isolated clinics where a few services are provided. To the best of my knowledge, only the Downtown Eastside of Vancouver has been able to begin to build a world where the harm-reduction philosophy has become a dispersed aspect of the ordinary life of that world. While syringe exchange is likely the most well-known harm-reduction practice, there are others that are just as significant even if less prevalent. For example, clean *works* (e.g., cotton, water, tourniquets, alcohol swabs, and Band-Aids), as far as I know, are always distributed along with syringes; condoms regularly are as well. Substitution therapy (e.g., methadone and buprenorphine) is also a fairly common harm-reduction practice but less so than syringe and works distribution. Even less common are supervised consumption sites, where people can use with a trained "supervisor" nearby. And even less common is heroin prescription, which allows users to get heroin without worry about such things as police harassment, the purchase of contaminated drugs, and violence in the context of purchasing from a dealer. Heroin prescription, as it is now being instituted in Copenhagen and Vancouver, is also regularly connected with supervised consumption sites and the provisioning of clean syringes and works and, as such, is likely the best example of what harm reduction can be.

There is no doubt that harm reduction in many places has become intertwined with the biopolitical therapeutic aspect of the drug war, and its implementation has thus resulted in the increased institutionalization of this philosophy, along with the consequent disciplinary effects of shaping specific kinds of persons. Much has been written on this.[19] In this section, however, I will focus on the potential of the harm-reduction philosophy despite these more pernicious, but not necessary, manifestations. In particular, I will focus on the essential core of harm reduction—without which the philosophy would lose all potentiality—that is, non-judgment. Nonjudgment is essential to harm reduction because unlike all other ways of addressing drug use today, harm reduction does not begin from the perspective that drug use is bad or evil and must be stopped. Rather, harm reduction begins with the acceptance that drug use occurs and will continue to occur and so worlds need to be built in which the possible dangers—note, by this it does not mean the evils—of drug use are minimized. Harm reduction as a philosophy begins with no judgment about drug use other than that it happens.

This, of course, does not mean that everyone who supports and puts into practice the harm-reduction philosophy supports drug use. Many, in fact, do not, and nearly every harm reductionist I have ever spoken with is fully aware of the possible health, social, and personal dangers of drug use. Nonjudgment, then, does not mean full-on support of drug use. Rather, I would like to make the case that nonjudgment, as the essence of harm reduction, is what I am trying to describe as disclosive freedom as open letting-be. For to be a harm reductionist entails that one does not exert his or her sovereign will on others and their worlds to impose certain notions of how or what should be. Rather, to be a harm reductionist is to accept that drug use happens and to attempt to build a world in which such use does not result in the dehumanization, ill-health, or death of those who do it. In other words, to practice harm reduction is to let-users-be and to build worlds that are open to this letting-be.

Here we can see how disclosive freedom as open letting-be is not a fatalistic stance of nonparticipation but rather necessitates an intense participation with the aim of transforming worlds to become places where such freedom is the nonnormative norm. That is, disclosive freedom necessitates a politics of worldbuilding as agonistic experimentation with an otherwise. This political work, at times, necessitates fairly intense self-work so one can become the kind of person who can enact the nonjudgment that is essential to this politics. Thus, for example, at a harm-reduction center in Honolulu, Hawaii,[20] a monthly meeting is held among staff with the purpose of training them on how to better enact nonjudgment. It is interesting to note that a good bit of these training meetings entails allowing the staff to complain judgmentally about the users with whom they work. In fact, this is a very common practice that I have witnessed and taken part in nearly everywhere my research has taken me, although in my experience it tends to be more ad hoc than the regular meetings in Honolulu. Such judgmental complaining should not be considered hypocritical, I suggest, but rather something like a cathartic necessity in the ongoing process of enacting nonjudgment. The starting point of harm reduction is nonjudgment, but in the everyday nitty-gritty of working with others and trying to train people in certain activities or getting them to be nonjudgmental in turn, frustration occurs. Rather than taking this frustration out on users or fellow harm reductionists, the Honolulu meetings and the ad hoc complaining offer an ethical release so that when it really "counts," the harm reductionist can keep going in her work.

Disclosive freedom as open letting-be is not a disengaged letting-go, and as such those who enact it must work on themselves to become capable of it. This process is that much harder given the fact that our contemporary condition is dominated by a notion of possessive mastery that seeks to judgmentally enframe all others in one's own projection. And indeed, it is just this attempt to be nonjudgmental in a condition that makes judgment the most normal way to be that regularly puts harm reductionists in a modality of what I have called *moral breakdown*.[21] But what should be clear is that this ethical work of complaint, as an example of ethics done in moments of breakdown, contrary to being a rupturing or transcendental experience as some have critiqued the concept of breakdown for supposedly being,[22] is part of the very ordinariness of everyday being-in-the-world for these harm reductionists.

For as I have made clear in *Disappointment* and elsewhere,[23] moral breakdowns are simply a part of ordinary social life, and the concept is only meant to indicate that ordinary social life is occasionally disrupted—but not ruptured or transcended—by "moments" when we become more or less reflective about our relationality with our world. To be a harm reductionist—in fact, to be an anti–drug war agonist of any kind and indeed, to be human—is difficult. We are regularly faced with problems and dilemmas of ethical, political, and existential import with which we must struggle. Indeed, I would argue that a good deal of ordinary life consists of this ethical struggle to existentially be-together-with-others comfortably, however moral comfort may be locally understood.[24] In other words, moral breakdown is just as ordinary to human life as is moral comfort, and for some, it may be more ordinary.[25]

But this does not entail that a moral breakdown must be so extreme that it results in "full" reflective awareness.[26] Rather, such breakdowns can be understood as nonconscious, mooded, affective processes of working through an ethical dilemma in the midst of everyday life, often-times without any awareness whatsoever other than "being in a mood."[27] In this sense, we can think of moral breakdowns variously occurring along a spectrum of reflection depending upon, for example, the intensity of the disruption that initiated the breakdown. Experiencing a moral breakdown, then, does not—somehow—force one "out of" the everyday or ordinary but rather shifts the modality of how this ordinary is experienced. As I put it in the original "Moral Breakdown" article,[28] the modality of the experience of being "in" the everyday shifts, but the ethical subject remains always being-in-the-world, which is, to be rather simplistic, merely a phenomenological term for describing ordinary life.

Terrance is one who has had to do a good bit of ethical work to become a nonjudgmental person who can be open and let go. When he first became acquainted with harm reduction, he once told me, he thought that it simply meant that one should use drugs safely; that it was a free pass to use drugs as long as it did no harm. This, he continued, was no good for him as all it did was allow him to give permission to himself to keep using and keep "being an asshole to everyone." Over time, though, and with a good bit of help from some people he knew already involved in harm reduction, Terrance learned that it was much more than a free pass to use safely, and now he claims that he has adopted a harm-reduction philosophy as his own. I asked what that philosophy is. He told me: "Respecting others; realizing that other opinions matter and I should acknowledge them and not just dismiss them. And if I'm going to respect others, I also need to respect myself. And it also means that just because someone else is in a shitty situation it doesn't mean I'm better than they are." All of this, he went on to tell me, "has helped me have better relations with others and with myself." Terrance, then, is an example of a drug user who at first didn't quite get the harm-reduction approach and as a result remained, by his own admission, an "asshole to everyone." In time, and with some help from friends and, as I argued the importance of in chapter two, by being *shown* what this philosophy is, Terrance has come to be one of the most respected harm reductionists in New York City and, increasingly, throughout the entire region as he travels the mid-Atlantic to give talks and seminars.

Notice that Terrance not only articulates how the harm-reduction philosophy allowed him to become one who can nonjudgmentally exercise disclosive freedom so as to remain open and let-be. He also points to how this has allowed him to begin to transform the world around him by having "better relations with others." In the following section, I want to begin to consider how this transformation occurs and how the anti–drug war movement in various locations is differentially experiencing and enacting this transformation. What I hope to begin to make clear is that disclosive freedom opens the potential for transforming persons and worlds because, as I started to show in this section, it necessitates an actively nonjudgmental and caring being-with-others.

EXPERIENCING DISCLOSIVE FREEDOM

New York

As already mentioned, when I first began research with VOCAL-NY, the leadership meetings consisted of just the few core leaders of the union who strategized and planned the aims and tactics that set the political agenda. In the winter of 2012, however, it was decided to try to expand the leadership, and as the calendar turned to 2013, this expansion was initiated. There were several reasons for this, among the most important being the recognition that the core leadership was increasingly busy with other responsibilities, as their positions had opened up new possibilities in terms of both careers and political activity. In other words, in order to address the potential that the union could one day in the not-so-distant future be left without a well-trained and experienced leadership, it was decided that it was time to open the leadership to new recruits from the general membership. This decision fundamentally changed the atmosphere of the leadership meetings. I would like to consider this atmospheric change in order to show that the very process of recruiting and training the next generation of leaders is best understood in terms of a disclosive freedom on the part of both the current and recruited leadership. In contrast to the expectations of sovereign freedom, by which recruited leaders would be expected to exercise self-mastery in conforming to an already established norm of behavior so as to achieve a certain position they chose to pursue, the disclosive freedom exhibited in these meetings reveal that this process of leadership training was one of open letting-be, whereby recruits would become what they do, and whatever that might be would not be judged.

If the leadership meetings had previously been small and intimate with a relaxed atmosphere well attuned to the political task at hand, the new leadership meetings nearly tripled in size, took on a classroom feel, and left many of the key decisions to be made outside of these meetings by the old core leadership. What had once been four to six persons sitting together around a table devising strategic aims and making tactical plans became at least fifteen people at any given meeting sitting in a half circle facing a white board with one of the core leadership or staff doing the talking and teaching. Although handpicked by the leadership to join these meetings, with the possibility that they themselves would one day become leaders in the union, the recruits neither understood the intricacies of political activity nor seemed to have the dispositions expected to take on such responsibilities. For although the core leadership was generally relaxed and quite capable of joking around, and at times became quite silly, they were a disciplined group who knew their issues well and thus always had a focused and intent approach to the meetings and the carrying out of political actions. The recruits, as a whole, exhibited none of this. Few of them knew with any depth any of the problematics VOCAL-NY addresses, and neither did they have any knowledge of the particularities of New York City or state politics nor any sense of how to organize, strategize, or carry out political action.

Because of this, rather than planning and organizing, these meetings became, for the most part, lessons on organizing and implementing political action and dealing with the primary problematics the union at that time was addressing. The "opioid overdose epidemic" was one such problematic addressed in these teaching meetings that because of an unexpected "attack" by a drug war foe in April 2013 quickly shifted to a planning meeting for a political action. The political demand for this shift arose because of a decision on the part of Hospira, the world's largest manufacturer of generic injectable pharmaceuticals and the only producer and distributer of naloxone, an overdose-reversal medication, in the United States. Although Hospira had already increased the price of naloxone by over 1000 percent in the past seven years, in April 2013 it further raised the price of naloxone to be purchased by the New York State Department of Health by another 43 percent, such that while in 2006 a single dose cost New York State $1.10, it would now cost $13.50, further reducing the availability of naloxone throughout the city and state. Because VOCAL-NY knew that heroin overdoses in New York had declined by 50 percent between 2006 and 2010 as the result of increased naloxone availability, it also knew that a reduction of this availability would result in more overdose deaths. Thus, it was time to act.

This political demand to act was even more pressing in a drug war situation in New York State and across the United States that was partly characterized by an "opioid overdose epidemic" and an already inadequate supply of naloxone to address it. Although this had been a topic of several teaching meetings prior to April, with the shift to political planning this event initiated, the teaching took on more urgency. Thus, for example, several weeks of teaching meetings were spent on overdose education, which included information on the rising number of opioid overdoses across the country and how overdoses commonly occur, as well as how naloxone works and how to administer it. They learned, for example, that as of 2013 opioid overdose had surpassed automobile accidents as a cause of death nationwide and that the Centers for Disease Control and Prevention (CDC) had reported that in 2010 there were 38,329 overdose deaths across the country.[29] If they had been doing this teaching meeting just a year later in 2014, they would have learned that this number had increased to 47,055, a new all-time yearly high in overdose deaths. This number, it should be noted, is very similar to the high point of HIV-related deaths in the United States in 1995,[30] an epidemic that was, and continues to this day to be, partly driven by drug war conditions. And as already described in chapter one, many of these overdose deaths are also the result of drug war conditions in which users rarely, if ever, know what they are actually using and what its potency is. Additionally, a high percentage of these deaths are from prescription pain medications taken by, predominantly, white suburban and rural persons who often, because of the drug war "mind-set," are too embarrassed or scared to seek help for their problematic use. For many in the room, all of this was very familiar since likely every person there had either survived an overdose and/or knew someone who had overdose and died. What was new, though, were the overwhelming numbers and rates at which this epidemic was growing; a drug war fact that few were aware of.

On May 8, 2013, Hospira was to hold its annual shareholder meeting in Washington, DC. The plan was, in collaboration with other unions and allies from across the country, to secretly infiltrate the meeting and then occupy the lobby, front entrance, and various rooms of the hotel where the meeting was to be held. The demand to be made was to get Hospira to agree to donate naloxone to all community-based overdose prevention programs across the country—a total amount, the recruits were informed, that would be only 1.5 percent of Hospira's total naloxone market and equal to about 5 percent of its chief executive officer's 2012 salary. From the perspective of VOCAL-NY and its allies, these minimal profit losses were more than reasonable considering the number of lives naloxone availability would save.

This kind of occupation and demand is pretty commonly practiced by VOCAL-NY, and many of the new recruits in leadership training had certainly taken part in actions just like this. They had not, however, planned and organized such actions. Not only did they need to learn to research and find all of the pertinent information that makes the demand for political action clear, they also needed the kind of information that would help make the action successful, such as where the shareholder meeting would be held and which shareholders might help them infiltrate the well-secured hotel. Furthermore, they needed to learn such political-organizing skills as transportation logistics to and from the action; securing last-minute funding for such an action from allied organizations; planning movements and tactics around the streets of the hotel and within its lobbies and corridors; and, perhaps most crucially, how to manage the eventual police response, which is primarily about how to delay it as long as possible before they finally move in to make arrests. This final crucial skill of managing the police is a matter of not only knowing the regulations that police are supposed to follow in such contexts and thus knowing what line the action can go up to before the police are required to make arrests but also, and perhaps more importantly, knowing how to emotionally manage and distract the police while the action continues.

All of this is what the new recruits did not know and had to learn on the fly as this action was quickly organized in response to what was understood by VOCAL-NY as Hospira's unacceptable attack on drug users in New York and across the country. Thus, for a little less than a month in the early spring of 2013, the new recruits found themselves in an advanced and accelerated course on planning and leading political action against drug war enemies. In the end, however, the action was cancelled at the last moment. During the final organizational meeting, before we were all scheduled to go to Washington, one of the leadership staff received a phone call from a mediator with Hospira. They had somehow found out that this action was planned and had decided that rather than having the embarrassment and chaos of their shareholder meeting disrupted, they would instead offer a twenty-four month deal to sell naloxone to community-based organizations for one dollar per unit. After a brief discussion, mostly among the core leadership, the staff member told the mediator on the telephone that VOCAL-NY would accept this deal. Once he hung up, smiles and congratulations circulated around the room about this specific anti–drug war win. Quickly, however, the core leadership brought everyone back to order, and they scheduled their next training meeting. Despite this win, the drug war continues.

This brief example shows the complexity of much of the anti–drug war political action and the speed with which it is often organized and carried out. It is, of course, expected that new recruits would not know the details and subtleties of how this is done. These are the kinds of training meetings, after all, that new recruits to any new endeavor, political or otherwise, would normally go through. But they seemed to lack what, at the time, I thought of as the discipline to learn any of this. As I sat in these meetings, I could not help but wonder why they had given up on the small, intimate meetings of the core leadership, which likely could have planned the entire Hospira action in two meetings. Instead, much extra time and effort was put into these new meetings, where most of the new recruits, so it often seemed, could not even handle sitting still for the two-plus hours they regularly lasted. Besides, how could anything get accomplished in these meetings, I wondered, when people were constantly going off on tangents that did not seem related to the task at hand, were oftentimes chatting with the person next to them or texting on their phones, or simply nodding off from the heroin they just took when they went to the restroom. It seemed to me that I was witnessing firsthand all the difficulties of politically organizing drug users that I had been regularly told about by experienced anti–drug war agonists around the globe.

What I did not realize at the time, however, is that this was simply an example of the kind of disclosive freedom characteristic of the anti–drug war movement. As characterized by the nonjudgmental approach of harm-reduction philosophy, these meetings, as the central component of building the future leadership of the union, had to be a process of letting-be so that the recruits could find their own way into possibly becoming leaders. The point was that there was no guarantee that anyone would eventually gain the necessary knowledge, skills, and savvy of political leadership, but if there were, it would only happen by letting it come about. There could be no projection of a prejudgment of what a political leader is and how one becomes one, followed by a judgment of some sort if one did not fulfill these expectations. Rather, as a process of open letting-be, these meetings *showed* the recruits what it would mean, entail, and be like to become a leader and left it open to see whether any of them would eventually become one.

This, of course, does not mean that recruits were simply allowed to do anything they wanted. Disclosive freedom as open letting-be is not disruptive, and neither does it give free reign for one to be, as Terrance discovered, an asshole. Disclosive freedom necessitates an attuned atmosphere in which all that inhabit it are mutually allowing such freedom to happen. As such, limits are necessary. In fact, it could be said that what needs to be limited is something like sovereign freedom, whereby one "feels" as if she has the "right" to impose her way of being by controlling the atmospheric mood and those who inhabit it and thus what is able to be done. Indeed, these limits were certainly imposed in the meetings. While there is no doubt there was much restlessness, distraction, tangents, and nodding off going on during these meetings, these were limited by the core leadership, who would occasionally step in quietly, in most cases, to tell a recruit that they were beginning to become too disruptive. That is, that they were allowing the disclosive freedom that was mutually experienced by all in the room to become imposed upon by their individualistic sovereign freedom that sought to control the mutuality. These meetings, then, were clearings in which freedom is not a property of individual human beings but rather an attuned atmosphere that emerges through the mutuality of letting each other be, from which becoming *any* kind of being is a possibility for any of those there.

As I have already indicated, this was not apparent to me at first. In time, however, and as I traveled to other locations of the anti–drug war movement around the globe and witnessed similar approaches, I began to see what it was that was trying to be shown through this disclosive freedom. When I returned to New York several months later after being in Vancouver, Denpasar, and Copenhagen, I was by then not all that surprised to see that several of the recruits had indeed become the kind of knowledgeable and skilled political leaders that I had—admittedly in my closed perspective—not expected them to become. Upon my return, the first union activity I joined was a monthly membership meeting like the one I described in the opening section of this chapter. But unlike the meeting I describe there, where Terrance and Martin and other core leaders led the meeting, now the meeting was almost entirely run by many of those who had been new recruits back in the winter and early spring of the year. As these new leaders stood in front of the nearly one hundred members who attended that evening, catching them up on and getting input to develop the ongoing focus on syringe access and public housing, I sat in the back with Terrance and Martin eating the chicken dinner normally served at such meetings. They were both proud of how these new leaders had developed and happy not to have to run yet another meeting.

As we sat there eating and listening, I leaned over to Terrance to tell him that I was pleasantly surprised to discover that Shanisha, an African American woman in her mid-thirties who had spent most of the first meetings she attended either nodding off or storming out in a rage, had clearly become one of the most articulate and savvy new leaders. Terrance, in fact, had been the one who had recruited her, and as he leaned toward me, he said, "She's really become something special." I told him again that I was surprised, and he said he understood but that he had always seen "potential in her." As he went on to put it: "She just needed to get into the right place." This is what all those meetings eventually brought Shanisha; they brought her to "the right place." Terrance likely meant this in the metaphorical way it is often used in the United States to indicate a mental or emotional "place" where one can come to realize or achieve certain things. For our purposes, however, it points to what I want to call a *site of potentiality*, or a clearing, where one is let-be to become within an atmospheric mood of freedom. The meetings, like the atmosphere in many of the user unions where I have done research, provided this openness where such disclosive freedom can be experienced.

Copenhagen

If the offices of VOCAL-NY are organized as, and have the feel of, a very intense political organization, then the BF in Copenhagen is more like a clubhouse, which in no way takes away from the political nature of this space but instead points to the political success of the union. This difference is in large part due to the different intensities of the drug war situation, as well as the political climate, of the two cities and their respective countries. This situated differential is manifest in the fact that many of the most basic problematics with which VOCAL-NY struggles intensely—for example, syringe access, housing, and mass incarceration, are simply not a problem for the BF. There are, of course, plenty of problems as a result of the drug war in Denmark and Copenhagen, but from the perspective of New York, they are "First World" problems. Thus, for example, while VOCAL-NY still struggles to get city police to respect the syringe access law that they are legally obliged to adhere to and enforce and that would help reduce the number of arrests for possession of trace amounts of heroin, the BF is fighting to get the currently experimental heroin prescription program to become a permanent part of the harm-reduction services already available, which include adequate syringe access and several supervised consumption sites.

These differences also result in different intensities of how disclosive freedom can be currently experienced. If in New York this experience is still primarily limited to individuals letting other individuals be to open the possibility that the latter could become politically active, then in Copenhagen the experience of disclosive freedom has opened up new possibilities for being-with and attuned care. In the following chapter, I will explore how being-with and attuned care become manifest in the anti–drug war movement as a result of the disclosive freedom I am describing in this chapter, but here I would like to briefly consider how the actual architectural space of the BF is a space of disclosive freedom that allows the possibility for being-with and attuned care to emerge and be enacted. It is possible to conceive of space in such a way, as what I am calling a *clearing*, because disclosive freedom does not indicate an inherent capacity or property that humans walk around with and instrumentally use—as the dominant notion of sovereign freedom could be characterized—rather, disclosive freedom always already is there for all beings but needs to be let go to manifest. As such, the political task is to deconstruct and rebuild worlds so that they do not cover over such freedom but rather are designed precisely as sites of potentiality where such clearings regularly emerge. This politics of worldbuilding is under-way in Copenhagen.

This politics of worldbuilding began in the early 1990s within the interstices of the biopolitical-therapeutic and the surveillance and con-trol aspects of the drug war situation in Denmark. Compared to most countries, Denmark's drug war situation has always been relatively less intense; nevertheless, since its beginnings in the interwar period, it has ambivalently shifted between an emphasis on control and welfare.[31] On the one hand, there has always been a surveillance, control, and punitive aspect that eventually became harshest in the mid-2000s.[32] Although primarily focusing on the supply side of drug use, this aspect of the Dan-ish drug war resulted in the dehumanized marginalization of many drug users who, when not imprisoned, were pushed to the precarious, albeit relatively comfortable, welfare margins of society. These relatively com-fortable welfare margins exist, in part, because, on the other hand, Den-mark also has always emphasized a biopolitical-therapeutic approach to the drug war, which is conceived and articulated as social rehabilitation or resocialization, or what we might call *normalizing care*. This latter approach has had several instantiations—from helping users adjust to the social upheavals caused by the war in the immediate postwar period, to the recognition of family and social problems as important causes of drug use in the 1960s and 1970s, to the increased acceptance of the addiction-as-a-disease model that ushered in the medicalization of drug treatment since the 1980s.[33] Unlike in New York, where the drug war situation has always been primarily a surveillance, control, and punitive focused war, in Denmark the situation has always leaned more toward the normalization of biopolitical-therapeutic care, although always having the potential to slip in a punitive-carceral direction.

But even normalizing care—or the kinder-sounding resocialization—has a significant amount of surveillance, control, and disciplining tied to it, and this, to a great extent, is what the BF responded to with its formation in 1993 and continues to offer drug users an alternative to with its space of freedom and attuned care. Indeed, the demand for politically building—or put another way, clearing—this space of freedom and attuned care was very well articulated in a survey of union members made in 1997 regarding their feelings toward the drug treatment biopolitical care regime of Denmark. The results of this survey showed that "69% of the members said that they did not feel that they were treated as 'adults' or in a 'correct manner' at the treatment institutions," "71% thought the treatment staff was too focused on resocialization," and "76% would choose heroin treatment if available."[34] In other words, this survey showed that the overwhelming majority of union members were of the opinion that the normalized care of the biopolitical-therapeutic approach was, in fact, focused on controlling and disciplining them into a certain kind of citizen-subject,[35] instead of allowing them the freedom to be drug users in a way that would remain, for the most part, harmless to themselves and others.

This is precisely what the BF tries to offer drug users. That is, it offers a space in which drug users can be treated "correctly," or like "adults," which is another way of saying nonjudgmentally letting them be to do and become what they will; it offers a space where the relationality, or the being-with, of the community of those without community is not narrowly predefined in its norms of belonging but instead by the mutually reciprocated gift of care, and it offers a place where heroin (and most other drug) use is considered perhaps the most normal thing to do and, for the most part, provides no impediment to the everyday communal and political activities of the union. Thus, although the Danish drug war situation is relatively nonintensive because of the welfare state of Denmark, it is precisely the normalized care of this welfare against which the BF politically fights and ethically experiments with an otherwise.

The very first time I went to the BF, I had a difficult time finding it. I had just spent several months in New York, where the union's building is located in a marginal area of an urban borderland between two highly gentrified Brooklyn neighborhoods with a prominent sign proudly hanging out front to let anyone who walks past on the littered sidewalk know the kind of politics being done inside. In contrast, once I found the city square where the BF is located, I could not find the actual entrance. After walking around the square several times, I finally decided to go into the children's library that sits in one of the corners of the square to ask. The person at the front desk told me that the user union was located on the top floor, and I should just take the stairs up. A drug user union that shares an entrance with a children's library! I immediately knew I was about to experience something different than VOCAL-NY.

As I walked onto the top floor, I entered a huge space of over six hundred square meters. When you first walk into the BF, you enter a very large hangout room with a long table, a couch and cushy chairs, a giant fish tank, and a projector television, where at any time of the day, union members can be found gathered together drinking coffee, chatting, reading the newspaper, or, as they were on this day, watching the Tour de France. Next to this room is a large kitchen, where communal meals are cooked nearly every day. As you walk down the long hall from here, you come to several offices for the administrators and rooms with computers for members to use. After these you would then find another long hall to your left with a number of rooms off of it, which include a workout room, a pool table room, two injection rooms that are also bathrooms, a conference room, a carpentry shop, a bike shop, a sewing room, a music room filled with instruments, a storage room, a small bedroom for guests, and an IT room. Along this long hall, inside a number of cabinets, you will also find a museum dedicated to the history of drug use. In addition to this space, the BF also has two vehicles, twelve bikes, and three scooters, which they use for everything from taking their monthly collective excursion, to picking up union members from such places as the hospital or the airport, to making their rounds in the city to pick up used syringes from public areas.

I want to focus here on the mooded atmosphere of this space and how it allows for an ethics and morality of letting-be.[36] For the BF has become a space of disclosive freedom. In this space, members, several of whom originate from other countries, come together to be together in an attuned manner. In so doing, they allow one another the freedom to openly be and become, which, as I have argued elsewhere, is what it means to be able to dwell in a world.[37] One of the first members I met when I first arrived, a Dutch man who has lived in Copenhagen for twenty years, told me that the BF is one of the main reasons he has stayed in Copenhagen because "it's about the only place where I feel at home, where I can be myself." Another example is William, a so-called methadone refugee from Sweden who has found a place to dwell at the BF. And of course, there are the eight hundred members of the union who reside throughout Denmark, approximately two hundred of whom come by every week to be in a communal space of freedom. In this space of letting-be, users from around the country and the region gather because here they can dwell openly with others in a communal space of mutually reciprocated attuned care.

As I already argued above in the New York example, however, this letting-be does not mean that the BF is a space of limitless disruption. Rather, it is a space where people come together to let each other be, which necessitates a mutual attunement to one another's being-there-openly. Indeed, for just this reason, they no longer allow cocaine users to be members because, as it was once put to me, "they are untrust-worthy" and "unreliable," and their past participation was ultimately too disruptive to the space of freedom the union seeks to maintain. As will become clearer in the next chapter, this "untrustworthiness" and "unreliability" is not a claim against the personhood of the individual drug users but rather an experientially and communally based conclusion that the effects of cocaine use oftentimes foreclose the ability to participate in the kind of attuned care that is expected of BF members. Thus, it is important to note that this exclusion was not made a priori as the exclusion of drug users is made within the conditions of the drug war. Rather, this exclusion only came about after several collective experiences of cocaine-using members having regularly disrupted both the letting-be atmosphere and the practices of attuned care within the union, disruptions that eventually had to be dealt with in order to guard and maintain the space of freedom the BF had brought into existence. Here, then, we see the way in which disclosive freedom necessitates both guardianship and maintenance, which, itself, can result in exclusion.

Despite the exclusion of those who disrupt its disclosive freedom, and similar to what we saw in the last chapter emerging in the Down-town Eastside of Vancouver, the BF enacts a kind of Derridian hospital-ity by which whoever "happens by" is welcome and cared for however she arrives,[38] and this hospitality continues as long as he who "happens by" reciprocally participates in this hospitable attuned care. As such, the BF is a localized manifestation of a community of those without community, an open collective for those who are excluded from all else—the nation, society, family—and where the only requirement for belonging is letting-others-be through attuned care. In this place of nonexclusion, exclusion is the last resort imposed on those who repeatedly disrupt its open nonexclusivity.

Indeed, as a researcher I experienced this hospitality myself. Of all the places my assemblic research took me, the BF was most welcoming. This is not to say others were not. In fact, most were very open and hospitable. But when I walked into the BF, like the Dutch man, I also immediately felt "at home." The very first thing anyone said to me when I first walked through the door was, "Hi, would you like a cup of coffee?" I was a stranger in a strange place. I just "happened by." The person who offered me the coffee had no idea that I was coming that day or who I was, but she and the rest of the members there treated me with hospitality. They were open to me, and unlike some other user unions who are quite skeptical of researchers, they let me be as a researcher. The approach to me was like it was with the cocaine users: of course you are welcome unless you disrupt the possibility of future hospitality and open letting-be. Within the first hour of my arrival, I was invited to dinner that evening, let-be to use the space as I wanted, and asked to participate in upcoming activities of the union.

William similarly experienced this hospitality as a methadone refugee. William came to Copenhagen and sought refuge with the BF because he could no longer get methadone in Sweden, which has a zero tolerance rule on relapse and some of the harshest drug policies in all of Europe. Because of these harsh policies, many refer to Sweden as the United States of Europe. For years the BF has been providing assistance in various ways to Swedish drug users, and so when William had his methadone cut off and did not want to return to regular heroin use, he sought help in the only place he could think of: the BrugerForeningen. At the time of my research, William was sleeping in a small room with a bed at the union—a room always available for any person, expected or not, who happens to come by—but was planning to move into an apartment with another member of the BF. I asked him once if he planned to stay in the city or return to Sweden: "I'll stay. Once they welcomed me here at the BF, I realized this is the only place where I can be now. It's the only place where I'm allowed to be me, whatever that is, and whatever 'mistakes' I might make." When I asked what he meant by "mistakes," he told me, "If I use heroin instead of methadone, for example" or "anything else that might happen, people don't judge each other here." To put it in a way that William probably would not, the BF is a place where he can dwell without predefined criteria by which his being and activity are judged. "Of course we took him in," Henrik told me. "We are all in this together, all of us, all of us users, so we have to help each other," perhaps perfectly articulating the community of those without community and the demand of hospitality and attuned care this entails. "And besides," Henrik continued, "he cooks well," indicating one of the ways in which William reciprocates the gift of care in return.

In the next chapter, I will consider in more detail this integral link between hospitality, disclosive freedom, and attuned care within the community of those without community. For now I only hope to have made clear that disclosive freedom is not a property of individual human beings but rather those clearings in our worlds that allow beings to become whatever it is they might; a potentiality opened and guarded with hospitality.

Vancouver

In chapter one I showed that the Downtown Eastside is becoming a safe zone for drug use in that harm reduction is being unknotted from singularly located centers and becoming an ordinary part of the world politically being built there. This is just one consequence of the politics of worldbuilding underway in the Downtown Eastside, a political process that is bringing into being a world that is characterized by attunement.[39] As I have already mentioned, this political activity in the Downtown Eastside and the world emerging there have become models for many within the global anti–drug war movement. What tends to get the most attention is the fact that a coalition of users, along with harm reduction and housing organizations, were able to establish the first and only legally sanctioned safe-injection site (Insite) in North America, which has become, let us say, the central core from which the ordinariness of harm reduction in this new world radiates.

Although the establishment of Insite is certainly a great accomplishment and a central aspect of the new world that has emerged there, it is just one aspect of this new world of the Downtown Eastside. Redesigned for the purpose of allowing drug users to dwell in a world of disclosive freedom, the Downtown Eastside now consists of, among other things, art galleries and studios, a bank, a grocery store, social housing, a dentist office, a community center, and a network of social enterprises where users can be trained for employment and work. This is the new world that I described in chapter one as attuned to itself because it is a world that is attuned to those and that which inhabit it, and thus in which they can dwell. As attuned, this world is also always open to becoming otherwise. For to be attuned and remain so, a world must always be open to becoming something that it is currently not. Here, then, we see that an attuned world is an open world that lets all of its inhabitants be to become, rather than impose a normative and a priori expectation, any deviation from which results in exclusion. An attuned world like the Downtown Eastside, in other words, is a world in which disclosive freedom is becoming the primary experience of freedom.[40]

What does this mean? Consider the bank that I briefly mentioned in chapter one. This bank is particularly intriguing because unlike most other banks, it is not an exclusionary space driven by profit but rather a site from which one could enter into the networked world of the Downtown Eastside and learn about or find access to such things as detox, dentistry, a job, housing, yoga classes, political activity, the Internet, a crack pipe, or free coffee. The bank, then, is an entry point into a range of possibilities that emerge because of the intertwined and open way in which this world has been built. But the bank is just one such site of potentiality in this world, and in the rest of this section, I will consider another with the intent of showing that the multiplicity of such sites in a world have made it one in which disclosive freedom is regularly experienced.

One of the social enterprise cafés in the Downtown Eastside is an artisan chocolate and coffee café that employs and trains residents of the same social housing unit for women that the vintage clothes shop that I discussed in the last chapter employs. Like the other social enterprises in the neighborhood, the chocolate café attunes itself to the lives of its employees. This means, among other things, being flexible with scheduling, taking a nonjudgmental approach to work experience and discipline, and viewing a job not as an end in itself but as an opening onto other possibilities for being-in-the-world. This opening, as both Teresa and the manager of the vintage shop put it, allows the possibilities of connection or being-with or the *cum-* of community for those who find themselves there. In addition to the connection between those beings—human or otherwise—who find themselves in this opening, the café, as with the bank and the other social enterprises, also connects employees to other possibilities available within the world of the Downtown Eastside—for example, different housing opportunities, various therapeutics or medical attention, events and activities, other jobs, or further education. This café, then, similar to the bank, is not simply a profit-driven enterprise but is primarily there as an opening for its employees to become something that they currently are not by becoming connected and attuned to a world built specifically for dwelling. And this openness was politically established not because, as we saw in chapter two, it is thought that drug users are shit, waste, and trash that need to change and become normal human beings. Rather, the openness of the café is there because of the recognition that to be at all is always to be in the process of becoming, and any business, city, state, politics, world, or ontological tradition that imposes an a priori limit on this is one that impedes disclosive freedom.

What makes the chocolate café unique in the Downtown Eastside is that it was specifically created with the intent of becoming intertwined with the broader world of Vancouver in the hope that through the process of a hermeneutic-political tactic of showing, the politics of world-building underway in the Downtown Eastside could begin to expand throughout the city. Unlike most of the social enterprises in the neighborhood that are primarily patronized by those who either live or work or regularly pass through it, the chocolate café sits right on the border with the highly gentrified neighborhood of Gastown and seeks to attract clientele from it. With hip décor, a prime location, coffee roasted on site, and boasting the only "bean to bar" chocolate in Vancouver, the café is a very attractive spot for the young professionals and hipsters that populate the area. Few customers know the idea behind the café, but those who did and with whom I spoke said that the café, as one person put it, "opened [their] eyes" to what is going on in the neighborhood and what drug users are capable of being and doing.

These singular revelations are of course important. But the possibilities this hermeneutic tactic of showing opens is most evident in the way this café has become intertwined with other businesses in Vancouver. Because the café is a "bean to bar" enterprise, this means that fair trade and organic cacao beans are brought in to the café, roasted and winnowed, and then made into chocolate and various chocolate products on-site. All of this work, including customer service, is either done by or assisted by the employed women from the social housing unit. Many restaurateurs, chefs, chocolatiers, and other such persons from around Vancouver and Canada have taken an interest in the café and regularly come by to observe the process, learn how it is done, and buy the products. This is important because this means they come to observe, learn from, and buy the products made by active and former drug users and sex workers—that is, the very people they normally would very likely never hire or expect to be capable of such work. For many, this is indeed an eye-opening and disruptive experience. Similar to the "shocking" transformational experience of the Danish politicians upon being told that Henrik is currently on heroin as he talks policy with them, those who come to the café to learn about chocolate making come away having had their way of being-in-the-world, at least slightly, transformed. Indeed, some have even started hiring active and former drug users in their own businesses and have tried to replicate, to some extent, the openness and letting-be of the café.

The café, then, is not only a site of potentiality within the world of the Downtown Eastside, it is also an opening into the broader world of Vancouver, explicitly for the political purpose of hermeneutically showing and making possible an otherwise. But within the Downtown Eastside, it is just one of many sites of potentiality that offer a clearing for an otherwise, and this is so because in their business practices, or banking practices, or the way they are infrastructurally designed, or the way they bring people together—in all of these ways these multiple sites have allowed the experience of disclosive freedom to regularly emerge within the Downtown Eastside.

In this section, then, I have tried to show that disclosive freedom as open letting-be is characteristic of the anti-drug war movement in general and is experienced in various ways in different locations depending on the situation of the drug war manifest at these locations. In New York, where the drug war is most intensely waged among these locations, this experience remains at the individual level because at the moment little more is possible. In Copenhagen disclosive freedom has become a normal experience for members of the BF and the small, intimate world they have built around their space. And in the Downtown Eastside of Vancouver, disclosive freedom has become characteristic of an entire neighborhood whose inhabitants are let-be to become what they might in the openings that are made available at multiple sites of potentiality. How this disclosive freedom is ultimately inextricably intertwined with the being-with of attuned care will become clear in the next chapter.

LETTING-BE, ATTUNED CARE, AND POSSIBILITIES

In this chapter I have tried to address the fact that no matter where my assemblic ethnography took me, people spoke about freedom in a way that at first could be easily heard in terms of the dominant contemporary understanding of freedom as sovereign freedom but that nevertheless seemed always to point to something else. I have tried to think this something else in terms of disclosive freedom as an open letting-be that gives way to the potential to become otherwise. In his close reading of Heidegger, the analytic philosopher John Haugeland concludes that the best way of understanding disclosive freedom as letting-be is in terms of enabling,[41] or what he describes as "permit[ing] in another way, as making possible."[42] This notion of letting-be as making possible in another way, Haugeland shows, is pertinent across various instantiations of our everyday social practices—from production to scientific practice—but he concludes that letting-be is perhaps most essential to the reconception and creation of what he calls another reality but what I will simply call an otherwise.[43] In the conclusion of this book, I will go into more detail about what I mean by the otherwise, but for now I will simply say that in this chapter I have tried to show how the tiny displacements that indicate the happening of an otherwise only become possible through the experience of letting-be. Or put another way: I have tried to show how political activity guided by disclosive freedom, as Hannah Arendt would put it, gives way to the "miracle" of "new beginnings" and is central to "establish[ing] a reality."[44]

Within the first two minutes of his opening ceremony speech at the anti–drug war conference, Ethan Nadelmann seemed to be conjuring the spirit of Arendt when he said, "What I find so wonderful about this [political movement] and this passion and life is the ways it requires each of us to open up; to open up to something new." In this chapter I have tried to show some of the ways in which anti–drug war agonists open up so as to allow something new to become. This opening up, I hope I have made clear, differs significantly from sovereign freedom in that it entails letting-be rather than (self)-mastery and control. Disclosive freedom as open letting-be, as the speaker who followed Nadelmann put it, gives way to "the infinite possibilities of life" and thus allows oneself and one's world to open up to these possibilities rather than mastering and controlling them through limitation and imposition.

Perhaps Frank, VOCAL-NY's staff organizer, described best the political imaginary that emerges from disclosive freedom when one day we were talking about the centrality of freedom to the anti–drug war movement, and I asked him to imagine what it might be like to live in post–drug war worlds. As he told me:

> You know, we will always have . . . (pause) . . . among the big elements of life is suffering, struggle, pain, you know. And loss and heartbreak too. That's not gonna go away. No matter how smartly organized we get with our societies and our structures and laws and policies, we're still human. I think in general [our political vision entails] deeper thinking about what human existence is, it brings us closer to understanding some of the deep questions, you know, what's the meaning of life, than [we can do] now. [Our new society would] calm us down in a lot of ways. It relaxes us. Our society relaxes in that scenario, in that utopian place. But still, we still will have troubled relationships, and loss; people will get hurt and killed and die. But I think it's a world where we're all much more at ease, much more creative, much more able to sort of find meaning in our life. Or at least given the room to run that journey in a real way. Not just after, like, go and do my shitty job to get home and study for six hours and wake up at six in the morning and go back to work again. I think it's a place where we, it's a world where people really are allowed to have peace, have some peace and contentment, you know. And more range.

Far from the individualized and autonomous assumptions behind sovereign freedom, and quite the opposite of the fatalistic passivity that open letting-be may conjure for some, this political imaginary of worlds characterized by disclosive freedom is articulated as an active process of opening up "to something new," with "infinite possibilities for life," where people can be "creative," "relax," and find "peace and contentment" while "running the journey" of life in a "real way." In this chapter I tried to give just a glimpse of how through the political activity of disclosive freedom by anti–drug war agonists, something new and otherwise is beginning to emerge as both individual and collective experience. But note that Frank is clear that this "utopian place," in fact, is not a place free of suffering, pain, and death. Thus, although it is possible to imagine and even bring about worlds of disclosive freedom, these are still worlds that necessitate care-ful being-with-others. In the next chapter, I consider much more closely how beginning from the experience of disclosive freedom, care-ful being-with follows. What becomes clear is that as the *cum-* of community emerges with disclosive freedom, so too does the attuned care of *munus*. As such, the community of whatever being—the community of whoever arrives—emerges and is enacted as the political imaginary of the anti–drug war movement.

CHAPTER 5

Attuned Care

We have neglected our primary duty: namely, to care for the
human (i.e., political) relations that can only come into
existence when men are free.

—Heinrich Blücher

Upon arriving at the BrugerForeningen (BF), Henrik asks if I want to go
for a ride. "We need to give Andreas a little bit of freedom," he tells me.
Andreas, a BF member in his sixties, had been in and out of the hospital
for several months as a result of multiple complicated operations on his
back and legs in an effort to counteract the effects of scoliosis. Despite
the seriousness of his condition, Andreas was able to leave the hospital
several hours a day, and Henrik thought it important that the union
help him do this, if for no other reason than that Andreas not "go crazy
in there not being able to smoke." It was unclear whether Henrik was
referring to cigarettes or heroin or both. Whatever the case may have
been, the point was clear: the hospital may be able to fix Andreas's
back, but only the BF provided the kind of care necessary for the singularity of his well-being.

As we walk out of the union, Henrik asks William to come along,
and the three of us hop into the BF's van and set off for the hospital.
After stopping by a trendy sandwich shop so Henrik could pick up a
sandwich he had ordered by phone, we arrive at the hospital, where
Andreas is waiting in his wheelchair on the street. William, who had
been quietly sitting in the back, helps Andreas into the van and puts his
wheelchair away. We then drive down to the docks, near the Little Mermaid and the flock of tourists the statue attracts, and slowly drive
around looking at the cruise ships, old sailing ships, and the queen's
yacht, occasionally stopping so Henrik can tell us the details of each

ship that he finds on the Ship Locator App on his phone: how tall each is, how far below the water they sit, where they are registered, and so on. We drive slowly past a giant ocean liner and stare silently at its enormity. Henrik and Andreas both point out to William and me the various buildings in the bay and the fort where taxes used to be levied on all ships leaving the harbor. We drive up to a snack stand and get Andreas an ice cream cone.

As we begin to head back to the BF, we first drive around a building with a patio overlooking the harbor. This is when Henrik tells us that he has had his eye on it for when they win the drug war. He tells us that his dream is that the BF can take it over and set up chairs on the balcony with little machines next to them that are hooked up to people's arms so they can push a button to get their fix as they sit back quietly and watch the sunset. For Henrik this is the image of what a certain kind of life could be like when the war is over and people are just let-be. After driving around for about an hour, we head back to the BF. William, who has hardly said a word this entire time, helps Andreas out of the van and into the union. Henrik and I carry in a few bags of supplies. As we walk in, Andreas talks for a bit with some other members sitting around drinking coffee in the main room. After a few minutes, he and another man head back in the direction of the consumption room.

I open with this vignette to illustrate the care, the hospitality, the being-with, and the ability to dwell that the BF provides. For a few short hours, Andreas was, as Henrik put it, free, and as such could feel at home in his world, be-with those others who care for one another, and use without concern or worry. All of this and more became possible because Andreas is part of a community. And because this is a community of those without community, it is a *cum-munus* that demands that anyone who arrives shall receive the gift of care. In this chapter, then, I will take up a consideration of just what kind of care this *cum-munus* demands and how it is enacted.

Henrik had already indicated the first step of care when he told me: "We need to give Andreas a little bit of freedom." For the freedom we provided Andreas that day was not simply an escape or "freedom from" the constraints of the hospital, and neither was it the enactment of an a priori capacity of self-determination or autonomy. Rather, the "little bit of freedom" we were able to allow Andreas that day emerged within the *cum-munus* of—at first—the four of us being-together in the van, each of us attuning to the "we" that we had become for that hour-long trip, allowing not only Andreas but all of us to freely become who we would in that time together. When we arrived at the BF, this attunement of the *cum-munus* continued as Andreas joined those drinking coffee and then with-an-other went elsewhere. As a first step, then, we can begin to see that the care of *cum-munus* is an attuned being-with that lets-be all of those who arrive to become attuned however they may—that is, as the singularity that they are.[1] Or to put it simply: attuned care is an onto-logical condition that allows for the letting-be of being-with; an onto-logical condition that emerges through the enactment of this form of care.

ATTUNED CARE

This may seem like a strange notion of care if it is contrasted with care as caring-for or taking-care-of. Indeed, with the contemporary domi-nance of biopolitics, this caring-for and taking-care-of life has too often become a process of normalization rather than an attunement to the singularity of whoever arrives.[2] Such normalization is particularly obvi-ous when it is realized that the life for which biopolitical care cares is life in general—or the life of the population as Foucault would put it—rather than any particular life at all. This regime of care,[3] and the anonymous care it provides,[4] is precisely one of the primary concerns of anti–drug war agonists in their fight against, for example, the institutionalization of harm-reduction programs.[5] Among other things, this institutionaliza-tion has resulted in harm-reduction programs around the globe now being organized, administered, and run by university-educated, nondrug using, lumpen-bureaucrats—or as Teresa calls them, "Nancy Drews"—who too often give the impression that they are more concerned with fulfilling the budgetary requirements of grants and government funding than with the everyday lives of drug users. This is, of course, not an indictment of the good intentions of many, if not most, of those who work in harm reduction. Rather, it is to point out that within the global conditions of biopolitical care, harm-reduction programs have too often become more akin to clinics for normalization than a community of users who care for one another in an attuned manner.

In her study of biopolitical responses to life and death in the Cana-dian Arctic, Lisa Stevenson has written about the "need to reimagine the political as something beyond biopolitics and beyond the ethics of professionalized caring."[6] This is something with which many anti–drug war agonists would most certainly agree. Indeed, Stevenson's notion of song has significant resonance with what I have so far been writing. Songs, Stevenson writes, are those "forms of address that seek the company of an other rather than those that attempt to identify, situate, or render an other intelligible,"[7] which is done in "those moments when it matters less *what* is being said (a name, proper or otherwise) than that *something* is being said,"[8] a notion strikingly similar to what I have elsewhere described as an *ethics of narrative*.[9] Song, then, could be understood as a possible intersubjective modality of the community of those without community that I have so far been describing.

Despite this ethical resonance, I suspect that many within the anti–drug war movement would have serious concerns about the political implications of the way Stevenson links this ethics of the song to her political reimagining, referred to as "the life-of-the-name" or alternatively, the "circulation of names,"[10] a reimagining that seems to foreclose any possibility of a community of those without community. For Stevenson, this reimagining becomes possible by recognizing that for the Inuit a life extends beyond the mere existence of a particular body and as such transcends multiple physical bodies over time by traversing the circulation of names.[11] This vision of a politics and community of the circulation of names works well for moving beyond the biopolitical fetishization of abstract life, but it also raises some significant questions regarding the potential conservative and exclusionary consequences of such a vision. For unlike the politics of worldbuilding and the community of those without community about which I have been writing in this book, the political vision that Stevenson imagines seems to be anchored in a community of those who *already do* belong because they have been born into the circulation of names. If the ethics of song somehow opens this seemingly closed community of the circulation of names to those who do not already belong, then Stevenson, unfortunately, falls short of showing how this might be the case. So, then, the question arises: How precisely is this community of the circulation of names less exclusionary than a normative biopolitics? Certainly, the focus is different: care of particular lives that matter because they belong rather than abstract bare life. But if care, community, and politics become focused on those who matter because they are already within—because they are born into—the circulation of names, does this not potentially, and perhaps even quickly, become quite exclusionary? History, after all, is pregnant with examples of just how easy it is to exclude those who are *not* born into such a circulation.

In contrast, the vision of anti–drug war agonists that I have been trying to articulate in this book seeks to go beyond the exclusionary normalization of biopolitics, the extreme of which is enacted through the deadly violence of wars on people, such as the drug war, by opening politics and community and worlds to whoever and however they arrive through the enactment of attuned care. As the example of the BF welcoming William shows, statuses of belonging are not prerequisites for care within these new worlds. Such examples proliferate in the global anti–drug war movement: the fact of the overwhelming number of drug users who are not from Vancouver or even Canada that are welcomed in the Downtown Eastside by those already there; the way in which VOCAL-NY has recently made significant attempts to welcome Russian-speaking users living, oftentimes undocumented, in Brighton Beach; the fact that the BF from its start consisted of several non-Danish users; and the fact that, as I have witnessed over and over again in many different places, a drug user from anywhere can show up at any user union or allied organization and be welcomed with and offered, among other things, food, shelter, and companionship, as well as the drugs he or she may need. These examples of attuned care attest not only to the nonnormative politics of the anti–drug war movement but also to its enactment of an open community of those who happen by. As such, they disclose the solidarity of those who share nothing other than their finitude within the precarious conditions of the widely diffused complexity of war, a condition that may have excluded them from a normalized humanity but has opened an onto-ethical-political possibility for the emergence of an otherwise.

This possibility for an otherwise (onto-) emerges through the enactment of attuned care (ethical-political). This is an important point. For unlike the way in which ontology is too often considered—and perhaps especially so today within the social humanities—ontological conditions are neither the culture-like walls within which certain practices and cosmologies are possible nor the background against which these make sense. Rather, ontological conditions emerge through everyday activity. Similar to how Agamben writes of the ontology of a form of life as "a being that is its mode of being, which is its welling up and is continually generated by its 'manner' of being," so too I intend ontological conditions as those that "well up," as Agamben puts it, "in that very instant" of everyday activity.[12] In this sense, ontological conditions are more like the affective forces that constrain habits than containers that mold their contents. And just as the affect emerges along with the enactment of the habit and does not precede it in a causal chain, so too do ontological conditions emerge along with those everyday activities they condition. Being, then, is more like a habit than a container, mold, idea, or horizon, and this holds true, I suggest, whether we are speaking of human-being or nonhuman-being.[13] The offshoot of this is that multiple ontological conditions regularly emerge. We live in worlds of constant flux and endless potentiality. That we almost never recognize this is a matter of the ways in which certain ontological traditions enframe particular possibilities while excluding others, the result of which are the habits of being that our environment, as well as ourselves, either do or do not acquire. Power, in one form or another, shapes habit, possibilities, and ultimately, being.[14] And this is why we must always speak in terms of the onto-ethical-political and why if we seek an otherwise, we must think and act accordingly.[15] In this chapter I will show that attuned care is the primary practice through which the anti–drug war movement is onto-ethical politically struggling to build new worlds.

This hospitality of attuned care could even be seen in the way that most anti–drug war agonists accepted me into their community. An example of this, one ripe with interpretive layers, is when I met Teresa at her apartment before we walked together to the park, a walk that I briefly described in chapter three. A few days earlier, I had just returned to Vancouver, so I went to the artisan chocolate and coffee café in the Downtown Eastside for a coffee and to see if anyone I knew was working or just hanging out. After talking with a few people who were indeed there that day, Teresa, who was working in the back and heard from the manager that I was there, came out to give me a giant hug. We chatted for a few minutes. I gave her an update on my research, and she told me about how things had been with her since we last spoke. Most significantly, she told me that after being homeless for three years and then living several more years in the single-room occupancy for women, she was able to find her own apartment in subsidized housing on the other side of town. She immediately invited me over to see it and, since it was just a few minutes from Stanley Park, to take a walk in the park together. Several days later I was knocking on her apartment door. Teresa let me in, and after showing me her studio apartment for a minute or so, she asked, "Can I get you anything? Tranquilizers, aspirin, weed, acid, coke?"

For many, this likely seems a very strange and perhaps inappropriate question. But I would like to suggest that this, in fact, is a question that is indicative of the hospitality and attuned care of an open community of whoever arrives. As she articulates with the first question, Teresa is trying to make me feel welcome. She is offering me "anything" within her capacity to give. As one who has arrived to where she has already been, she feels obliged to give me *(munus)* what I need to feel welcome with her *(cum-)*. In other words, with this simple question she is already beginning to enact the hospitality of a *cum-munus* and the ontological condition of attuned care by which we can be-together-comfortably. But the full expression of this attuned care only comes with the second question: "Tranquilizers, aspirin, weed, acid, coke?" For anyone who knows a bit about drug use, this will immediately seem like an odd collection of possibilities. Some, like weed and acid, could certainly go well together; others, like tranquilizers and cocaine, not so well. Aspirin seems like the odd one out altogether. But, as I hope to show, Teresa's offer of aspirin is actually the key to understanding the question.

It is important not to read Teresa's question too literally. Certainly, if I had wanted any of these and more, I know that Teresa had them to give, and she would have. Despite this fact, however, the intent of the question, I want to suggest, was not a mere matter of fulfilling my potential desire to take a drug but, much more importantly, to enact the hospitality of attuned care. How is this so? If we set aside the literal interpretation of the question and read it instead as the enactment of attuned care, we can understand the question as doing several things that are ultimately necessary for bringing into being the ontological conditions of an open community.

First, by offering this diverse range of possible substances, Teresa is letting-me-be whoever it is that I may be or become as he who has arrived. Because the substances she offered are so diverse, each having their own distinct effect, my response will indicate who and how I am at that moment and how this being-now may proceed. Second, by making such an offer, Teresa is also in the process of becoming attuned to me, for my response will allow her to respond to me in certain ways. For example, if I had accepted her offer of acid, our way of being-together in the park that day would have been very different, and she would have attuned accordingly. Third, and following from the second, her attunement allows me, in turn, to become attuned to her, and this co-attunement is another way of articulating the relational process of how it is that two beings become intertwined as the multiple singularity of being-with. For the *cum-* of being-with is not a "natural" process, and neither is it two individual beings simply standing alongside one another. Rather, being-with, and the care that conditions it, is a hermeneutic process of co-attunement, by which those who happen to come alongside one another must attune so as to become-with. In other words, through these two simple questions, Teresa opened the possibility for an ontological condition of attuned care, and whether or not this condition stuck, as it were, was a matter of the two of us co-attuning so as to allow this way of being-together to be.

Teresa offering the aspirin, I want to suggest, is key to understanding these questions as an attempt to enact the condition that would allow for our co-attunement. Aspirin clearly does not belong with the other options she offers. In this context, I read "aspirin" as the placeholder, the X factor, the et cetera of the hospitable offer. In other words, to offer me aspirin in this context is more or less equivalent to saying something like "or anything else you might need and that I can provide." And this "anything else," I suggest, is another way of saying, "You are welcome in this place, you can feel comfortable here, and because we are being-here-together let's care for one another in whatever way becomes necessary,"[16] which of course would be very strange to actually say so instead Teresa just offers me aspirin. "Aspirin," then, in this instance is the signifier of attuned care as the necessary accompaniment of being-with.

What this example of a simple interaction shows is a very particular and singular instance of how those in the anti–drug war movement are trying to create the worlds they are building around the globe. Some of these worlds may only emerge in the kind of intersubjective moments I just described between Teresa and myself; some may gather more but yet remain quite small, perhaps limited to just a few rooms in a building that agonists have been able to secure in the midst of a war waged on them; and some are much larger, as in the case of the Downtown Eastside, which has grown to map onto an entire neighborhood. But in all of these cases, the political aim is to build worlds conditioned by attuned care, within which communities open to whoever arrives can emerge. This political imaginary was perhaps best articulated by that Downtown Eastside agonist who told me that "we wanted to offer the possibility for people to just be whatever they are, the opportunity to breathe, and be accepted no matter what. We wanted, for example, to let someone scream if they need to scream because sometimes you need to scream and that has to be okay." To put it plainly, in an open community conditioned by attuned care, whether one needs to scream or wants aspirin, that is simply okay, and the community and those who constitute it accept this and try to offer what they can in response as the gift of care.

BUILDING WORLDS OTHERWISE

On a globe increasingly characterized by wars on people, building worlds where such open communities of attuned care can gather has become a political and existential imperative. In this book I have been trying to show how the anti–drug war movement has responded to the demand of this imperative, and that perhaps contrary to how most perceive drug users, the political activity that some of them are now doing provides a model for imagining how others can also respond and begin to build worlds otherwise. In the rest of this final chapter, I will once again show this politics of worldbuilding through three vignettes, each one illustrating how new ontological conditions for being are emerging in worlds through various practices of attuned care.

New York City

"Come here darling, give me a hug," Ann says to nearly everyone she interacts with at any VOCAL-NY event. Ann is a hugging machine. Well over six feet and with a frame to match, it is always just a little amusing to watch people who have never met Ann react to her when she says this as she is already initiating the hug. Ann says this is because they are afraid of human touch. For as Ann knows well, many of the users who are VOCAL-NY members or who the union tries to recruit or simply work with—in fact, many users all around the globe—have been systematically excluded from the intimacy of human touch. Whether because their parents gave up on them because of their use, or their spouses left because of the hardships drug use can sometimes cause, or because they have been incarcerated for years, or because of the precarious housing or homelessness many of them endure, there are many reasons why drug users in New York City and elsewhere rarely have the opportunity for the intimacy that is essential to being-human. Here I do not intend intimacy in terms of what Elizabeth Povinelli calls the intimate event of love,[17] which can be understood as central to liberal heteronormative hegemony. Rather, by intimacy I intend what I take to be an essential existential need for the intertwining connectivity of being-with that touch, perhaps most particularly, opens a possibility for. Intimate touch, then, can be considered as the felt materiality through which being-with emerges.

Not unlike how Cheryl Mattingly has shown that what she calls the care of the intimate other can be central to the development of communities of care, I have been trying to make clear that the *cum-* of being-with that intimacy can initiate is central to the political project of the anti–drug war movement, and this is so because it entails the *munus* of the obligation and the gift of attuned care, together which found the possibility for the community of whoever arrives.[18] Why this particular kind of political project is so vital to the anti–drug war movement becomes clearer when we better understand the theory of addiction that is at the core of the drug war and the way in which the drug war actually perpetuates the very conditions in which problematic drug use occurs. As I showed in chapter two, the drug war is driven by the "mind-set" that a drug user as "addict" is consubstantially enslaved to an evil drug that renders the "addict" less than human and akin to shit, trash, and waste. The result is the drug war imaginary of the stereotypical "addict" who sits alone outside train stations or on park benches, oftentimes in his own filth, looking to steal your money when he is not nodding off in some corner. This imaginary feeds into the normalizing desire of our contemporary condition, resulting in the fact that the only kind of care available for the "addict," when any care is available at all, is that biopolitical care that demands that the "addict" become "clean." But this is only part of the ideological story behind the drug war. For the question remains as to why a person actually becomes addicted to a substance in the first place. The ideological answer lies in the evilness of the drug. For according to Bruce Alexander, a critic of the drug war and a psychologist of addiction who has taught and done research in Vancouver since the 1970s, the theory of addiction that founds the drug war is what he calls the *myth of demon drugs.*[19]

According to this myth, drugs are evil because they are modern-day demons that after having been ingested just once, will possess the user and consubstantially enslave him, rendering the "addict" more akin to a zombie than a human. Thus, zero tolerance is necessary—so the myth goes—because the substance itself is so demonically dangerous that any use at all will very likely result in addiction. With this foundational myth, then, the only way to prevent the demon drugs from spreading evil and destroying our way of life is to make the world drug free, as the United Nations declared its drug war goal to be in 1998. Thus, the myth of the demon drug and the zombie "addicts" it produces has resulted in the international attempt to eradicate all drugs, which almost by definition entails the eradication of those who have become possessed by them.

As with most exclusionary projects, drug warriors have found justification for this foundational myth in scientific research, most famously so in research on the self-administration of drugs by experimental animals such as caged rats.[20] Scientists and drug warriors conclude from these tests that if rats (as well as mice and monkeys) isolated in small laboratory cages continue to self-administer drugs to the detriment of their health, then there must be something about the drug as a substance that compels this self-destructive behavior. Thus, as one prominent American scientist concluded from this research, "I have to infer that if heroin were easily available to everyone, and if there were no social pressure of any kind to discourage heroin use, a very large number of people would become heroin addicts."[21] In other words, the claim being made here is that scientific research supports the violent waging of the drug war, here euphemistically articulated as "social pressure" and "discouragement," to protect populations from these demon drugs.

Alexander and his colleagues, however, began to wonder if perhaps these rats continued to self-administer the drug offered them not because they could not resist the evil demon drug once they had been exposed to it but rather as a pharmacological relief to the distress of being "housed in isolated metal cages, subjected to surgical implantations, and tethered to a self-injection apparatus."[22] In other words, they asked if the problematic overusage of drugs by these caged animals was a consequence of their isolated, torturous, and thus existentially distressful conditions and not the drug itself. In an attempt to answer this question, Alexander and his colleagues built Rat Park, a spacious laboratory environment about two hundred times the size of a standard laboratory cage, with empty cans, wood scraps, and other rat-friendly goodies spread about, which held sixteen to twenty rats of both sexes.[23] Running a series of experiments to compare the self-administration of morphine by rats living in Rat Park with those isolated in small laboratory cages, Alexander and his colleagues found that at no point did the rats of Rat Park exhibit "anything that looked to [them] like addiction."[24] Although some of the Rat Park rats occasionally self-administered morphine, the rats in isolated cages continued to administer at much higher and frequent rates and under some conditions as much as twenty times more than those in Rat Park.[25] This outcome remained the case even when the researchers forced the rats of Rat Park to consume morphine for weeks, thus assuring that when given the opportunity to self-administer, they would be experiencing withdrawal and thus, theoretically, would be more likely to continue a high use of morphine in order to avoid withdrawal symptoms. But even this did not work, as ultimately no matter what Alexander and his colleagues did to get the rats of Rat Park "addicted," they simply could not do so as these rats seemed to prefer the sociality, fun, and sexual pleasure of an environment attuned to their ratness over the effects of the so-called demon drug. In Rat Park, rats simply had no need to pharmacologically relieve themselves from physical or existential pain because their social and living conditions caused very little of this pain. The Rat Park experiments, then, seem to confirm the interpretation that problematic overuse of drugs by rats in isolated laboratory cages is more the result of the conditions of their being isolated and under constant distress than that of the drug itself.

The results of the Rat Park experiments, however, were just too radical and disruptive for the "mind-set" of the drug war, and eventually, Alexander and his colleagues had their funding cut because of it.[26] And although since then the results of these experiments have been replicated several times,[27] governments, the biomedical-pharmaceutical complex, the mass media, and most of the scientific establishment to this day refuse to acknowledge and in some cases, to publish, these findings.[28] For to do so would be to acknowledge that the foundational myth that supports the violent exclusion of the drug war is false. If this myth appears to remain plausible, then, perhaps this is because the drug war itself brings into being and perpetuates human versions of those isolated cages—what I have called *zones of uninhabitability*, or Martin calls the *void*, or others call a *carceral society*—in which self-medication to cope with the fact of anxiety-ridden isolation remains one of the few possibilities available to survive these conditions.

In fact, Alexander concludes that it is the conditions of late-liberal consumer capitalism in general that provide the isolating conditions that drive high rates of addictive behavior around the globe, which includes not only drug and alcohol use but also excessive gambling, gaming, and even the pursuit of money.[29] Perhaps he is right. But what certainly appears to be the case is that like these rats, drug users around the globe continue to find themselves in conditions of extreme isolation, loneliness, and distress to a great extent because these are perpetuated through the violently exclusionary practices of the drug war. As Dean Wilson, the well-known Downtown Eastside anti–drug war agonist once put it, "Addiction is a disease of loneliness,"[30] and thus the "cure" is not more exclusion and violence but instead the rebuilding of worlds conditioned by attuned care, within which the intertwined connectivity of being-with can become the new nonnormative norm.[31] This is the political project of the anti–drug war movement, and Ann is participating in its realization one hug at a time.

In fact, Ann has become one of the most familiar faces and effective leaders of VOCAL-NY. She runs meetings, she recruits new members, she meets with politicians, and she is front and center at nearly every action. At each of these, she is giving hugs. For example, when she is introduced at a membership meeting to give a talk on a particular topic such as stop-and-frisk policing, she begins by asking all the members present to stand up and hug the persons near them. Or when she goes to a local harm-reduction center to recruit new members for VOCAL-NY, she begins by giving each person present a hug. When I asked her once why she does this, she said: "Everybody can always talk, but it's better—(pause)—you know you can't help nobody when everybody talks at one time, but if everybody sings together and hugs each other, you notice that there's a calmness in the air." In contrast to talking "at one time," a phrase that suggests the banality of endless opinion and idle chatter, Ann here wants to emphasize how the intimacy of the hug and the harmony of singing allow connectivity, or being-with, to emerge. The calmness that this connectivity carries with it is a mood that, as Ann described to me on another occasion, makes people more comfortable, which allows them in turn to open up, to trust her enough to tell her what they may not tell others, and to hear what she has to say in return. This intimate mood brought about through the hug can be understood as the atmospheric condition of attuned care.

Moods are not subjective or psychological states. Rather, moods are an "all-enveloping force that comes over us and things together,"[32] and they go a long way toward conditioning the way we are in a world at any particular moment.[33] In this sense, moods are more akin to an atmosphere than an emotion or one's character. Furthermore, moods are not permanent; they do not define one's way of being-in-the-world from here on out forever. But as Jason Throop has argued, moods' affects do have lasting effects,[34] and it is in this sense that I want to say that Ann's hugs have lasting political, ethical, and ultimately ontological effects. For these hugs bring about intimately mooded moments in which people become open and trusting in their being-together-there and in so doing open the possibility for attuned care to become central to the everyday ways of being within the worlds Ann is helping to build. Indeed, I would suggest that it is just this intimate mood that Ann conjures that has made her not only VOCAL-NY's most effective recruiter but also increasingly one of its most recognizable and effective political agonists. For the trust she is able to conjure with the intimate mood can open the possibility for the attuned care of another user just as much as it can be an expedient tactic in a political confrontation.

While Ann and her hugs may be the most obvious example of how an intimate mood gives way to attuned care at VOCAL-NY, such intimacy is enacted regularly by others, even if in brief interactions. Thus, for example, I once observed the following very brief but important interaction at a planning meeting for a political action on hepatitis C (HCV). As usual I was sitting near the back of the room so I could observe everyone in attendance. Directly in front of me sat Jonathan, one of the union leaders, Terrance, and Brenda, an African American woman in her early sixties who had recently become a more active member, especially around issues of HCV, from which she suffered. About the time I started research with them, VOCAL-NY began to make HCV treatment a political priority because it was becoming increasingly obvious that an overwhelming majority of its members had the virus and were not receiving treatment. Indeed, globally about 90 percent of those who have HCV are injecting drug users, and the vast majority of these go untreated, oftentimes due to a drug war "mind-set" that considers users too irresponsible or too troubled to adhere to treatment.[35] The result is that in the United States, for example, HCV mortality has surpassed that of HIV, and VOCAL-NY's membership is disproportionately affected by this fact.[36] Brenda's struggles to be treated, the lack of care she receives from doctors and others in the medical and social services of the city, and the kind of isolation she experiences because of this are typical of many VOCAL-NY members and drug users across the country. She was at this meeting to offer her experiences in shaping the political response.

About halfway through the meeting, Brenda was telling us about how badly she is treated at the hospital where she must go to try to access HCV treatment and how this has led her not only to postpone her treatment but to feel as if she has no place to turn for help and support. As she was telling us this, she began to cry and just audibly said between sobs, "They don't care about me." It was at this point that I saw Jonathan lean over to Brenda, touch her gently on her arm, and say quietly, "You're here with us now," as Terrance, from her other side, touched her other arm and nodded. These simple but deeply significant touches and words seemed to matter to Brenda because she was able to stop crying just enough to continue telling us about how she is treated at the hospital and the kinds of demands she and others treated there would like to make. The meeting then continued, and an action was organized in response to these demands.

With this brief interaction, we see how the intimate mood conjured through the touch of Terrance and Jonathan, along with the latter's words, assured Brenda that the isolating noncare she experiences at the hospital, and within the general conditions of the drug war, do not pertain to VOCAL-NY. Rather, at the union and in the, at this point primarily still, intersubjective worlds VOCAL-NY is able to build, attuned care conditions the being-with of those already there and the hospitality offered to whoever arrives. And it is oftentimes the intimacy of these little touches or Ann's big enveloping hugs that first creates the atmospheric mood that allows for such care and the otherwise worlds it is helping to bring about.

Terrance once told me that he thought the most important mission of the user union is to help people overcome the dehumanizing effects of the drug war. As he put it, "We have to see what we can do to help individuals address this, and make them feel comfortable in their whole." To become "comfortable in their whole," or as I would rather put it, to become comfortable in one's being, this is the political vision Terrance articulates. This existential comfort, this trust, this openness is largely made possible by the attuned care enacted through the kinds of intimate moods I briefly described here. Against the dehumanizing and isolating conditions of drug war situations like Brenda experiences at the hospital, VOCAL-NY, like anti–drug war agonists around the globe, is attempting to show politicians, police, medical staff, and nearly everyone else that the "fantasy" the drug war is based upon actually creates a nightmare for those it claims to help. But before that political showing can take place, before any political activity against the drug war can begin at all, the first step for many within the anti–drug war movement is to help drug users escape the loneliness they experience, the self-loathing spiral many have fallen into, and the general lack of existential comfort many have as a result of the isolating and dehumanizing conditions of the drug war. This attuned care becomes possible because of the intimate moods conjured in the various communities these political agonists are building. And it is through these intimate moods, the attuned care they give way to, and the intertwined connectivity of being-with that this care conditions that drug users in New York City and around the globe are able to begin to build worlds otherwise.

Copenhagen

It was not for nothing that when introducing William to me, Henrik mentioned that he was a good cook. For a significant aspect of the attuned care of the BF is the shared cooking and meals. Every morning, breakfast is served at ten o'clock and left out for a couple of hours for anyone who comes by. Three days a week, dinner is communally prepared and eaten, and in the summer Henrik regularly has groups of BF members out to his summer cottage for barbeques. It is expected that anyone who eats the meals also help with its preparation or cleanup. Indeed, this expectation of active membership holds for all activity around the union, whether it be cleaning the space of the BF, managing its activities, helping another member in a time of need, participating in the syringe cleanup program BF runs in certain neighborhoods, preparing for political rallies, or hosting political guests. None of these other activities, however, would have the significance they do without the shared meals. For it is with the meals that the *cum-* of BF is most clearly manifest and solidified through the enactment of attuned care.

Just one of the dehumanizing consequences of the drug war is the poor nutrition of many drug users around the globe.[37] This is especially so for the most precarious and isolated of drug users. The lack of money as the result of being excluded from most employment, the lack of a place to cook as the result of being excluded from adequate housing, the lack of a support system as the result of being excluded from family and loved ones—all of these lacks have a number of significant deleterious consequences but perhaps the most basic one is that many drug users must survive on whatever food they can get their hands on, much of which is seriously deficient in any kind of nutritional value. But the deficiency in nutrition is not the only negative consequence. For this situational conditioning of eating also means that many of the most precarious drug users often eat in an ad hoc and solitary manner. When they get their hands on some food, they eat it. Having a meaningful shared meal with others is for many of these most precarious drug users around the globe simply not a possibility most of the time. For those drug users in the worst of conditions and suffering through some of the worst health consequences of hard-core drug use, this lack of nutrition, and the isolation of being forced scavengers, only adds an extra burden to the hardships of making it through any given day. It is for this reason that at every single place my assemblic research took me, regular attempts were made to provide at the very least a basic and somewhat healthy meal that could be shared with others.

Although drug users in Denmark are on the whole in a better situational condition than most users around the globe because of the social welfare system of the country, still, as Henrik told me, many Danish drug users suffer from poor nutrition, and the attempt to address this fact is, in part, a reason for the shared meals at the BF. But it would be incorrect to reduce these shared meals to biopolitical care that simply seeks to address a biological necessity. For in contrast to a humanitarian soup kitchen, these shared meals are more akin to how Levinas in *Otherwise than Being* argues that the very possibility of ethics is the giving of "bread," by which we not only care for the other but, perhaps more importantly, offer the conditions for enjoyment out of which the possibility of ethics arises.[38] If a soup kitchen can be understood as providing the sustenance for survival, which no doubt is oftentimes necessary and important but is also regularly done in a mode of anonymous care, then the shared meals of the BF are better understood as opening the possibility of being-together in enjoyment.

For these shared meals are primarily an instance of attuned care, which allows for the *cum-* of the community of whoever arrives to emerge through the very sharedness, the relational sociality and enjoyment, of the preparation and the eating. Thus, on dinner days at least four to six people will be in the large kitchen preparing the meal. Others will be rearranging the tables in the communal room and setting them for dinner. Others will be preparing drinks—lemonade is a favorite in the summer, and coffee is a favorite every day and at all times—while others will make a quick run to one of the local vegetable shops to pick up something to add at the last minute or because a key ingredient may not be available in the pantry. Afterward, everyone cleans. This, then, is a simple but healthy meal prepared as a collective to be shared and eaten as a community in enjoyment. This is a process of attuned care by which the community cares for itself not simply by providing collectively for the most basic biological necessity but by doing so together and openly, as anyone who happens to come along that day can join in and participate however they are able.

These shared meals, then, can be understood as a political-ethical act by which an ontological condition of attuned care as the possibility for being-with emerges. We should not expect, of course, that attuned care as the condition for being-with would be openly articulated, or even something about which most participants are likely aware. Rather, these shared meals are simply what are done at the BF. They are part of the everydayness of being-there. Participating in the preparation and eating the meals together is simply what it is to be a member of the BF, to be a part of this community. Thus, in contrast to the kind of care offered by the biopolitical-therapeutic aspect of the drug war assemblage, which we can understand as anonymous, normative, and overtly regulative, the attuned care that is a condition for the being-with of the BF is singular, open, and immanent to the everydayness of union activity. As I put it above, attuned care is an ontological condition that emerges along with everyday activity, none of which, once it becomes habit, need be done overtly or with conscious awareness.

Certainly, however, instances of overt attuned care do occur on occasion. For example, one day in the spring of 2015 Jeppe, an older member who also has a long history of heavy alcohol use, attended a dinner. Despite the fact that he was experiencing serious shakes and tremors from trying to stay off the drink, Jeppe participated the best he could in the meal's preparation by helping to set the table. Although this went fine, when Jeppe went to get himself a glass of lemonade, he dropped it, and the glass shattered and lemonade spilled across the floor. As he awkwardly started to clean this up, two other members, Sofie and Bernard, went over and kindly told him to sit down and let them clean it. At this point Jeppe went to get himself a cup of coffee, most of which he spilled on the floor as he walked to the table. Bernard cleaned it up without saying a word. As usual the dinner was served buffet style, and when Jeppe walked back to the table with his full plate he dropped that too, at which point a few of the members joked a bit about Jeppe not getting any more bacon and having to eat plain mashed potatoes. As Jeppe walked to get the mop, others cleaned the mess from the floor. At this point Jeppe was quite embarrassed and went to the kitchen to make himself a simple sandwich. Morten, another BF member, went over to Jeppe and told him to stop being silly and to go sit down while Morten prepared a plate of food for him. When Jeppe finished eating, Morten took his plate and put it in the dishwasher.[39]

This is an example of an overt act of attuned care within the everydayness of life at the BF. At some point it became very clear to everyone that Jeppe needed assistance in a very singular manner, and his fellow unionists felt obliged to offer him that care in a way that attuned to him at that moment. Thus, the obligation of care and how to enact it emerged in the singularity of this moment and among those who were there; to care for Jeppe then and there was a matter of attuning to that singularity. But for the most part, the attuned care of the shared meals is not, should we say, so obvious. Rather, the attuned care is perhaps better understood as what we might call the condition of being for these shared meals and for the BF in general.

As with all conditions of being, attuned care is immanent to the very practices and activity it allows—in this case, the process of communally preparing and eating meals together. Planning a menu together, shopping together, prepping and cooking the food together, moving tables and setting them together, cleaning up after one another together—the attuned care is enacted in the togetherness of activity. This sharedness of the process, and the intertwined connectivity that emerges with it, is what opens possibilities for being-with as a community of those without community. For those whom "normal society" has systematically excluded from almost every possibility of being-with another human in ways that matter, these shared meals are significant for the openness of being-with offered at the BF. Unlike a soup kitchen or other instances of humanitarian meals provided as anonymous care, the shared meals provide a possibility for those who happen to come by to be accepted in their singular capacity to contribute and thus to enjoy and participate in the gift of care with others. Whoever they are and whatever they can do to participate in the meal is welcome. The attuned care enacted through the shared meals, then, makes it clear that whoever arrives matters as who they are,[40] and this mattering matters for the BF as a whole because it is in this particular way, this time, that this person will be a part of the community that has emerged there.

Vancouver

Throughout this book I have been emphasizing that the political activity in the Downtown Eastside has become, to a great extent, a model for the anti–drug war movement. This is so not only because of the tactics used and their interstitial focus but, perhaps most importantly, because of the long-term vision of the political activity and the world that has emerged as a result. I have been describing this world as an intertwined one, in which its labor, service, housing, entertainment, and health/therapeutic sectors are all networked such that by entering this world at any point—for example, getting a job at one of the social enterprises—one can easily access any other—for example, good and adequate housing. Because of this, I have been describing the Downtown Eastside as an attuned world.[41] We could also say that as a result of the politics of worldbuilding done there, the Downtown Eastside is best described as having an ontological condition of attuned care.

In the previous chapters, I tried to show how this condition of attuned care within the Downtown Eastside emerged and the kinds of possibilities it allows. Thus, for example, I have argued that the Downtown Eastside can, for the most part, be understood as a world in which harm reduction has become a part of ordinary everyday life. This world, to a great extent, can be characterized as one that is now a (relatively) safe zone for drug use. Unlike most other harm-reduction services around the globe that can only be found at relatively isolated—that is, disconnected—clinics, which tend to put a lot of emphasis on the responsibilization of the "participants" who go there, the Downtown Eastside has become an entire world in which harm-reduction services are easily accessed within minutes of anywhere one may be and accessed in a way that lets-be whoever does.

The social enterprise jobs are another example of how the onto-infrastructure of the Downtown Eastside gives way to the condition of attuned care. Recall that these jobs are by definition attuned to those who work them. Thus, for example, working at the chocolate café or the vintage clothes shop or the grocery store or the arts and crafts shop or any of the other social enterprise jobs does not entail that the employee conform to the rigid standards of a "responsible" nine-to-five worker. Rather, these jobs attune to the ways of being of those who work them. But similar to how I argued in the previous chapter that disclosive freedom does not mean that one's freedom can become disruptive, so too must employees attune themselves to the ways of being of a job. This co-attunement, then, provides the conditions in which work is a possibility for anyone who might happen by. This condition opens the possibility that anyone is able to get a paycheck, which is indeed important within the larger drug war condition that excludes drug users from most job opportunities. But more importantly, this condition of attuned care allows for what Teresa and the vintage clothes shop manager called *connectivity*.

In chapter three we saw how Teresa emphasizes the importance of connectivity as an essential condition of being-human. What I hope to have made clear throughout this book is that being-connected in an attuned manner is not simply a matter of standing over and against some other person or thing and feeling a connection because of an understood shared interest or obligation. Rather, an attuned connectivity—or simply attunement—is better understood as an ontological responsivity through which the being of diverse existents becomes intertwined such that what is at stake is not interest or obligation but the very existence of this intertwinement.[42] That is to say, what is at stake is being as such, an at stakeness that entails care. I have been trying to argue throughout this book that it is precisely because of this attuned connectivity and the condition of attuned care this entails that Teresa and so many others finally feel that they now have a place to dwell despite the difficulties that remain in the Downtown Eastside. In other words, this condition of attuned care is one in which those who dwell there are regularly caught up in what I have been calling in this chapter an atmospheric mood of intimacy. Therefore, I would like to finish this chapter with one last example of how the attuned care of the Downtown Eastside gives way to such an atmospheric mood and the being-together-with that this condition and mood allow.

As already mentioned in the previous chapters, more or less at the geographical center of the Downtown Eastside sits a bank. For years those living in the neighborhood had no bank, as all the big commercial banks shut down their branches in the Downtown Eastside, and those in surrounding neighborhoods increasingly hired security guards to keep so-called undesirables out. Being a resident of the Downtown Eastside is for most others in Vancouver, by definition, being an undesirable. This evacuation of the banking industry from the neighborhood, for the most part, resulted in a situation in which most of the residents of the Downtown Eastside had no access to financial institutions other than cash-checking and money order companies that charged a hefty fee for any transaction. Thus, thousands of residents who already lived quite precarious lives were further marginalized. Left without the possibility of having a savings account, which for many in the neighborhood who live in precarious housing or are homeless is very important so as not to have all your cash easily stolen or used on a binge, or without the possibility of having a checking account from which to pay bills, economic precarity for many Downtown Eastside residents became even more systemically established. Eventually, one of the main anti–drug war organizations working in the Downtown Eastside convinced a Vancouver-area credit union to provide the banking infrastructure for a new bank in the neighborhood, which the organization now operates with its own personnel. Today the bank offers basic banking services for a low monthly fee, does not require a permanent address for its customers, and welcomes all who arrive no matter how they look or smell.

Having been planned, organized, established, and run to be attuned to those who arrive rather than to exclude those who do not fit a pre-conceived idea of who counts as a proper bank customer, the bank is an opening into the world of the Downtown Eastside where new possibilities for becoming regularly emerge. Part of what allows for this attunement is that the bank is more than simply a financial institution seeking profit and where one goes to do a banking transaction. Rather, the bank is also a place where, during the time of my research, people could hang out in the lobby or in front of the bank and socialize with friends or anyone who might pass by; or have a free cup of coffee offered in the lobby and read announcements of political, artistic, or other events going on in the neighborhood; or even, for a short period, get a crack pipe from the crack-pipe vending machine in the lobby. In other words, the bank is not predefined in its exclusionary and limited possibilities of what it could be but rather was designed as an open and attuned space that allowed for potentialities to emerge as realizable possibilities. Thus, this bank provides conditions of attuned care by means of its financial services. But perhaps more significantly, the bank also offers an intimate atmosphere that gives way to attuned connectivity because it is an open space that welcomes all who arrive to be together in a communal manner.

An example of how this is so and thus why the bank is central to the attuned care of a community of whoever arrives is the opera performed in the bank lobby at least once a year. Every Christmas season a local opera company performs in the lobby, and occasionally, additional performances are put on throughout the year. One such additional performance was a celebration of May Day in 2015. Yes, to be clear, this was an opera held in a bank to celebrate International Worker's Day. In addition to the free performance that started at seven in the evening, a free dinner was provided to anyone who happened by. This is perhaps the most obvious example of how the political activity of the Downtown Eastside is a creative and experimental politics of worldbuilding attempting to bring about an otherwise. For the very idea of performing an opera and providing a free meal in the lobby of a bank is not one that normally occurs, let alone one that is enacted. This is an experimental politics that does not begin, for example, with either an "is" or an "ought" but instead with "Why not?" This is politics as creative experimentation with an otherwise.

As I walked down Hastings Street toward the bank, I could already see traces of the operatic event several blocks away because nearly everyone I passed on the street was eating a bowl of chili. As I mentioned above, drug users the globe over struggle with access to proper nutrition, and those living in the Downtown Eastside, unfortunately, are no different.[43] So if for no other reason, the operatic event provided the possibility that at least on this day, anyone who might pass by would be offered a free hot meal. Although this hot meal, in and of itself, might be more akin to the biopolitical-humanitarian meals that I contrasted with the Copenhagen shared meals, it is important to recognize that the attuned care of the bank that day was the *entirety* of the operatic event and not the meal on its own. For it was the communal experience of the performance, the being-with-in-the-midst-of-creativity, and indeed the shared experience of eating a meal together-there-and-then that, I want to suggest, was the enactment of attuned care that gave way to an intimate atmospheric mood that day.

When I walked into the bank, the lobby was packed with people sitting on folding chairs, as the operatic performance was already underway. Just in front of the tellers' desks and surrounded on all other sides by the audience, the four-person performance, accompanied by a small band, transformed the space into an intimate musical theater. People of all ages, some First Nations peoples, some black, some Asian, and some white, sat transfixed on the performers. Occasionally, a young child jumped off his father's lap and ran toward the performance, stopping just before crashing into one of the singers, and then ran back to the open arms of his father. While most watched intently, some nodded off in their seats. Did they do so from the calming effect of the music, boredom, or the effects of heroin? The answer was not particularly obvious, and no one seemed to care.

Throughout the performance, people walked in and out of the lobby: some just out of curiosity, some realizing after a period of time that this was not their cup of tea, and others looking to see if there was any chili left. Out front on the sidewalk, just as many people gathered as had inside. Standing outside, still able to hear the performance, they talked about it, and the food, and any number of other topics of conversation. They, like those inside, simply seemed to enjoy the possibility of being-together in the atmosphere of the operatic performance. When the performance was over and the standing ovation died down, some went home, but many remained in the lobby chatting and—for quite some time afterward—outside the bank and on the surrounding streets. They talked with one another, some got high, and they talked about which part they liked most and which performer they thought sang and danced the best. Some sang themselves and others laughed. The next day as I walked down the street, I heard a few still talking about the performance, as the atmospheric mood conjured by it still lingered.

The bank for those couple of hours was both bank and not-bank; it was a bank in the process of becoming something else that tomorrow would become bank again. The politics of worldbuilding underway in the Downtown Eastside has been as successful as it is because it has focused on this kind of creative and experimental political activity meant to enact attuned care and provide the conditions for an otherwise world.[44] This is a politics as a process of poetic building.[45] That is, it is a political poetic building of a world where a community of those without community can gather and dwell and in so doing, be-with-one-another in conditions of attuned care. The result of the political activity that has built this world of the Downtown Eastside is that there now exists a world, as one of the key political actors there has said, where one can "be a human being with other human beings," where no one tells anyone "how to live their fricking life," where nonjudgment is perhaps the primary ethical value, and where, collectively, people try to "be there" with and for one another.[46] This is perhaps the best description of what a world conditioned by attuned care looks like.

This world of the Downtown Eastside is not a utopia realized, however. As Frank put it at the end of the last chapter while describing his post–drug war imaginary, in the Downtown Eastside there remains much suffering, pain, death, and exclusion from the larger world of Vancouver. What is politically significant about what is happening in the Downtown Eastside is not that people have somehow magically discovered how to eradicate suffering—far from it—but that through political activity such as building a bank that can also sometimes be an opera theater and through which one can also be connected to housing or employment or artistic or recreational or health possibilities around the neighborhood, through building such a world that is intertwined and attuned to itself and its constituents, this political activity has also built a world in which those dwelling there can find care as the singularity that they are. In other words, this politics of worldbuilding is creatively experimenting with ways in which a world can become a place where those who dwell there need not be in some predefined a priori manner but instead are let-be in their singularity and, as such, become intertwined within a relationality that offers the gift of care.

ATTUNED CARE AND THE HUMAN CONDITION

I began this chapter with the story of Andreas and his day with us away from the hospital. With that vignette I tried to show that the care offered

Andreas gave way to an attuned being-with that lets-be. If that is indeed the case, then it is so because, as I have shown in the rest of this chapter, this kind of attuned care is the ontological condition not only of community—*cum-munus*—but also for the emergence of otherwise worlds and beings. That is, in this chapter I showed that attuned care is the condition that allows for the ontological differentiation of an otherwise. To argue that attuned care must be understood first and foremost as an ontological condition may seem strange in a time when care has primarily become manifest as a biopolitically framed practice of caring-for. Within this biopolitical framework, left-liberal politics has too often been reduced to a reformism that seeks more robust social welfare systems through which the sick, the marginalized, and all the others who suffer can be cared-for. But as I showed in the last chapter, in the country where this kind of robust social welfare system is already perhaps the most well established on the planet, Denmark, we see that this kind of care is not enough. Or perhaps better put, this biopolitical care is oftentimes *too much* in the sense that through a very narrow definition of what counts as caring-for, the result is more often the oppression of normalization than the letting-be of attuned care.

Certainly, attuned care as an ontological condition can take the form of explicit acts of caring-for, and I have tried to give a few examples of this throughout the chapter. For there is little doubt that even in the locales of the most fully manifest condition of attuned care—for example, the Downtown Eastside or at the BF, explicit practices of caring-for are a significant aspect of the new worlds emerging there. Think, for example, of the safe-consumption sites in both of these worlds. But the point I have been trying to make throughout this chapter, and to a great extent throughout this book, is that attuned care as an ontological condition is first and foremost that which allows for the possibility of the *cum-* of being-with. That is, attuned care provides the conditions for the intertwined relationality of being-human-together, grounded in an openness that welcomes whoever and however one arrives.

This attuned care, then, is not explicit care for this pain or that suffering, although it can certainly manifest as this at times. Rather, attuned care is that which allows for the very possibility of being-human-together. Being-human, that is, as a being always already intertwined in relations with other beings—human and nonhuman alike—for whom we have, because of this ontological intertwining, obligations of care. As such, the long-term political project of the anti–drug war movement can be articulated as the onto-ethical-political enactment of worlds of attuned care. Perhaps here at the end, then, we can see that the political hope—that is, the political vision—offered by this project is that attuned care can be the human condition if and when we are finally able to escape the laboratory cage of our biopolitically enforced contemporary condition of war.

Epilogue

Otherwise

Everything will be as it is now, just a little different.

—Walter Benjamin

Only a crisis—actual or perceived—produces real change. When that crisis occurs, the actions that are taken depend on the ideas that are lying around. That, I believe, is our basic function: to develop alternatives to existing policies, to keep them alive and available until the politically impossible becomes the politically inevitable.

—Milton Friedman

In this time of perpetual war as governance, we may have to accept that the only political and existential recourse is experimenting with the otherwise. Reformism is exhausted. Prefigurative horizontalism alone does not work in any lasting manner. Insurrection against technologically advanced militarized states is pointless. Our last, best hope is that despite everything, we remain worldbuilders. The beings that we call human—when not destroying worlds—are fundamentally builders of worlds. Such building does not begin at the level of the state or through governance and neither will it emerge from mere prefiguration. Rather, new worlds emerge over the long term through the everydayness of our political and ethical activities with one another, as well as those other beings with whom we are inextricably intertwined.

    In this time of perpetual war, confronted by the overwhelming and technologically superior force of power that wages this war on people, we must accept that political change on the model of the French or Bolshevik

Revolutions is no longer a viable option and instead begin to think of political activity more in line with the worldbuilding activity of early pre-Constantinian Christian communities or those incipient capitalists who chiseled their worlds out of the foundations of feudalism. For it was from the interstices of their conditions of being, where they discovered and created spaces of potentiality, that these future rulers of the globe, each in their own way and time, began their worldbuilding activity, eventually creating networks of relationality by which over the long durée they came to transform theirs and everyone else's worlds in unimaginable ways.

Similarly, the political and existential imperative of our time is to search, discover, and create, within the interstices of the complexity of our contemporary condition, potentialities with which we can experiment in order to release new possibilities that may allow an otherwise to emerge. In other words, the imperative of our time is "the long-term redefinition of the possible," through both the theoretical and practical engagement and experiment with "new modes of being and new modes of sociality."[1] This is fundamentally a human project—but not a humanist project—because, as Hannah Arendt would put it,[2] we are the kinds of beings characterized by the capacity for bringing about new beginnings, and it is this ontological capacity of being-human that allows us to be both political and ethical beings.

In this book I have tried to show one example of a global political movement that is attempting to build new worlds, to create new beginnings, and to bring about an otherwise. Although those involved, at times, engage in political activity aimed at legislation and policy—an engagement I largely did not show in this book but in the introduction described as planting potentiality time bombs that clear further sites of potentiality for future experimentation—the truly revolutionary character of their politics is the worldbuilding they do in their everyday onto-ethical-political activity. The otherwise, these anti-drug war agonists know, is ultimately not possible through legislation alone but rather by being-with one another differently. The political and existential hope this offers all of us is that this otherwise, or perhaps another like it, will someday become a new nonnormative norm for other worlds and other beings.

This book—as an example of what an anthropology of potentiality could be—has been an attempt to articulate such an otherwise and its nonnormative norms currently being created by this politics of worldbuilding. Here it is important to note that although it has been beyond the limitations of this book to explicitly draw out the implications of this politics of worldbuilding for addressing other political demands within our contemporary condition, I hope it is clear that the kind of otherwise the anti–drug war movement is enacting could also address, for example, such concerns as migration and refugees; racial, ethnic, and sexual inequalities; climate change; economic crises and inequalities; and the question of human/nonhuman relations. I leave it to others to creatively imagine and enact these possibilities. What I hope I have made clear in this book, however, is that such worldbuilding projects can only begin when these are no longer conceived as individual issues but instead are understood and acted upon as the widely diffused complex phenomena that they are.

The question of what precisely constitutes the otherwise, however, needs be asked. To be clear: throughout this book when I write of the otherwise, I do not intend it in terms of a radical rupture or the ushering in of the unrecognizably new. Neither is the otherwise a utopian state or perfection. Indeed, it need not even be "better" than the current state of affairs. For this "better," we can only hope. In fact, for many, the emergence of an otherwise may not even be recognizable at first. In his analysis of Walter Benjamin's retelling of a parable of the Kingdom of the Messiah, Giorgio Agamben offers an analysis of the otherwise that I think best captures the kind of otherwise I have been trying to describe in this book.[3] That is, the otherwise is best considered, as Benjamin put it at the end of his telling, as "everything will be as it is now, just a little different."

Agamben tells us that it is this "just a little different," this, as he puts it, "tiny displacement," that is particularly difficult to explain. This is especially so in his analysis since he is trying to explain the little difference that is the otherwise of the perfection of what he calls the *Absolute*. But even in the imperfect otherwise that I have been trying to describe in this book, this "tiny displacement" is difficult to articulate. For this difference is not empirically verifiable—again, at least at first— and therefore is not simply a matter of ethnographically describing how what was once done or said or limited in a certain way is now done or said or limited in slightly other ways. The otherwise is not simply change. As Agamben puts it, the "just a little different" cannot refer to the fact "that the dog outside will stop barking" or put in terms of the topic of this book, for example, that police will stop harassing, raping, torturing, and incarcerating drug users.[4] These may be the consequence of the otherwise, but they do not constitute the otherwise.

Elizabeth Povinelli warns of the potential naivety, sadism, and exhaustion of seeking the otherwise in what I call *zones of uninhabitability*.[5] But to be clear: neither I nor the anti–drug war movement are attempting to discover an otherwise within these zones of uninhabitability. Rather, the otherwise is being experimented with at the interstices of the widely diffused complexity of the drug war that conditions and renders these zones uninhabitable. It is only because this complexity is manifest with such intensity at these zones that the latter are a particularly apt—but not a necessary—situated place to begin a politics of worldbuilding. This is so because such political activity does not begin with "the state of things" but rather with the potentiality already waiting to be opened within the interstices of such complexity. Therefore, the "tiny displacement" of the otherwise that this politics seeks to initiate does not, as Agamben puts it, "refer to the state of things, but to their sense and their limits. It does not take place in things, but at their periphery, in the space of ease between every thing and itself."[6] This "space of ease" that allows the otherwise to emerge is perhaps best described as what I have been calling a *clearing*—Agamben describes it as a threshold—but no matter what metaphor we use, the otherwise becomes possible because of an opening already there to receive and make way for it. The political task today must be imagining, articulating, and actually creating such openings.

In this book I have been trying to show an example—and to the best of my knowledge a unique one—of how this politics can be done. For above all else, the political activity of the anti–drug war movement is primarily aimed at creating clearings or openings at the interstices of their drug war situations, through which an otherwise can emerge. Those involved do this precisely because they recognize that the widely diffused complexity that conditions the zones of uninhabitability in which most of these agonists try to survive does not allow for changes to the states of things in any kind of immediate manner. Again, legislative reform alone is not going to do it, prefigurative horizontalism is ineffective in the long term, and insurrection is impossible. Meanwhile, the sense and limits that constitute the conditions of their worlds, for lack of a better way of putting it, are nonsense and suffocating. Because of this, the anti–drug war movement has developed a form of politics that creatively experiments with opening the sense and limits of these uninhabitable worlds so that an otherwise can begin to emerge. As of yet the worlds, neighborhoods, streets, and buildings in which this otherwise is emerging may look as they once did. But the sense and limits of the possibilities that now exist there have radically altered because of this political activity. As a result, the otherwise worlds emerging are real, experienced as such, and sticking.

This expansive alteration of the sense and limits of possibilities is what I have tried to show throughout this book. Using a critical hermeneutic approach, I have tried to participate in this emergence of possibilities by articulating and conceptualizing the experimental onto-ethical-political activity as the not-yet of the new worlds the anti–drug war movement is attempting to build. I have called this an *anthropology of potentiality*. In doing so, I have tried to trace the contours of the otherwise to which this politics of worldbuilding is giving way. This otherwise, so far, can be characterized as communities of whoever arrives, within which those who arrive can dwell and are let-be to experience the disclosive freedom of being their singularity. They are able to do so because of the onto-logical condition of attuned care in these new worlds. This political attempt to create openings is also evident in the hermeneutic-political tactic of showing that is a primary tactic of the anti–drug war movement in its engagement with others. For hermeneutic politics—as is all herme-neutic practice—is a process of opening up so to disclose an otherwise that was always already there as potential but not yet possible.

In other words, the political activity that I have been describing in this book seeks to conjure tiny displacements of the sense and limits of what and how it might be possible to exist in emerging worlds today. By creating openings so that an otherwise community, an otherwise free-dom, and an otherwise care emerge, the anti–drug war movement has offered a glimpse of how other worlds can be brought into being right here in the midst of the most dehumanizing situations. These other worlds may look and sound and smell just like the broken-down worlds we have grown accustomed to. But the tiny displacements anti–drug war agonists have enacted have already opened possibilities for what these exhausted worlds could become. Those openings await anyone who might happen by; Ann, no doubt, will give each of you a hug when you arrive.

Notes

INTRODUCTION—ON WAR AND POTENTIALITY

1. See, for example, Alain Badiou, *Saint Paul: The Foundation of Universalism* (Stanford, CA: Stanford University Press, 2003); Simon Critchley, *Infinitely Demanding: Ethics of Commitment, Politics of Resistance* (London: Verso, 2007); Jarrett Zigon, *Disappointment: Toward a Critical Hermeneutics of Worldbuilding* (New York: Fordham University Press, 2018).

2. See, for example, David Graeber, "The Globalization Movement and the New Left," in *Implicating Empire: Globalization and Resistance in the 21st Century World Order*, ed. Stanley Aronowitz and Heather Gautney (New York: Basic Books, 2003), 325–38; Jeffrey S. Juris, *Networking Futures: The Movements against Corporate Globalization* (Durham, NC: Duke University Press, 2008); Jodi Dean, *Democracy and Other Neoliberal Fantasies: Communicative Capitalism and Left Politics* (Durham, NC: Duke University Press, 2009); Mark Fisher, *Capitalist Realism: Is There No Alternative?* (Winchester, UK: Zero Books, 2009); Jane Bennett, *Vibrant Matter: A Political Ecology of Things* (Durham, NC: Duke University Press, 2010); Elizabeth A. Povinelli, *Economies of Abandonment: Social Belonging and Endurance in Late Liberalism* (Durham, NC: Duke University Press, 2011); William E. Connolly, *The Fragility of Things: Self-Organizing Processes, Neoliberal Fantasies, and Democratic Activism* (Durham, NC: Duke University Press, 2013); Timothy Morton, *Hyperobjects: Philosophy and Ecology after the End of the World* (Minneapolis: University of Minnesota Press, 2013); Ghassan Hage, *Alter-Politics: Critical Anthropology and the Radical Imagination* (Melbourne: Melbourne University Press, 2015); Maple Razsa, *Bastards of Utopia: Living Radical Politics after Socialism* (Bloomington: Indiana University Press, 2015); Nick Srnicek and Alex Williams, *Inventing the Future: Postcapitalism and a World without Work* (London: Verso, 2015); Elizabeth A. Povinelli, *Geontologies: A Requiem to*

Late Liberalism (Durham, NC: Duke University Press, 2016); Kabir Tambar, "Brotherhood in Dispossession: State Violence and the Ethics of Expectations in Turkey," *Cultural Anthropology* 31, no. 1 (2016): 30–55; Zigon, *Disappointment: Toward a Critical Hermeneutics.*

3. For a more sustained critique along these lines, see Srnicek and Williams, *Inventing the Future.*

4. I use the term *agonist* instead of *activist* in order to emphasize the agonistic nature of the political activity I describe in this book.

5. For the need for a pluralist assemblage of nonidentitarian political allies, see Connolly, *Fragility of Things;* for the need to build an ecology of organizations and provide a counterhegemonic alternative, see Srnicek and Williams, *Inventing the Future,* chap. 7 and 8; for the now classic post-Marxian articulation of hegemony and counterhegemony, see Ernesto Laclau and Chantal Mouffe, *Hegemony and Socialist Strategy: Towards a Radical Democratic Politics* (London: Verso, 2001).

6. For my conception of worlds and their transformation, see Zigon, *Disappointment: Toward a Critical Hermeneutics.*

7. Juris, *Networking Futures,* 300.

8. Hannah Arendt, *On Revolution* (New York: Viking Press, 1965), 284.

9. Democratic centralism is strongly associated with Leninism, though it is characteristic of much party-based political organization. That much of the anti–drug war organizational activity I observed and participated in was organized as such is not surprising since some agonists spoke to me of their Leninist sympathies or tendencies when it comes to organizing. Such self-definitions almost always came in the context of contrasting their organizational activity with that of such anarchist-inspired groups as Occupy, which these anti–drug war agonists found incredibly frustrating to work with because—according to them—the latter were seemingly incapable of making a decision and acting on it. I should also note that those anti–drug war groups who claim to be anarchist in nature also tended to have a core "committee" that made decisions for the rest of the group. The vast majority of those in the anti–drug war movement, however, have no history of past political activity and have very little if any knowledge of the history of political organizing.

10. Zigon, *Disappointment: Toward a Critical Hermeneutics.*

11. See, by way of comparison, Michel Foucault, *"Society Must Be Defended": Lectures at the Collège de France 1975–1976* (New York: Picador, 2003).

12. For excellent examples of work on security within anthropology, see Carlo Caduff, "The Semiotics of Security: Infectious Disease Research and the Biopolitics of Informational Bodies in the United States," *Cultural Anthropology* 27, no. 2 (2012): 333–57; Caduff, "On the Verge of Death: Visions of Biological Vulnerability," *Annual Review of Anthropology* 43 (2014): 105–21; Joseph Masco, *The Theater of Operations: National Security Affect from the Cold War to the War on Terror* (Durham, NC: Duke University Press, 2014).

13. See, for example, Bryan Stevenson, "Drug Policy, Criminal Justice and Mass Imprisonment" (working paper, First Meeting of the Global Commission on Drug Policies, Geneva, 2011), 1–10.

14. United Nations Office on Drugs and Crime (UNODC), *World Drug Report 2014* (New York: UNODC, 2014), 3. In fact, this report gives a very minimal estimation on the death toll of the drug war since it only reports what it calls "drug-related deaths" (183,000 in 2012). It defines these deaths in a footnote: "The definition of drug-related deaths varies among Member States but includes all or some of the following: fatal drug overdoses, deaths due to HIV acquired through injecting drug use, suicide, and unintentional deaths and trauma, due to drug use." Thus, drug-related deaths as defined by the United Nations are a result of what I am calling, perhaps inappropriately, the passive violence of the drug war. What is missing from this definition is the number of deaths as a result of the active violence of the drug war. Thus, for example, this definition does not account for the over one hundred thousand people killed in Mexico since 2006 as a result of the drug war or the number of persons in such places as the United States, Russia, Indonesia, the Philippines, and Thailand (to name only some of the most violent locations) killed every day as a result of drug war violence. Perhaps, then, it would be more accurate to refer to drug war–related deaths in order to account for all of these.

15. Giorgio Agamben, *Stasis: Civil War as a Political Paradigm* (Stanford, CA: Stanford University Press, 2015).

16. Michael Hardt and Antonio Negri, *Multitude: War and Democracy in the Age of Empire* (New York: Penguin, 2004).

17. See, for example, Judith Butler, *Frames of War: When Is Life Grievable?* (London: Verso, 2010); Etienne Balibar, "In War," *openDemocracy*, November 16, 2015, opendemocracy.net; Hage, *Alter-Politics: Critical Anthropology*, 18–24; Brian Massumi, *Ontopower: War, Powers, and the State of Perception* (Durham, NC: Duke University Press, 2015); Franco Berardi Bifo, "The Coming Global Civil War: Is There Any Way Out?," *E-Flux* no. 69, January 2016, e-flux.com; David Armitage, *Civil Wars: A History in Ideas* (New Haven, CT: Yale University Press, 2017).

18. In the context of the drug war, an example of chemical warfare would be the dangerous contaminants that are mixed with drugs as they pass through the illegal global drug commodity chain. But we can also consider such things as government approval of certain kinds of processed foods or genetically modified seeds as forms of chemical warfare in reference to food politics or the refusal on many governments' parts to regulate industrial waste pollution as yet another example in the context of climate change and environmental politics.

19. Foucault, *"Society Must Be Defended."*

20. Carl von Clausewitz, *On War* (Princeton, NJ: Princeton University Press, 1984), 605.

21. For an interesting, if not overly narrow, reading of Clausewitz as concerned primarily with resistance, see Howard Caygill, *On Resistance: A Philosophy of Defiance* (London: Bloomsbury, 2013).

22. Clausewitz, *On War*, 87.

23. Ibid., 75.

24. Ibid., 80.

25. Ibid., 80–81.

26. Ibid., 81.

27. Ibid.

28. Paul Rabinow and Nikolas Rose, "Biopower Today," *BioSocieties* 1 (2006): 195–217.

29. Povinelli, *Geontologies: A Requiem to Late Liberalism.*

30. Talal Asad, "The Concept of Cultural Translation in British Social Anthropology," in *Writing Culture: The Poetics and Politics of Ethnography,* ed. James Clifford and George E. Marcus (Berkeley: University of California Press, 1986), 141–64.

31. See, by way of comparison, Giorgio Agamben, *The Coming Community* (Minneapolis: University of Minnesota Press, 2009), 85–87.

32. Zigon, *Disappointment: Toward a Critical Hermeneutics.*

33. See, for example, João Pina-Cabral, "World: An Anthropological Examination (Part 1)," *HAU: Journal of Ethnographic Theory* 4, no. 1 (2014): 49–73; "World: An Anthropological Examination (Part 2)," *HAU: Journal of Ethnographic Theory* 4, no. 3 (2014): 149–84; Tim Ingold, "One World Anthropology," paper presented at The Human Condition: Reinventing Philosophical Anthropology Conference, Aarhus University, 2015.

34. Andrew J. Mitchell, "The Fourfold," in *Martin Heidegger: Key Concepts,* ed. Bret W. Davis (Durham, NC: Acumen, 2010), 215.

35. See, by way of comparison, Jean-Luc Nancy, *The Creation of the World or Globalization,* trans. François Raffoul and David Pettigrew (Albany: SUNY Press, 2007).

36. Elizabeth A. Povinelli, "Routes/Worlds," *E-Flux Journal* 27 (September 2011): 7.

37. Zigon, *Disappointment: Toward a Critical Hermeneutics,* chap. 3 (italics in original).

38. Hardt and Negri, *Multitude: War and Democracy,* 94–95.

39. Jarrett Zigon, "Human Rights as Moral Progress? A Critique," *Cultural Anthropology* 28, no. 4 (2013): 716–36; Zigon, "Maintaining the 'Truth': Performativity, Human Rights, and the Limitations on Politics," *Theory and Event* 17, no. 3 (2014); Zigon, *Disappointment: Toward a Critical Hermeneutics.*

40. Elsewhere I have argued that ethics can never be separated from its particular ontology. See Jarrett Zigon, "Attunement and Fidelity: Two Ontological Conditions for Morally Being-in-the-World," *Ethos* 42, no. 1 (2014): 16–30; Zigon, *Disappointment: Toward a Critical Hermeneutics;* see also Martin Heidegger, "Letter on Humanism," in *Basic Writings,* ed. David Farrell Krell (London: Routledge, 2011), 141–81.

41. Srnicek and Williams, *Inventing the Future,* chap. 1.

42. Juris, *Networking Futures,* 238–39.

43. For an important argument on this point, see Wendy Brown, *Politics Out of History* (Princeton, NJ: Princeton University Press, 2001), chap. 2.

44. David Graeber, "The New Anarchists," *New Left Review* 13 (January–February 2002): 61–73; Juris, *Networking Futures;* Marianne Maeckelbergh, *The Will of the Many: How the Alterglobalisation Movement Is Changing the Face of Democracy* (London: Pluto Press, 2009), chap. 2.

45. Juris, *Networking Futures.*

46. Srnicek and Williams, *Inventing the Future,* 8.

47. Lauren Berlant, *Cruel Optimism* (Durham, NC: Duke University Press, 2011), 182, fn25.

48. For the centrality of a political vision or imaginary to political theory and activity, see Sheldon S. Wolin, *Politics and Vision*, expanded (Princeton, NJ: Princeton University Press, 2004).

49. Srnicek and Williams, *Inventing the Future*, 3; see also Alex Williams and Nick Srnicek, "#ACCELERATE MANIFESTO for an Accelerationist Politics," *Critical Legal Thinking*, May 14, 2013, criticallegalthinking.com.

50. On changing habits to change conditions, see, for example, William James, *Habit* (New York: Henry Holt, 1890); Andrew Dilts, *Punishment and Inclusion: Race, Membership, and the Limits of American Liberalism* (New York: Fordham University Press, 2014), 215; Wendy Hui Kyong Chun, "On Hypo-Real Models or Global Climate Change: A Challenge for the Humanities," *Critical Inquiry* 41, no. 3 (2015): 675–703.

51. Hannah Appel, for example, shows that the Alternative Banking Working Group that emerged from Occupy Wall Street imagines other possibilities of banking, but it is rather clear that as of yet they have done very little other than meet on a weekly basis to discuss and debate such possibilities and occasionally engage in protests. (This assessment is based solely on Appel's article and a thorough reading of their website on March 30, 2017. If they have actually started an alternative bank, then I retract this contrast.) In contrast, the politics of worldbuilding about which I will write in this book actually enacts imagination in worlds as experiments for building those worlds anew in ways that stick and endure. Hannah Appel, "Occupy Wall Street and the Economic Imagination," *Cultural Anthropology* 29, no. 4 (2014): 602–25.

52. On the Paris Commune as a form of prefigurative politics, see Kristin Ross, *Communal Luxury: The Political Imaginary of the Paris Commune* (London: Verso, 2015). For the worldbuilding potential of councils and assemblies, see Arendt, *On Revolution*.

53. David Graeber, *Fragments of an Anarchist Anthropology* (Chicago: Prickly Paradigm Press, 2004), 84–85.

54. V.I. Lenin, *Report on the Unity Congress of the R.S.D.L.P.: A Letter to the St. Petersburg Workers*, 1906, www.marxists.org/archive/lenin/works/1906 /rucong/viii.htm.

55. On the limitations of prefiguration for a politics of becoming, see Razsa, *Bastards of Utopia*, 202–3.

56. Here I do not necessarily intend to contrast an anthropology of potentiality with what Paul Rabinow has called an anthropology of the actual but rather with the broader founding assumption of the discipline that focuses its research and most particularly its analysis solely on the Now of the empirically observable. For his description of the anthropology of the actual, see Paul Rabinow, *Anthropos Today: Reflections on Modern Equipment* (Princeton, NJ: Princeton University Press, 2003).

57. See also José Esteban Muñoz, *Cruising Utopia: The Then and There of Queer Futurity* (Durham, NC: Duke University Press, 2009).

58. Michael Jackson, *As Wide as the World Is Wise: Reinventing Philosophical Anthropology* (New York: Columbia University Press, 2016), 62.

59. Vincent Crapanzano, *Imaginative Horizons: An Essay in Literary-Philosophical Anthropology* (Chicago: University of Chicago Press, 2004).

60. Jonathan Lear, *Radical Hope: Ethics in the Face of Cultural Devastation* (Cambridge, MA: Harvard University Press, 2006), 6–10.

61. Thomas Schwarz Wentzer, "'I Have Seen Königsberg Burning': Philosophical Anthropology and the Responsiveness of Historical Experience," *Anthropological Theory* 14, no. 1 (2014): 27–48; Rasmus Dyring, "Freedom, Responsiveness and the Place of the Ethical: Toward a Philosophical Anthropology of Ethics" (PhD diss., Aarhus University, Denmark, 2015).

62. For an example of using historical material that documents the "lived" experience of persons as a starting point for conceptual analysis and creativity, see Ross, *Communal Luxury.*

63. Robert Desjarlais, "Picturing Homelessness: A Glossary of Perceptions," *MAT: Medicine Anthropology Theory*, 2016, www.medanthrotheory.org/read /6122/picturing-homelessness.

64. Cheryl Mattingly, *Moral Laboratories: Family Peril and the Struggle for a Good Life* (Berkeley: University of California Press, 2014); C. Jason Throop, "Moral Moods," *Ethos* 42, no. 1 (2014): 65–83.

65. Hage, *Alter-Politics: Critical Anthropology*; Povinelli, *Economies of Abandonment*; Povinelli, *Geontologies: A Requiem to Late Liberalism.*

66. Anand Pandian, *Reel World: An Anthropology of Creation* (Durham, NC: Duke University Press, 2015); Stuart McLean, "Stories and Cosmogonies: Imagining Creativity beyond 'Nature' and 'Culture,'" *Cultural Anthropology* 24, no. 2 (2009): 213–45; *Fictionalizing Anthropology: Encounters and Fabulations at the Edges of the Human* (Minneapolis: University of Minnesota Press, 2017).

67. Joel Robbins, "Beyond the Suffering Subject: Toward an Anthropology of the Good," *Journal of the Royal Anthropological Institute* 19, no. 3 (2013): 457.

68. For example, Graeber, "Globalization Movement and the New Left"; Juris, *Networking Futures*; Dean, *Democracy and Other Neoliberal Fantasies*; Bennett, *Vibrant Matter*; Povinelli, *Economies of Abandonment*; Connolly, *Fragility of Things*; Morton, *Hyperobjects*; Razsa, *Bastards of Utopia.*

69. For a few exceptions, see, for example, Povinelli, *Economies of Abandonment*; Paul Rabinow, *The Accompaniment: Assembling the Contemporary* (Chicago: University of Chicago Press, 2011); Martin Holbraad, *Truth in Motion: The Recursive Anthropology of Cuban Divination* (Chicago: University of Chicago Press, 2012); Povinelli, *Geontologies: A Requiem to Late Liberalism*; Martin Holbraad and Morten Axel Pedersen, *The Ontological Turn: An Anthropoogical Exposition* (Cambridge: Cambridge University Press, 2017); Zigon, *Disappointment: Toward a Critical Hermeneutics.*

70. Michel Foucault, "So Is It Important to Think?," in *Power*, ed. James D. Faubion (New York: New Press, 2000), 456.

71. By responsive process I intend an ontological claim that all beings are in a constant process of responding and adjusting to that with which they have become intertwined. We might prefer to call such responsiveness *attunement.* Similarly, philosophers at Aarhus University have been developing a philosoph-

ical anthropology of responsiveness, although it is much more grounded in a humanist first-person perspective than the responsive attunement of which I write here. See, for example, Wentzer, "'I Have Seen Königsberg Burning'"; Dyring, "Freedom, Responsiveness and the Place of the Ethical."

72. The classic articulation of this is Martin Heidegger's *Being and Time*, though it remained central to his hermeneutic project until his death. See *Being and Time*, trans. Joan Stambaugh (Albany: SUNY Press, 1996); see also John D. Caputo, *Radical Hermeneutics: Repetition, Deconstruction, and the Hermeneutic Project* (Bloomington: Indiana University Press, 1987); Reiner Schürmann, *Heidegger On Being and Acting: From Principles to Anarchy* (Bloomington: Indiana University Press, 1990).

73. Caputo, *Radical Hermeneutics*, 37; Schürmann, *Heidegger On Being and Acting*.

74. It is interesting to note that some of the most recent ethnographies of social movements claim that their movements are creating new worlds, and yet what they seem to be doing is either temporarily prefiguring a hoped-for world or actually seeking to be "included" in the already-is. This is particularly clear in Jeffrey S. Juris, *Networking Futures: The Movements against Corporate Globalization* (Durham, NC: Duke University Press, 2008); Naisargi Dave, *Queer Activism in India: A Story in the Anthropology of Ethics* (Durham, NC: Duke University Press, 2012). But see also Deborah B. Gould, *Moving Politics: Emotion and ACT UP's Fight against AIDS* (Chicago: University Of Chicago Press, 2009); Marianne Maeckelbergh, *The Will of the Many: How the Alterglobalisation Movement Is Changing the Face of Democracy* (London: Pluto Press, 2009); Angelique Haugerud, *No Billionaire Left Behind: Satirical Activism in America* (Stanford, CA: Stanford University Press, 2013); Maple Razsa, *Bastards of Utopia: Living Radical Politics after Socialism* (Bloomington: Indiana University Press, 2015).

75. See, by way of comparison, Graeber, "Globalization Movement and the New New Left," 11–12; on militant ethnography, see Juris, *Networking Futures*, 19–24; on affirmative anthropology, see Razsa, *Bastards of Utopia*, 209–17.

76. David Graeber writes about one role of a radical intellectual being that "one observes what people do, and then tries to tease out the hidden symbolic, moral, or pragmatic logics that underlie their actions; one tries to get at the way people's habits and actions make sense in ways that they are not themselves completely aware of. One obvious role for a radical intellectual is to do precisely that: to look at those who are creating viable alternatives, try to figure out what might be the larger implications of what they are (already) doing, and then offer those ideas back, not as prescriptions, but as contributions, possibilities—as gifts." See Graeber, "Globalization Movement and the New New Left," 11–12.

77. See, for example, Manuel DeLanda, *A New Philosophy of Society: Assemblage Theory and Social Complexity* (London: Continuum International, 2006); Oliver Human and Paul Cilliers, "Towards an Economy of Complexity: Derrida, Morin and Bataille," *Theory, Culture and Society* 30, no. 5 (2013): 24–44; Srnicek and Williams, *Inventing the Future*, 13–16.

78. Connolly, *Fragility of Things*; Srnicek and Williams, *Inventing the Future.*

79. Srnicek and Williams, *Inventing the Future*, chap. 1.

80. Srnicek and Williams, *Inventing the Future.*

81. Just a few examples are Joel Robbins, *Becoming Sinners: Christianity and Moral Torment in a Papua New Guinea Society* (Berkeley: University of California Press, 2004); Charles Hirschkind, *The Ethical Soundscape: Cassette Sermons and Islamic Counterpublics* (New York: Columbia University Press, 2006); Jarrett Zigon, "Moral Breakdown and the Ethical Demand: A Theoretical Framework for an Anthropology of Moralities," *Anthropological Theory* 7, no. 2 (2007): 131–50; Zigon, *HIV Is God's Blessing: Rehabilitating Morality in Neoliberal Russia* (Berkeley: University of California Press, 2011); Omri Elisha, "Moral Ambitions of Grace: The Paradox of Compassion and Accountability in Evangelical Faith-Based Activism," *Cultural Anthropology* 23, no. 1 (2008): 154–89; Gregory M. Simon, "The Soul Freed of Cares? Islamic Prayer, Subjectivity, and the Contradictions of Moral Selfhood in Minangkabau, Indonesia," *American Ethnologist* 36, no. 2 (2009): 258–75; Hayder Al-Mohammad, "Towards an Ethics of Being-with: Intertwinements of Life in Post-invasion Basra," *Ethnos* 75, no. 4 (2010): 425–46; Michael Lambek, *Ordinary Ethics: Anthropology, Language, and Action* (New York: Fordham University Press, 2010); C. Jason Throop, *Suffering and Sentiment: Exploring the Vicissitudes of Experience and Pain in Yap* (Berkeley: University of California Press, 2010); James D. Faubion, *An Anthropology of Ethics* (Cambridge: Cambridge University Press, 2011); Didier Fassin, ed., *A Companion to Moral Anthropology* (Malden, MA: Wiley-Blackwell, 2012); "On Resentment and Ressentiment: The Politics and Ethics of Moral Emotions," *Current Anthropology* 54, no. 3 (2013): 249–67; Girish Daswani, "On Christianity and Ethics: Rupture as Ethical Practice in Ghanaian Pentecostalism," *American Ethnologist* 40, no. 3 (2013): 467–79; Michael Lempert, "No Ordinary Ethics," *Anthropological Theory* 13, no. 4 (2013): 370–93; James Laidlaw, *The Subject of Virtue: An Anthropology of Ethics and Freedom* (Cambridge: Cambridge University Press, 2014); Mattingly, *Moral Laboratories*; China Scherz, *Having People, Having Heart: Charity, Sustainable Development, and Problems of Dependence in Central Uganda* (Chicago: University of Chicago Press, 2014); Webb Keane, *Ethical Life: Its Natural and Social Histories* (Princeton, NJ: Princeton University Press, 2015).

82. Jarrett Zigon, "An Ethics of Dwelling and a Politics of World-Building: A Critical Response to Ordinary Ethics," *Journal of the Royal Anthropological Institute*, n.s., 20 (2014): 746–64; Zigon, *Disappointment: Toward a Critical Hermeneutics.*

83. Michael Lambek, "Toward an Ethics of the Act," in *Ordinary Ethics: Anthropology, Language, and Action* (New York: Fordham University Press, 2010), 40.

84. On anthropology's current focus on suffering, see Robbins, "Beyond the Suffering Subject"; for liberalism's longstanding concern with pain and suffering, see Wolin, *Politics and Vision*; for a critique of liberalism's concern with pain and suffering, see Talal Asad, "Thinking about Agency and Pain," in *Formations*

of the Secular: Christianity, Islam, Modernity (Stanford, CA: Stanford University Press, 2003), 67–99; for how liberalism's humanitarian concerns to alleviate suffering enacts an antipolitics that ultimately reproduces the conditions of suffering, see Miriam Ticktin, *Casualties of Care: Immigration and the Politics of Humanitarianism in France* (Berkeley: University of California Press, 2011).

85. See, for example, Zigon, "Moral Breakdown and the Ethical Demand"; Zigon, "Within a Range of Possibilities: Morality and Ethics in Social Life," *Ethnos* 74, no. 2 (2009): 251–76; Zigon, "On Love: Remaking Moral Subjectivity in Postrehabilitation Russia," *American Ethnologist* 40, no. 1 (2013): 201–15; Zigon, "An Ethics of Dwelling"; Zigon, "Attunement and Fidelity"; Zigon, "Temporalization and Ethical Action," *Journal of Religious Ethics* 42, no. 3 (2014): 442–59; Zigon, *Disappointment: Toward a Critical Hermeneutics*. On the necessity of anthropology doing recursive analysis, see Holbraad, *Truth in Motion*.

86. Agamben, *Coming Community*, 54.

87. Ibid., 53–56.

CHAPTER 1. THE DRUG WAR AS WIDELY DIFFUSED COMPLEXITY

1. See *World Drug Report 2014* (New York: United Nations Office on Drugs and Crime, 2014), 3; Drug Policy Alliance, "Drug War Statistics," accessed March 28, 2016, http://www.drugpolicy.org/drug-war-statistics.

2. See, by way of comparison, Johann Hari, *Chasing the Scream: The First and Last Days of the War on Drugs* (London: Bloomsbury Circus, 2015), 42.

3. See, by way of comparison, Ernesto Laclau and Chantal Mouffe, *Hegemony and Socialist Strategy: Towards a Radical Democratic Politics* (London: Verso, 2001); Wendy Brown, *Politics out of History* (Princeton, NJ: Princeton University Press, 2001); Simon Critchley, *Infinitely Demanding: Ethics of Commitment, Politics of Resistance* (London: Verso, 2007); William E. Connolly, *The Fragility of Things: Self-Organizing Processes, Neoliberal Fantasies, and Democratic Activism* (Durham, NC: Duke University Press, 2013).

4. Alain Badiou, *Ethics: An Essay on the Understanding of Evil* (London: Verso, 2001); Brown, *Politics out of History*; Connolly, *Fragility of Things*.

5. Patricia Hill Collins and Sirma Bilge, *Intersectionality* (Cambridge: Polity Press, 2016), 2.

6. Anna Lowenhaupt Tsing, *Friction: An Ethnography of Global Connections* (Princeton, NJ: Princeton University Press, 2005).

7. See, by way of comparison, Connolly, *Fragility of Things*.

8. George E. Marcus, "Ethnography In/Of the World System: The Emergence of Multi-Sited Ethnography," *Annual Review of Anthropology* 24 (1995): 95–117.

9. Jarrett Zigon, *HIV Is God's Blessing: Rehabilitating Morality in Neoliberal Russia* (Berkeley: University of California Press, 2011).

10. VOCAL-NY is the organization's actual name. Throughout this book, when I give the name of an organization or group of agonists, it will be the actual name, and it will have been used with permission.

11. Tsing, *Friction: An Ethnography*.

12. This style of writing and analysis, though done with less subtlety and sophistication, can be seen in the recently popular book on the drug war by the investigative journalist Johann Hari. See Hari, *Chasing the Scream*.

13. This is the real name of the organization, and Javier Sicilia is the real name of its founder.

14. Drug Policy Alliance, "Drug War Statistics."

15. See, by way of comparison, Hari, *Chasing the Scream*, 139.

16. Because he is known around the globe for his political activity in Vancouver, I am using Bud Osborn's real name. Throughout this book, however, I will use pseudonyms for all those who are neither famous nor public figures.

17. Recited at the event "Voices of the Drug War: Mexico and Canada," which took place at SFU Woodward's in Vancouver on October 28, 2013. Any mistakes in the transcription of the recording are entirely my own.

18. Giorgio Agamben, *Homo Sacer: Sovereign Power and Bare Life* (Stanford, CA: Stanford University Press, 1998).

19. See, for example, Liz Goodwin, "Police Turn Routine Traffic Stops into Cavity Searches," *Yahoo News*, November 8, 2013; Jacob Sullum, "Why Is That Cop's Finger in Your Butt?: The War on Drugs Now Features Roadside Sexual Assaults," *Reason*, May 11, 2015.

20. Sara L.M. Davis and Agus Triwahyuono, "Police Abuse of Injection Drug Users in Indonesia," in *At What Cost? HIV and Human Rights Consequences of the Global "War on Drugs"* (New York: Open Society Institute, 2009), 18–34.

21. Nick Perry, "Winning a Battle, Losing the War: Drug Users in Indonesia Are Made Vulnerable by Current Drug Laws," *Inside Indonesia*, ed. 96, 2009.

22. See, for example, Joanne Csete and Jonathan Cohen, "Lethal Violations: Human Rights Abuses Faced by Injection Drug Users in the Era of HIV/AIDS," in *War on Drugs, HIV/AIDS, and Human Rights*, ed. Kasia Malinowska-Sempruch and Sarah Gallagher (New York: IDEA, 2004), 214–16.

23. This was done on January 18, 2015.

24. See Zigon, *HIV Is God's Blessing*.

25. See, for example, Bankole A. Johnson, "We're Addicted to Rehab: It Doesn't Even Work," *Washington Post*, August 8, 2010; Lance Dodes and Zachary Dodes, *The Sober Truth: Debunking the Bad Science behind 12-Step Programs and the Rehab Industry* (Boston: Beacon Press, 2014).

26. See, for example, Kenneth Anderson, "Death after Treatment for Heroin Dependence," Rehabs.com, May 14, 2015.

27. See, for example, Bruce K. Alexander, *The Globalization of Addiction: A Study in Poverty of the Spirit* (Oxford: Oxford University Press, 2008), chap. 8; Hari, *Chasing the Scream*, pt. IV.

28. Michelle Alexander, *The New Jim Crow: Mass Incarceration in the Age of Colorblindness* (New York: New Press, 2012), 63–71.

29. For this and other information, see "Stop-and-Frisk Data," New York Civil Liberties Union, http://www.nyclu.org/content/stop-and-frisk-data; and "Analysis Finds Racial Disparities, Ineffectiveness in NYPD Stop-and-Frisk Program; Links Tactic to Soaring Marijuana Arrest Rate," May 22, 2013 http://

www.nyclu.org/news/analysis-finds-racial-disparities-ineffectiveness-nypd-stop
-and-frisk-program-links-tactic-soar.

30. For an ethnographic description of this in Philadelphia, see Alice Goffman, *On the Run: Fugitive Life in an American City* (New York: Picador, 2014).

31. Bryan Stevenson, "Drug Policy, Criminal Justice and Mass Imprisonment," in *First Meeting of the Global Commission on Drug Policies* (Geneva: Global Commission on Drug Policy, 2011), 3; see also Alexander, *New Jim Crow*; Andrew Dilts, *Punishment and Inclusion: Race, Membership, and the Limits of American Liberalism* (New York: Fordham University Press, 2014), 9; Goffman, *On the Run*, xii, 3; Hari, *Chasing the Scream*, 93–96, 109–10.

32. Daniel Wolfe and Roxanne Saucier, "Introduction," in *At What Cost? HIV and Human Rights Consequences of the Global "War on Drugs"* (New York: Open Society Institute, 2009), 13.

33. Campaign to Stop Torture in Health Care, *China: Brutality and Forced Labor as Treatment* (New York: Open Society Foundations, 2011), 5.

34. Campaign to Stop Torture in Health Care, *Russia: When Vigilantes Step In* (New York: Open Society Foundations, 2011).

35. Goffman, *On the Run*, xiii.

36. These statistics come from the Drug Policy Alliance website unless otherwise noted. See Drug Policy Alliance, "Drug War Statistics."

37. Corrections Corporation of America, "2010 Annual Report on Form 10-K," *Annual Report Pursuant to Section 13 or 15(d) of the Securities Exchange Act of 1934*, December 31, 2010, 2, 19.

38. See The Sentencing Project, www.sentencingproject.org.

39. Radley Balko, *Rise of the Warrior Cop: The Militarization of America's Police Forces* (New York: PublicAffairs, 2013), 157.

40. William L. Marcy, *The Politics of Cocaine: How U.S. Foreign Policy Has Created a Thriving Drug Industry in Central and South America* (Chicago: Lawrence Hill, 2010), 88; Alexander, *New Jim Crow*, 74; Balko, *Rise of the Warrior Cop*, xii, 145, 157–58, 178–79, 207, 209–10.

41. Balko, *Rise of the Warrior Cop*, xii.

42. Ibid., 207, 222, 250, 321–22.

43. Ibid., 308.

44. Ibid., xi–xiv.

45. Marcy, *Politics of Cocaine*, 10.

46. Marcy, *Politics of Cocaine*; Winifred Tate, "Congressional 'Drug Warriors' and U.S. Policy towards Colombia," *Critique of Anthropology* 33, no. 2 (2013): 214–33.

47. Marcy, *Politics of Cocaine*, 135.

48. Quoted in ibid., 137.

49. Michael Kenney, "From Pablo to Osama: Counter-Terrorism Lessons from the War on Drugs," *Survival* 45, no. 3 (2003): 187–206; Vanda Felbab-Brown, "Counterinsurgency, Counternarcotics, and Illicit Economies in Afghanistan: Lessons for State-Building," in *Convergence: Illicit Networks and National Security in the Age of Globalization*, ed. Jacqueline Brewer, Michael Miklaucic, and James G. Stavridis (Washington, DC: National Defense University Press, 2013), 189–209.

50. Thomas M. Sanderson, "Transnational Terror and Organized Crime: Blurring the Lines," *SAIS Review of International Affairs* 24, no. 1 (2004): 52; see also Balko, *Rise of the Warrior Cop*, 250–52.

51. Sanderson, "Transnational Terror and Organized Crime," 55–58; Felbab-Brown, "Counterinsurgency, Counternarcotics, and Illicit Economies."

52. For example, Karen Barad, *Meeting the Universe Halfway: Quantum Physics and the Entanglement of Matter and Meaning* (Durham, NC: Duke University Press, 2007); Jane Bennett, *Vibrant Matter: A Political Ecology of Things* (Durham: Duke University Press, 2010); Connolly, *Fragility of Things*; Timothy Morton, *Hyperobjects: Philosophy and Ecology after the End of the World* (Minneapolis, MN: University of Minnesota Press, 2013).

53. Morton, *Hyperobjects*, 1.

54. For example, Graham Harman, *Tool-Being: Heidegger and the Metaphysics of Objects* (Chicago: Open Court, 2002).

55. For example, Morton, *Hyperobjects*, 149–54.

56. Alain Badiou, *Logic of Worlds: Being and Event, 2* (London: Bloomsbury, 2013).

57. Ibid., 37–38.

58. Ibid., 101.

59. Ibid.

60. Ibid., 113, 118–19.

61. For a book-length critique of metaphysical humanism, see Jarrett Zigon, *Disappointment: Toward a Critical Hermeneutics of Worldbuilding* (New York: Fordham University Press, 2018).

62. For example, Martin Heidegger, ". . . Poetically Man Dwells . . .," in *Poetry, Language, Thought* (New York: Harper Colophon, 1975), 211–29; Maurice Merleau-Ponty, *The Visible and the Invisible* (Evanston, IL: Northwestern University Press, 1997).

63. Aihwa Ong and Stephen J. Collier, *Global Assemblages: Technology, Politics, and Ethics as Anthropological Problems* (Malden, MA: Blackwell, 2005).

64. Ibid., 11.

65. See, for example, Jarrett Zigon, "Within a Range of Possibilities: Morality and Ethics in Social Life," *Ethnos* 74, no. 2 (2009); Zigon, *Making the New Post-Soviet Person: Moral Experience in Contemporary Moscow* (Leiden: Brill, 2010); Zigon, "Moral and Ethical Assemblages: A Response to Fassin and Stoczkowski," *Anthropological Theory* 10, no. 1–2 (2010): 3–15; Zigon, *HIV Is God's Blessing*; Zigon, "On Love: Remaking Moral Subjectivity in Postrehabilitation Russia," *American Ethnologist* 40, no. 1 (2013): 201–15.

66. See, for example, Jarrett Zigon, "What Is a Situation?: An Assemblic Ethnography of the Drug War," *Cultural Anthropology* 30, no. 3 (2015): 501–24; Zigon, *Disappointment: Toward a Critical Hermeneutics*.

67. Paul Rabinow, *Anthropos Today: Reflections on Modern Equipment* (Princeton, NJ: Princeton University Press, 2003), 56; *The Accompaniment: Assembling the Contemporary* (Chicago: University of Chicago Press, 2011), chap. 5.

68. See, by way of comparison, Akhil Gupta and James Ferguson, "Beyond 'Culture': Space, Identity, and the Politics of Difference," *Cultural Anthropology*

7, no. 1 (1992): 18; Critchley, *Infinitely Demanding;* Elizabeth A. Povinelli, *Economies of Abandonment: Social Belonging and Endurance in Late Liberalism* (Durham, NC: Duke University Press, 2011), 109–10.

69. Max Gluckman, *Analysis of a Social Situation in Modern Zululand* (Manchester: Manchester University Press, 1940).

70. See also T.M.S. Evens, "Some Ontological Implications of Situational Analysis," *Social Analysis* 49, no. 3 (2005): 46–60; John Kelly, "Seeking What?: Subversion, Situation, and Transvaluation," *Focaal—Journal of Global and Historical Anthropology* 64 (2012): 51–60.

71. For example, Raoul Vaneigem, *The Revolution of Everyday Life* (Welcombe, UK: Rebel Press, 2001).

72. For example, Guy Debord, *Report on the Construction of Situations and on the International Situationist Tendency's Conditions of Organization and Action,* 1957, www.bopsecrets.org/SI/Report.htm.

73. See, by way of comparison, Laclau and Mouffe, *Hegemony and Socialist Strategy;* Tsing, *Friction: An Ethnography;* Connolly, *Fragility of Things.*

74. Connolly, *Fragility of Things,* 11, 137, 41.

75. Susan Boyd, Donald MacPherson, and Bud Osborn, *Raise Shit!: Social Action Saving Lives* (Halifax and Winnipeg: Fernwood, 2009), 37; Larry Campbell, Neil Boyd, and Lori Culbert, *A Thousand Dreams: Vancouver's Downtown Eastside and the Fight for Its Future* (Vancouver: Greystone Books, 2009), 111.

76. Jarrett Zigon, "An Ethics of Dwelling and a Politics of World-Building: A Critical Response to Ordinary Ethics," *Journal of the Royal Anthropological Institute* (N.S.) 20 (2014): 746–64; *Disappointment: Toward a Critical Hermeneutics.*

77. Zigon, *Disappointment: Toward a Critical Hermeneutics.*

78. See Jarrett Zigon, "Human Rights as Moral Progress? A Critique," *Cultural Anthropology* 28, no. 4 (2013); *Disappointment: Toward a Critical Hermeneutics.*

79. See, for example, Zigon, *HIV Is God's Blessing;* "Human Rights as Moral Progress?"; "On Love."

CHAPTER 2. "ADDICTS" AND THE DISRUPTIVE POLITICS OF SHOWING

1. See, for example, Bruce K. Alexander, *The Globalization of Addiction: A Study in Poverty of the Spirit* (Oxford: Oxford University Press, 2008), especially chapter 2; Susan Zieger, *Inventing the Addict: Drugs, Race, and Sexuality in Nineteenth-Century British and American Literature* (Amherst: University of Massachusetts Press, 2008).

2. Judith Butler, *Frames of War: When Is Life Grievable?* (London: Verso, 2010).

3. For a sustained critique of a closed and totalizing ontology and the politics of the a priori it tends to support, see Jarrett Zigon, *Disappointment: Toward a Critical Hermeneutics of Worldbuilding* (New York: Fordham University Press, 2018).

4. See Michel Foucault, *"Society Must Be Defended": Lectures at the Collège de France 1975–1976* (New York: Picador, 2003).

5. Butler, *Frames of War,* 29.

6. Ibid. See particularly, the introduction.

7. Jarrett Zigon, "An Ethics of Dwelling and a Politics of World-Building: A Critical Response to Ordinary Ethics," *Journal of the Royal Anthropological Institute,* n.s., 20 (2014); Zigon, *Disappointment: Toward a Critical Hermeneutics.*

8. The supposedly most dangerous are Schedule I and include heroin, cocaine, and marijuana, among others.

9. A description of the complexities of the international drug control regime is beyond the scope of this book. For some interesting insights into the current transformation and fracturing of this regime, see David R. Bewley-Taylor, *International Drug Control: Consensus Fractured* (Cambridge: Cambridge University Press, 2012).

10. Natasha Maguder, "Addicts Shoot Up in Safe Haven in Canada," *CNN International Edition,* April 12, 2013, http://edition.cnn.com/2013/04/11/world/americas/wus-canada-drug-safe-haven/.

11. Count the Costs, "The War on Drugs: Promoting Stigma and Discrimination," *The War on Drugs: Count the Costs,* n.d., 3–4, www.countthecosts.org. The *Irish Independent* article is referenced in this publication.

12. For discussions of addiction and the addict as slavery and slave, see Alexander, *Globalization of Addiction,* chap. 2; Zieger, *Inventing the Addict,* 6–7, part I.

13. My italics.

14. John Locke, *Second Treatise of Government* (Indianapolis: Hackett, 1980), chap. 3 and 4; Andrew Dilts, *Punishment and Inclusion: Race, Membership, and the Limits of American Liberalism* (New York: Fordham University Press, 2014), 89–101.

15. Dilts, *Punishment and Inclusion,* 106, chap. 2.

16. Drug Policy Alliance, "New York City: Marijuana Arrest Capital of the World," press release, New York, n.d.

17. New York Penal Law Section 220.45, which prohibits possessing or selling a hypodermic syringe or needle, was amended in 2007 as a direct result of the political activity of VOCAL-NY. This amendment "explicitly provide[s] that it is not a violation of Section 220.45 when a person obtains and possesses a hypodermic syringe or hypodermic needle pursuant to Public Health Law Section 3381," which "permits pharmacies, health care facilities or health care practitioners to sell or furnish any individual, 18 and over, with a hypodermic instrument or needle without a prescription" and also permits any members of sanctioned syringe exchange programs "to possess hypodermic instruments and are not subject to arrest for possession" even if there are residual amounts of a controlled substance within them. Operations Order #38 of the New York City Police Department, from which these quotes are taken, furthermore states that as a result of this amendment, "it is not necessary to determine whether or not an individual is a SEP [syringe exchange program] participant for this purpose." Meaning, that a New York City police officer should not and legally cannot arrest anyone for carrying syringes even if those syringes contain trace or resid-

ual amounts of a controlled substance. Unfortunately, the New York City police continue to do just this. See New York City Police Department, "Operations Order #38," October 25, 2012.

18. Bruce Alexander similarly writes about "the myth of the demon drugs" that has dominated popular, scientific, and governing understandings of addiction since the mid- to late nineteenth century. The essence of this myth, no matter how "scientifically" it may be rendered, is that once one has tried certain drugs—and heroin, cocaine, crack, and now crystal meth are the most dangerous or demonic of the drugs—the user is transformed not only into a slave of the drug but into a demonic being himself. See Alexander, *Globalization of Addiction*, chap. 8.

19. Both quotes from Radley Balko, *Rise of the Warrior Cop: The Militarization of America's Police Forces* (New York: PublicAffairs, 2013), 166.

20. Felipe Villamor and Richard C. Paddock, "Nearly 1,800 Killed in Duterte's Drug War, Philippine Police Official Tells Senators," *New York Times*, August 22, 2016, online edition.

21. Zigon, "An Ethics of Dwelling"; Zigon, *Disappointment: Toward a Critical Hermeneutics*.

22. Just one of many examples is John Shiffman and Kristina Cooke, "Exclusive: U.S. Directs Agents to Cover Up Program Used to Investigate Americans," *Reuters*, August 5, 2013.

23. For excellent ethnographic descriptions of this everyday incarcerated life, see Alice Goffman, *On the Run: Fugitive Life in an American City* (New York: Picador, 2014).

24. For excellent work on the everydayness of the carceral society, see Loïc Wacquant, *Punishing the Poor: The Neoliberal Government of Social Insecurity* (Durham, NC: Duke University Press, 2009); Elizabeth Bernstein, "Militarized Humanitarianism Meets Carceral Feminism: The Politics of Sex, Rights, and Freedom in Contemporary Antitrafficking Campaigns," *Signs* 36, no. 1 (2010): 45–71; Michelle Alexander, *The New Jim Crow: Mass Incarceration in the Age of Colorblindness* (New York: New Press, 2012); Lisa Marie Cacho, *Social Death: Racialized Rightlessness and the Criminalization of the Unprotected* (New York: New York University Press, 2012); Dilts, *Punishment and Inclusion: Race, Membership, and the Limits of American Liberalism*; Goffman, *On the Run: Fugitive Life in an American City*.

25. Georges Bataille, *The Accursed Share: Volume I* (New York: Zone Books, 1991), 59.

26. Ibid., 171–72.

27. Count the Costs, "The War on Drugs: Wasting Billions and Undermining Economies," *The War on Drugs: Count the Costs*, n.d., 3, www.countthecosts.org.

28. *World Drug Report 2014* (New York: United Nations Office on Drugs and Crime, 2014), 3.

29. Eugene Oscapella, *Changing the Frame: A New Approach to Drug Policy in Canada*, Canadian Drug Policy Coalition, January 2012, 12.

30. For a more detailed explication of moral breakdown, see Jarrett Zigon, "Moral Breakdown and the Ethical Demand: A Theoretical Framework for an

Anthropology of Moralities," *Anthropological Theory* 7, no. 2 (2007): 131–50; Zigon, *HIV Is God's Blessing: Rehabilitating Morality in Neoliberal Russia* (Berkeley: University of California Press, 2011); Zigon, "On Love: Remaking Moral Subjectivity in Postrehabilitation Russia," *American Ethnologist* 40, no. 1 (2013): 201–15; Zigon, "Attunement and Fidelity: Two Ontological Conditions for Morally Being-in-the-World," *Ethos* 42, no. 1 (2014): 16–30. For a detailed response to critiques of moral breakdown, see Zigon, *Disappointment: Toward a Critical Hermeneutics*, chap. 5.

31. Susanne Lüdemann, *Politics of Deconstruction: A New Introduction to Jacques Derrida* (Stanford, CA: Stanford University Press, 2014), 95.

32. See, by way of comparison, Hannah Arendt, *The Human Condition* (Chicago: University of Chicago Press, 1998).

33. Simon Critchley, *The Ethics of Deconstruction: Derrida and Levinas*, 3rd ed. (Edinburgh: Edinburgh University Press, 2014), 32, 40.

34. William James, *Habit* (New York: Henry Holt, 1890), 51.

35. Wendy Hui Kyong Chun, "On Hypo-Real Models or Global Climate Change: A Challenge for the Humanities," *Critical Inquiry* 41, no. 3 (2015): 675–703, 698.

36. Ibid., 703.

37. Jonathan Lear, *Radical Hope: Ethics in the Face of Cultural Devastation* (Cambridge, MA: Harvard University Press, 2006).

CHAPTER 3. A COMMUNITY OF THOSE WITHOUT COMMUNITY

1. These numbers given by the speaker more or less reflect those given in official reports, which list 6,100 deaths in Europe and 183,000 globally. In fact, the speaker did reference the *World Drug Report* when giving the global number, but to the best of my knowledge, the report he would have had access to would have only provided numbers for 2010. In any case, the numbers given by the speaker are accurate. See "Perspectives on Drugs: Preventing Overdose Deaths in Europe," European Monitoring Centre for Drugs and Drug Addiction, Lisbon, Portugal, 2014, 2; United Nations Office on Drugs and Crime (UNODC), *World Drug Report 2014* (New York: UNODC, 2014), 3.

2. See, by way of comparison, Benedict Anderson, *Imagined Communities: Reflections on the Origin and Spread of Nationalism* (London: Verso, 1999), 7.

3. See, by way of comparison, Roberto Esposito, *Communitas: The Origin and Destiny of Community* (Stanford, CA: Stanford University Press, 2010), 2.

4. According to costofwar.org, approximately 350,000 persons have died from direct violence since 2001 in the so-called global war on terrorism (website accessed June 1, 2015). As mentioned in footnote 1 of this chapter, in 2012 alone the drug war situation provided the conditions for 183,000 deaths, a number that, as I have indicated above, does not reflect the complete body count of drug war–related deaths.

5. Esposito, *Communitas: The Origin and Destiny*, 8; Esposito, *Terms of the Political: Community, Immunity, Biopolitics* (New York: Fordham University Press, 2013), 123.

6. Georges Bataille, *Oeuvres complètes V* (Paris: Éditions Gallimard, 1973), 483.

7. Similarly, in his study of the emergence of the category of transgender and the political activism around this emergence, David Valentine emphasizes that community is not a natural fact but an achievement. See David Valentine, *Imagining Transgender: An Ethnography of a Category* (Durham, NC: Duke University Press, 2007), 73; see also Anderson, *Imagined Communities*.

8. Michael Javen Fortner, *Black Silent Majority: The Rockefeller Drug Laws and the Politics of Punishment* (Cambridge, MA: Harvard University Press, 2015).

9. Sheldon S. Wolin, *Politics and Vision,* expanded (Princeton, NJ: Princeton University Press, 2004).

10. Anderson, *Imagined Communities,* 7; David Harvey, *Paris, Capital of Modernity* (New York: Routledge, 2003), chap. 13.

11. Ferdinand Tönnies, *Community and Society* (East Lansing: Michigan State University Press, 1957); Zygmunt Bauman, *Community: Seeking Safety in an Insecure World* (Cambridge, MA: Polity Press, 2001), chap. 1.

12. Robert Redfield, *The Little Community and Peasant Society and Culture* (Chicago: University of Chicago Press, 1971); Bauman, *Community: Seeking Safety.*

13. Bauman, *Community: Seeking Safety;* see also Esposito, *Terms of the Political,* 123.

14. For example, Akhil Gupta and James Ferguson, "Beyond 'Culture': Space, Identity, and the Politics of Difference," *Cultural Anthropology* 7, no. 1 (1992).

15. Rupert Stasch, *Society of Others: Kinship and Mourning in a West Papuan Place* (Berkeley: University of California Press, 2009). See, especially, his discussion in the introduction.

16. Bauman, *Community: Seeking Safety;* Peter Geschiere, *The Perils of Belonging: Autochthony, Citizenship, and Exclusion in Africa and Europe* (Chicago: University of Chicago Press, 2009), 77.

17. See, by way of comparison, Michel Foucault, *"Society Must Be Defended": Lectures at the Collège de France 1975–1976* (New York: Picador, 2003). Giorgio Agamben, *Homo Sacer: Sovereign Power and Bare Life* (Stanford, CA: Stanford University Press, 1998); Agamben, *The Coming Community* (Minneapolis: University of Minnesota Press, 2009).

18. Jean-Luc Nancy, *The Inoperative Community* (Minneapolis: University of Minnesota Press, 1991), 15.

19. Ibid (italics in original).

20. Ibid.

21. By way of comparison, see Hayder Al-Mohammad, "What Is the 'Preparation' in the Preparing for Death?: New Confrontations with Death and Dying in Iraq," *Current Anthropology,* forthcoming. In this important article, Al-Mohammad offers another phenomenologically inspired anthropological account of the relationality of death and dying in terms of being-with. Note, however, that he does this primarily through the work of Levinas, rather than that of Nancy, Blanchot, and Bataille, and in so doing remains primarily at the

intersubjective "level" of oneself and an Other (and, perhaps, a few intimates), rather than the community to which the being-with of Nancy brings us.

22. Maurice Blanchot, *The Unavowable Community* (Barrytown, NY: Station Hill Press, 1988), 9.

23. Although—to the best of my knowledge—neither Nancy nor Blanchot wrote of the open community as also including nonhuman finite beings and explicating this possibility in any significant manner is beyond the limitations of this book, it is of the utmost importance to recognize the open community of finite beings as comprising all finite beings, human and nonhuman alike. As such, the freedom as letting-be and the attuned care that in the following chapters I will show are essential to this community pertain just as much to nonhuman finite beings as they do to humans. For it is only in this way that we can begin to truly speak of an open community of finite beings and begin to build new worlds in an existentially sustainable manner.

24. Esposito, *Terms of the Political*, 25–26, 48–49, 59.

25. See, for example, Esposito, *Communitas: The Origin and Destiny*; Esposito, *Terms of the Political*. See also Thomas Lemke, *Biopolitics: An Advanced Introduction* (New York: New York University Press, 2011), 89–91.

26. Esposito, *Communitas: The Origin and Destiny*; Esposito, *Terms of the Political*, 25–26; see also, for example, Martin Heidegger, *Being and Time*, trans. Joan Stambaugh (Albany: SUNY Press, 1996), 115.

27. Simon Critchley, *The Ethics of Deconstruction: Derrida and Levinas*, 3rd ed. (Edinburgh: Edinburgh University Press, 2014), 223, 225.

28. For a wonderful philosophical description of such being-with that has ethnographic-like resonance, see Alphonso Lingis, *The Community of Those Who Have Nothing in Common* (Bloomington: Indiana University Press, 1994).

29. See, by way of comparison, Jacques Derrida and Elisabeth Roudinesco, *De Quoi Demain* (Paris: Fayard/Galilée, 2001); Derrida, "The Principle of Hospitality," *Parallax* 11, no. 1 (2005): 6–9; see also Critchley, *Ethics of Deconstruction*.

30. Heidegger, *Being and Time*, 115.

31. Esposito, *Terms of the Political*, 25–26.

32. Jarrett Zigon, "An Ethics of Dwelling and a Politics of World-Building: A Critical Response to Ordinary Ethics," *Journal of the Royal Anthropological Institute*, n.s., 20 (2014); Zigon, *Disappointment: Toward a Critical Hermeneutics of Worldbuilding* (New York: Fordham University Press, 2018).

33. For a more Foucaldian take on thanatopolitical motivation, see Stuart J. Murray, "Thanatopolitics: On the Use of Death for Mobilizing Political Life," *Polygraph* 18 (2006): 191–215.

34. I would like to thank Elinor Ochs for her help in analyzing this narrative. The interpretation—as well as any mistakes—are entirely my own.

35. Esposito, *Communitas: The Origin and Destiny*; Esposito, *Terms of the Political*.

36. C. Jason Throop, "On the Problem of Empathy: The Case of Yap, Federated States of Micronesia," *Ethos* 36, no. 4 (2008): 402–26.

37. See, by way of comparison, Douglas Hollan, "Being There: On the Imaginative Aspects of Understanding Others and Being Understood," *Ethos* 36, no. 4 (2008): 475–89.

38. See, by way of comparison, C. Jason Throop, "Latitudes of Loss: On the Vicissitudes of Empathy," *American Ethnologist* 37, no. 4 (2010): 771–82.

39. Although there are clear differences between our positions, what I am claiming here for the role of empathic attunement and imagination is not—ultimately— all that different from what Joseph Hankins calls sympathetic engagement and imagination. The difference, I suggest, essentially arises from our differing ontological assumptions. See Joseph D. Hankins, *Working Skin: Making Leather, Making a Multicultural Japan* (Oakland: University of California Press, 2014), 157. For another outstanding ethnography on the role of sympathy in political activity, see Catherine Fennell, *Last Project Standing: Civics and Sympathy in Post-welfare Chicago* (Minneapolis: University of Minnesota Press, 2015).

40. Miriam Ticktin, *Casualties of Care: Immigration and the Politics of Humanitarianism in France* (Berkeley: University of California Press, 2011), 3.

41. For this and similar critical engagements with the politics of the a priori, most particularly around rights-based politics, see Jarrett Zigon, *HIV Is God's Blessing: Rehabilitating Morality in Neoliberal Russia* (Berkeley: University of California Press, 2011); Zigon, "Human Rights as Moral Progress? A Critique," *Cultural Anthropology* 28, no. 4 (2013); Zigon, "Maintaining the 'Truth': Performativity, Human Rights, and the Limitations on Politics," *Theory and Event* 17, no. 3 (2014); Zigon, *Disappointment: Toward a Critical Hermeneutics of Worldbuilding*.

42. Throughout these paragraphs I refrain from "siding" with either the empathy or the sympathy "crowd" within anthropology. For ultimately— despite their differences and their attempts to formulate nonsubjectivist notions—both seem to me to ultimately rely upon the assumption of a self-same subject that has certain capacities to "connect" with other self-same subjects standing over and against them. In other words, they assume beings that can make connections but that are not relational to begin with.

43. For an example of this, see Zigon, *Disappointment: Toward a Critical Hermeneutics*, chap. 5.

44. Benedict Anderson has famously articulated the centrality of imagination to the creation of national communities. Here, however, I want to emphasize that imagining dying-with an other allows one to recognize she or he has always already been a part of the community of those without community, or what might be better put as the nontotalizable being-with of finite being. See Anderson, *Imagined Communities*; See also Valentine, *Imagining Transgender*.

45. Alexei Yurchak, *Everything Was Forever, Until It Was No More: The Last Soviet Generation* (Princeton, NJ: Princeton University Press, 2006).

46. For a historical analysis of the coming to equate geographical location with community, see Harvey, *Paris, Capital of Modernity*, chap. 13; See also: Anderson, *Imagined Communities*, 7; chap. 10.

47. See Zigon, *Disappointment: Toward a Critical Hermeneutics*, chap. 5.

48. Esposito, *Terms of the Political*, 123.

49. Hannah Arendt, *The Human Condition* (Chicago: University of Chicago Press, 1998).

50. See, for example, Charles Taylor, "The Politics of Recognition," in *Multiculturalism: Examining the Politics of Recognition*, ed. Amy Gutmann (Princ-

eton, NJ: Princeton University Press, 1994), 25–74; Elizabeth A. Povinelli, *Economies of Abandonment: Social Belonging and Endurance in Late Liberalism* (Durham, NC: Duke University Press, 2011).

51. Hankins, *Working Skin*.

52. Taylor, "Politics of Recognition." For an excellent ethnography on the difficulties of avoiding these homogenizing effects, see Kabir Tambar, *The Reckoning of Pluralism: Political Belonging and the Demands of History in Turkey* (Stanford, CA: Stanford University Press, 2014).

53. Agamben, *Coming Community*.

54. Ibid., 1–2 (italics in original).

55. Zigon, "An Ethics of Dwelling"; Zigon, *Disappointment: Toward a Critical Hermeneutics*.

56. Agamben, *Coming Community*, 86.

57. See, by way of comparison, Jacques Derrida and Anne Dufourmantelle, *Of Hospitality* (Stanford, CA: Stanford University Press, 2000); Esposito, *Communitas: The Origin and Destiny*; Esposito, *Terms of the Political*.

58. See Bruce K. Alexander, *The Globalization of Addiction: A Study in Poverty of the Spirit* (Oxford: Oxford University Press, 2008), 18; Larry Campbell, Neil Boyd, and Lori Culbert, *A Thousand Dreams: Vancouver's Downtown Eastside and the Fight for Its Future* (Vancouver: Greystone Books, 2009).

CHAPTER 4. DISCLOSIVE FREEDOM

1. See, by way of comparison, Vincent Crapanzano, *Imaginative Horizons: An Essay in Literary-Philosophical Anthropology* (Chicago: University of Chicago Press, 2004).

2. Consider how Edith Wyschogrod describes Foucault's notion of freedom in relation to homosexuality: "When Foucault speaks of homosexuality as liberating, his remarks are not directed toward establishing a new gay profile, but rather as a move toward defining a new way of life, '[as] an historic occasion to reopen affective and relational virtualities not so much through the [homosexual's] intrinsic qualities but, due to the biases against the position that he occupies.'" Edith Wyschogrod, "Heidegger, Foucault, and the 'Empire of the Gaze': Thinking the Territorialization of Knowledge," in *Foucault and Heidegger: Critical Encounters*, ed. Alan Milchman and Alan Rosenberg (Minneapolis: University of Minnesota Press, 2003), 286–87.

3. Isaiah Berlin, "Two Concepts of Liberty," in *Four Essays on Liberty* (Oxford: Oxford University Press, 1969), 131.

4. Leslie Paul Thiele, *Timely Meditations: Martin Heidegger and Postmodern Politics* (Princeton, NJ: Princeton University Press, 1995), 81, 90–91.

5. Ibid., 90–91.

6. Jarrett Zigon, "An Ethics of Dwelling and a Politics of World-Building: A Critical Response to Ordinary Ethics," *Journal of the Royal Anthropological Institute*, n.s., 20 (2014); Zigon, *Disappointment: Toward a Critical Hermeneutics of Worldbuilding* (New York: Fordham University Press, 2018).

7. I borrow this term from Thiele, *Timely Meditations*, 81–91.

8. Quoted in ibid., 78.

9. Tracy B. Strong, *Politics without Vision: Thinking without a Banister in the Twentieth Century* (Chicago: University of Chicago Press, 2012), 89.

10. Ibid., 306.

11. Martin Heidegger, *Discourse on Thinking,* trans. John M. Anderson and E. Hans Freund (New York: Harper and Row, 1966), 55.

12. Hannah Arendt, "What Is Freedom?," in *Between Past and Future* (New York: Penguin, 2006), 163.

13. Hannah Arendt, *The Human Condition* (Chicago: University of Chicago Press, 1998, 235.

14. The rare reference and engagement with Arendt within anthropology tends to do so as a latter-day Aristotelian, which matches well with the discipline's recent Aristotelian craze. But this interpretation completely elides the much more obvious and essential influence on her thinking and work, that of Heidegger. For a key text for understanding the Heideggerian influence on Arendt, see Dana R. Villa, *Arendt and Heidegger: The Fate of the Political* (Princeton, NJ: Princeton University Press, 1996).

15. On my reading, a good deal of the work of the anthropologist Hayder Al-Mohammad shows precisely this necessity of understanding care as central to Heidegger's project and just how pertinent it is to anthropological analysis. See, for example, Hayder Al-Mohammad, "Towards an Ethics of Being-with: Intertwinements of Life in Post-invasion Basra," *Ethnos* 75, no. 4 (2010): 425–46; Al-Mohammad, "A Kidnapping in Basra: The Struggles and Precariousness of Life in Postinvasion Iraq," *Cultural Anthropology* 27, no. 4 (2012): 597–614.

16. Martin Heidegger, "On the Essence of Truth," in *Existence and Being,* trans. R. F. C. Hull and Alan Crick (Chicago: Henry Regnery, 1949), 306.

17. Thiele, *Timely Meditations,* 83.

18. See, for example, Webb Keane, "Freedom, Reflexivity, and the Sheer Everydayness of Ethics," *HAU: Journal of Ethnographic Theory* 4, no. 1 (2014): 443–57; James Laidlaw, *The Subject of Virtue: An Anthropology of Ethics and Freedom* (Cambridge: Cambridge University Press, 2014).

19. For example, Philippe Bourgois, "Disciplining Addictions: The Bio-Politics of Methadone and Heroin in the United States," *Culture, Medicine and Psychiatry* 24 (2000): 165–95; Gordon Roe, "Harm Reduction as Paradigm: Is Better than Bad Good Enough? The Origins of Harm Reduction," *Critical Public Health* 15, no. 3 (2005): 243–50; Katherine McLean, "The Biopolitics of Needle Exchange in the United States," *Critical Public Health* 21, no. 1 (2011): 71–79; Zigon, "Human Rights as Moral Progress? A Critique," *Cultural Anthropology* 28, no. 4 (2013): 716–36.

20. I would like to thank one of my masters students for drawing my attention to these meetings, which she described in her thesis. I followed up on these meetings in the summer of 2012 while doing some short-term research in Honolulu. See Guusje Bressers, "Share Aloha, Nothing Else: Exclusion and Non-judgment within a Harm Reduction Program in Hawaii" (Masters thesis, University of Amsterdam, 2012).

21. Jarrett Zigon, "Moral Breakdown and the Ethical Demand: A Theoretical Framework for an Anthropology of Moralities," *Anthropological Theory* 7,

no. 2 (2007): 131–50; Zigon, *HIV Is God's Blessing: Rehabilitating Morality in Neoliberal Russia* (Berkeley: University of California Press, 2011); Zigon, "On Love: Remaking Moral Subjectivity in Postrehabilitation Russia," *American Ethnologist* 40, no. 1 (2013): 201–15.

22. For example, Laidlaw, *Subject of Virtue*, 119; Veena Das, "What Does Ordinary Ethics Look Like?," in *Four Lectures on Ethics: Anthropological Perspectives* (Chicago: HAU Books, 2015), 113.

23. Zigon, *Disappointment: Toward a Critical Hermeneutics*; see also, for example, Zigon, "Moral Breakdown and the Ethical Demand"; Zigon, *HIV Is God's Blessing*; Zigon, "On Love."

24. Elsewhere I have argued in detail that moral comfort should not be considered as something like "feeling good" or bourgeois comfort. Indeed, moral comfort may, in some cases, actually feel quite "bad" (perhaps "negative" would be less misleading). See Zigon, *Disappointment: Toward a Critical Hermeneutics*, chap. 5.

25. For some very clear examples of how moral breakdowns only occur in the ordinariness of everyday life, see Zigon, "Within a Range of Possibilities: Morality and Ethics in Social Life," *Ethnos* 74, no. 2 (2009): 251–76; Zigon, *Making the New Post-Soviet Person: Moral Experience in Contemporary Moscow* (Leiden: Brill, 2010); Zigon, *HIV Is God's Blessing*; Zigon, "On Love."

26. See, for example, Zigon, "On Love"; Zigon, "Attunement and Fidelity: Two Ontological Conditions for Morally Being-in-the-World," *Ethos* 42, no. 1 (2014): 16–30; *Disappointment: Toward a Critical Hermeneutics.*

27. See C. Jason Throop, "Moral Moods," *Ethos* 42, no. 1 (2014): 65–83.

28. Zigon, "Moral Breakdown and the Ethical Demand," 138.

29. This information and the information on Hospira comes from various handouts provided at the educational and organizational meetings at the union in April 2013.

30. Haeyoun Park and Matthew Bloch, "How the Epidemic of Drug Overdose Deaths Ripples across America," *New York Times*, January 19, 2016, online edition.

31. Lau Laursen and Jorgen Jepsen, "Danish Drug Policy—An Ambivalent Balance between Repression and Welfare," *Annals of the American Academy of Political and Social Science* 582 (2002): 20–36; Esben Houborg, "Control and Welfare in Danish Drug Policy," *Journal of Drug Issues* 40, no. 4 (2010): 783–804; Esben Houborg and Bagga Bjerge, "Drug Policy, Control and Welfare," *Drugs: Education, Prevention and Policy* 18, no. 1 (2011): 16–23.

32. See Houborg, "Control and Welfare in Danish Drug Policy"; Esben Houborg and Vibeke Asmussen Frank, "Drug Consumption Rooms and the Role of Politics and Governance in Policy Processes," *International Journal of Drug Policy* 25, no. 5 (2014): 972–77.

33. Houborg, "Control and Welfare in Danish Drug Policy"; Houborg, "The Political Pharmacology of Methadone and Heroin in Danish Drug Policy," *Contemporary Drug Problems* 39, no. 1 (2012): 155–92; Houborg, "Methadone, a Contested Substance: Danish Methadone Policy in the 1970s," *International Journal of Drug Policy* 24, no. 6 (2013): 73–80.

34. Houborg, "Political Pharmacology of Methadone," 171.

35. For an ethnography of the ethical disciplining of citizen-subjects within the context of biopolitical-therapeutic drug rehabilitation, see Zigon, *HIV Is God's Blessing.*

36. For the centrality of mood to ethics, see Throop, "Moral Moods."

37. Zigon, "An Ethics of Dwelling"; *Disappointment: Toward a Critical Hermeneutics.*

38. See, by way of comparison, Jacques Derrida, *Rogues: Two Essays on Reason*, trans. Pascale-Anne Brault and Michael Naas (Stanford, CA: Stanford University Press, 2005), 86.

39. For an extended analysis of the DTES in terms of attunement, see Zigon, *Disappointment: Toward a Critical Hermeneutics*, chap. 5.

40. See, by way of comparison, Jean-Luc Nancy, *The Experience of Freedom* (Stanford, CA: Stanford University Press, 1993).

41. We should note the disruptive potential in characterizing as enabling the kind of freedom active drug users enact in their political activity since this is the term usually used within the drug war "ideology" to describe how "loved ones" make it possible for people who use drugs to continue "to feed their addiction," or what this really means, to remain enslaved. The disruption to this "ideology" comes precisely when the enabling of disclosive freedom discloses the absurd fantasy of the drug war "mentality" and the notion of sovereign freedom often used to buttress it.

42. John Haugeland, "Letting Be," in *Dasein Disclosed: John Haugeland's Heidegger* (Cambridge, MA: Harvard University Press, 2013), 167–78.

43. Ibid., 178.

44. Arendt, "What Is Freedom?," 168–69.

CHAPTER 5. ATTUNED CARE

1. Angela Garcia writes about "watchfulness" in a way that has some resonance with what I am calling *attuned care*. But while Garcia's watchfulness, at least as she articulates it, remains at the interpersonal level of individual or a network of relationships, the attuned care of which I write is an ontological condition for being-with that emerges through the sustained and systematic political enactment of everyday forms of attuned care, some of which may be similar to "watchfulness." See Angela Garcia, *The Pastoral Clinic: Addiction and Dispossession along the Rio Grande* (Berkeley: University of California Press, 2010), 182.

2. See Jarrett Zigon, *HIV Is God's Blessing: Rehabilitating Morality in Neoliberal Russia* (Berkeley: University of California Press, 2011).

3. Miriam Ticktin, *Casualties of Care: Immigration and the Politics of Humanitarianism in France* (Berkeley: University of California Press, 2011).

4. Lisa Stevenson, *Life beside Itself: Imagining Care in the Canadian Arctic* (Oakland: University of California Press, 2014), 82.

5. For a more nuanced look at the ambiguity between the normalizing and institutional aspects of harm reduction and the potentialities of openness it holds, see Jarrett Zigon, *Disappointment: Toward a Critical Hermeneutics of Worldbuilding* (New York: Fordham University Press, 2018).

6. Stevenson, *Life beside Itself*, 126.

7. Ibid., 165.
8. Ibid., 158.
9. Jarrett Zigon, "Narratives," in *A Companion to Moral Anthropology*, ed. Didier Fassin (Malden, MA: Wiley-Blackwell, 2012), 204–20.
10. Stevenson, *Life beside Itself*, 158.
11. Ibid., 126.
12. Giorgio Agamben, *The Use of Bodies* (Stanford, CA: Stanford University Press, 2015), 224.
13. See, by way of comparison, William James, *Habit* (New York: Henry Holt, 1890).
14. See, for example, Brian Massumi, *Ontopower: War, Powers, and the State of Perception* (Durham, NC: Duke University Press, 2015).
15. For a book-length explication of this argument, see Zigon, *Disappointment: Toward a Critical Hermeneutics*.
16. Angela Garcia might articulate this as watchfulness. See Garcia, *Pastoral Clinic*, 182.
17. Elizabeth A. Povinelli, *The Empire of Love: Toward a Theory of Intimacy, Genealogy, and Carnality* (Durham, NC: Duke University Press, 2006).
18. Cheryl Mattingly, *Moral Laboratories: Family Peril and the Struggle for a Good Life* (Oakland: University of California Press, 2014).
19. Bruce K. Alexander, *The Globalization of Addiction: A Study in Poverty of the Spirit* (Oxford: Oxford University Press, 2008), chap. 8.
20. Ibid., 193.
21. Quoted in ibid., 194.
22. Ibid.
23. Ibid., 195.
24. Ibid.
25. Ibid.
26. Johann Hari, *Chasing the Scream: The First and Last Days of the War on Drugs* (London: Bloomsbury Circus, 2015), 179.
27. Alexander, *Globalization of Addiction*, 203, fn. 132.
28. See David F. Musto, *The American Disease: Origins of Narcotic Control* (New York: Oxford University Press, 1987), chap. 11; Richard DeGrandpre, *The Cult of Pharmacology: How America Became the World's Most Troubled Drug Culture* (Durham, NC: Duke University Press, 2006); Hari, *Chasing the Scream*, 177–80.
29. Alexander, *Globalization of Addiction*.
30. Hari, *Chasing the Scream*, 175.
31. Ibid., 181. The journalist Johann Hari makes a similar claim.
32. Quoted in Michael Inwood, *A Heidegger Dictionary* (Malden, MA: Blackwell, 1999), 131.
33. Martin Heidegger, *Being and Time*, trans. Joan Stambaugh (Albany: SUNY Press, 1996).
34. C. Jason Throop, "Moral Moods," *Ethos* 42, no. 1 (2014): 65–83.
35. Margaret Hellard, Rachel Sacks-Davis, and Judy Gold, "Hepatitis C Treatment for Injection Drug Users: A Review of the Available Evidence," *Clinical Infectious Diseases* 49, no. 4 (2009): 561–73.

36. Kathleen N. Ly et al., "The Increasing Burden of Mortality from Viral Hepatitis in the United States between 1999 and 2007," *Annals of Internal Medicine* 156, no. 4 (2012): 271–78.

37. See, for example, F. J. Santolaria-Fernández et al., "Nutritional Assessment of Drug Addicts," *Drug and Alcohol Dependence* 38, no. 1 (1995): 11–18; Aranka Anema et al., "Hunger and Associated Harms among Injection Drug Users in an Urban Canadian Setting," *Substance Abuse Treatment, Prevention, and Policy* 5, no. 20 (2010): 1–7; Alice M. Tang et al., "Malnutrition in a Population of HIV-Positive and HIV-Negative Drug Users Living in Chennai, South India," *Drug and Alcohol Dependence* 118, no. 1 (2011): 73–77.

38. Emmanuel Levinas, *Otherwise than Being, or beyond Essence* (Pittsburgh: Duquesne University Press, 2011), 74.

39. This example was provided by one of my masters students who also did research with the Copenhagen Union. See Renee Michels, "Care from the Perspective of People Using Drugs: Biopolitical Care vs. Everyday Forms of Care in Copenhagen, Denmark" (Masters thesis, University of Amsterdam, 2015).

40. For more on care and mattering, see Stevenson, *Life beside Itself*.

41. For a more detailed description of the attunement of the DTES, see Zigon, *Disappointment: Toward a Critical Hermeneutics*, chap. 5.

42. Jarrett Zigon, "Attunement and Fidelity: Two Ontological Conditions for Morally Being-in-the-World," *Ethos* 42, no. 1 (2014): 16–30; Zigon, *Disappointment: Toward a Critical Hermeneutics*. On responsivity, see also Thomas Schwarz Wentzer, "'I Have Seen Königsberg Burning': Philosophical Anthropology and the Responsiveness of Historical Experience," *Anthropological Theory* 14, no. 1 (2014): 27–48; Wentzer, "The Meaning of Being," in *The Routledge Companion to Phenomenology*, ed. Sebastian Luft and Søren Overgaard (New York: Routledge, 2014), 307–17; Rasmus Dyring, "Freedom, Responsiveness and the Place of the Ethical: Toward a Philosophical Anthropology of Ethics" (PhD diss., Aarhus University, Denmark, 2015).

43. Anema et al., "Hunger and Associated Harms."

44. This could be contrasted with the Alternative Banking Working Group of Occupy Wall Street that Hannah Appel describes. For although Appel convincingly shows how this working group imagines other possibilities of banking, it is rather clear that as of yet they have done very little other than meet on a weekly basis to discuss and debate such possibilities and occasionally engage in protests. (This assessment is based solely on Appel's article and a thorough reading of their website on March 30, 2017. If they have actually started an alternative bank, then I retract this contrast.) In contrast, the politics of worldbuilding about which I have been writing actually enacts imagination in worlds as experiments for building those worlds anew in ways that stick and endure. This would seem to be an imperative for our times. See Hannah Appel, "Occupy Wall Street and the Economic Imagination," *Cultural Anthropology* 29, no. 4 (2014): 602–25.

45. Zigon, *Disappointment: Toward a Critical Hermeneutics*.

46. Quoted in Hari, *Chasing the Scream*, 157.

EPILOGUE—OTHERWISE

1. Nick Srnicek and Alex Williams, *Inventing the Future: Postcapitalism and a World without Work* (London: Verso, 2015), 59, 83.

2. Hannah Arendt, *The Human Condition* (Chicago: University of Chicago Press, 1998).

3. Giorgio Agamben, *The Coming Community* (Minneapolis: University of Minnesota Press, 2009), 53.

4. Ibid., 54.

5. Elizabeth A. Povinelli, *Economies of Abandonment: Social Belonging and Endurance in Late Liberalism* (Durham, NC: Duke University Press, 2011), 128; Jarrett Zigon, "An Ethics of Dwelling and a Politics of World-Building: A Critical Response to Ordinary Ethics," *Journal of the Royal Anthropological Institute*, n.s., 20 (2014); Jarrett Zigon, *Disappointment: Toward a Critical Hermeneutics of Worldbuilding* (New York: Fordham University Press, 2018).

6. Agamben, *Coming Community*, 54.

Index

Made in the USA
Middletown, DE
28 February 2019